Americanism

Edited by Michael Kazin & Joseph A. McCartin

Ameri⋆

canism

New Perspectives on the History of an Ideal

THE UNIVERSITY OF NORTH CAROLINA PRESS   Chapel Hill

Set in Cycles and Quadraat Sans by
Keystone Typesetting, Inc.
Manufactured in the United States of America

This book was published with the assistance of
the Thornton H. Brooks Fund of the University of
North Carolina Press.

The paper in this book meets the guidelines for
permanence and durability of the Committee on
Production Guidelines for Book Longevity of the
Council on Library Resources.

Library of Congress
Cataloging-in-Publication Data
Americanism : new perspectives on the history of an
ideal / edited by Michael Kazin and Joseph A. McCartin.
    p. cm.
Includes bibliographical references and index.
ISBN-13: 978-0-8078-3010-9 (cloth : alk. paper)
ISBN-10: 0-8078-3010-0 (cloth : alk. paper)
1. National characteristics, American. 2. United States—
Politics and government. 3. United States—Foreign
relations. I. Kazin, Michael, 1948– II. McCartin, Joseph
Anthony III. Title.
E169.1.A52   2006
973—dc22   2005031396

10 09 08 07 06 5 4 3 2 1

Contents

Americanism

MICHAEL KAZIN & JOSEPH A. McCARTIN

★ Introduction

> *It has been our fate as a nation not to have ideologies but to be one.*
> *—Richard Hofstadter*

> *Just because you're in this country doesn't make you an American. No,*
> *you've got to go farther than that before you can become an American.*
> *You've got to enjoy the fruits of Americanism.—Malcolm X*

> *They also must understand that what took place in [Abu Ghraib]*
> *prison does not represent the America I know. The America I know*
> *is a compassionate country that believes in freedom. The America I*
> *know cares about every individual.—George W. Bush*

The topic of this book is vast, protean, and famously contested—
and so a definition may be helpful. "Americanism" has two different meanings. It signifies both what is distinctive about the United States (and the
colonies and territories that formed it) *and* loyalty to that nation, rooted in
a defense of its political ideals. Those canonic ideals—self-government,
equal opportunity, freedom of speech and association, a belief in progress—were first proclaimed during the era of the Revolution and the early
republic and have developed more expansive meanings since then. Thanks
to a powerful civil rights movement, full *social* equality, for example, finally
entered the canon in the decades after World War II. But the bundle of
ideals we call Americanism has proved remarkably supple over time, which
helps to account for its enduring appeal to people in other lands as well as
at home.

Its shifting content is not the only thing that distinguishes Americanism
from the patriotisms generated by other powerful nation-states. Love of
any country requires attachment to its supposed virtues, past and present.
Affection for "Holy Russia"—its fields and forests and Orthodox Church—
long predated the Soviet Union and easily survived it. Traditional Japanese
patriots revere the uniqueness of their national tongue and of Shinto, a
pantheistic faith linked closely with an unbroken imperial house. Americanism, by contrast, has been rooted less in a shared culture than in shared
political ideals.

Like Americans, French patriots may pay homage to the Enlightenment-born ideals of their revolution—liberty, equality, fraternity—but French patriotism includes a stronger cultural component than does America's national creed. Americans have always fought more over how to define and apply their national ideals than about the merits of their language or cuisine. The resulting battles to define Americanism have alternately divided the nation and unified it, producing both internal strife and solidarity against foreign enemies. These two tendencies have often crested together during wartime. Americanism's propensity to generate both conflict and cohesion continues in the early twenty-first century, a time when the United States has no rival on the world stage but when "Americanism" is fought about nearly everywhere.

The concept itself is nearly as old as the first European settlements to endure on the landmass of North America. John Winthrop was thinking about his church, not a nation, when, in 1630, he told those fellow Puritans who sailed with him to a new world, "We must consider that we shall be as a city upon a hill, the eyes of all people are upon us." But Winthrop's notion that America ought to be a model for Christendom and beyond soon transcended the intra-Protestant dispute that had led to the founding of the Massachusetts Bay Colony. In 1763, another New Englander, John Adams, wrote that America's settlement was "the opening of a grand scene and design in Providence." Adams believed his young land was destined to break the grip of feudal laws and customs, thus showing how individuals could free themselves from an irrational, often tyrannical past. During and just after the war for independence, such thinking was commonplace in sermons, pamphlets, and even the diaries of ordinary men and women. The new nation had the potential to be more than what Tom Paine called "an asylum for mankind." It had a mission to liberate the world.[1]

For many Americans, that messianic ambition was fused with religious meaning. The Second Great Awakening of the early nineteenth century spawned thousands of new Protestant churches and made the passion of evangelicalism the common discourse of most inhabitants, whether free or slave. Since that spiritual upsurge, the idea that anyone, regardless of learning or social background, can "come to Christ" has dovetailed with the belief in equal rights emblazoned in the Declaration of Independence. This synthesis of evangelical Protestantism and republicanism was found in no other nation—at least not with such passionate conviction and for such a long period of time.[2]

Over the past two centuries, Americanism has been put to a variety of uses, benign and belligerent, democratic and demagogic. During the first decades of the nineteenth century, that quasi-religious ideal took luxuriant, imperial form. It inspired the notion of Manifest Destiny, which legimitized the conquest of lands occupied by Native American tribes as well as by Mexicans in the Southwest. It was omnipresent among both Jacksonian Democrats—who defined it as the gospel of rough-hewn, self-made men in conflict with "the rich, the proud, [and] the privileged"—and their Whig opponents, whose "American system" called for higher tariffs and a national bank.[3] It also animated, in the 1850s, the attempt by the new American Party (the "Know-Nothings") to drive Irish immigrants from political power wherever the "papists" had established a foothold.

At the same time, the national faith was provoking an equally prophetic critique. In the forefront were abolitionists, both black and white, who scored the hypocrisy of a slave-holding republic. In 1829, David Walker demanded that white citizens "compare your own language" in the Declaration of Independence "with your cruelties and murders inflicted . . . on our fathers and on us—men who have never given your fathers or you the least provocation!!!!!!"[4] In the 1850s, William Lloyd Garrison called the Constitution "a covenant with death," and Frederick Douglass asked, "What to the slave is the Fourth of July?"

Yet few radicals rejected the ideals themselves. At the end of his famous Independence Day speech, Douglass predicted the abolition of slavery in his lifetime. He drew his optimism from "the great principles" of that same Declaration "and the genius of American institutions" as well as from an enlightened spirit he believed was swelling on both sides of the Atlantic.[5] Such figures initiated a vital countertradition. Since the antebellum era, dissidents have routinely cited the gap between America's utopian promise and its disappointing reality.

The Civil War brought two contending versions of Americanism into bloody conflict, the terms of which were not finally settled until Reconstruction had run its course in the mid-1870s. In many ways, the war's "new birth of freedom" renewed the national faith. Yet no sooner had Reconstruction begun to wane—as whites North and South started to "shake hands across the bloody chasm"—then anxiety grew about the weakness of Americanism in the fast-growing, culturally fragmented land. On the eve of the war, Carl Schurz, a German-born reformer and foe of slavery, had confidently predicted that "True Americanism, tolerance and equal rights will peacefully overcome all that is not reconcilable." By the 1870s, it seemed that jagged splits along lines of region, race, religion, class, and immigrant status could tear the industrializing society apart.[6]

For the nation's leaders, it thus seemed essential to Americanize the population if Americanism were to prosper. Never before had patriots engaged in so self-conscious an attempt "to make a religion out of citizenship," as Michael Walzer puts it. The massive Grand Army of the Republic created the ritual of Memorial Day to associate love of country with selfless loyalty in battle. Veterans, ministers, and teachers urged that the flag be displayed in every public building and many private ones.

In 1891, Francis Bellamy, a devout Christian attracted to socialism, wrote a short pledge to the Stars and Stripes that he hoped would bind American children to a shared set of convictions. An admirer of the French Revolution, Bellamy mused about including "equality and fraternity" in the pledge but decided that would be too controversial in a society riven by differences of race and ideology. So he restricted himself to a single phrase defining the republic: "one nation indivisible, with liberty and justice for all." His Pledge of Allegiance was quickly adopted by schools throughout the land (Congress added "under God" in 1954).

As that example suggests, a reassertion of Americanism was not always intended to produce political conformity at the turn of the twentieth century. Dissenters could appropriate the national faith as readily as conservatives. Three years after the Pledge was drafted, Eugene Debs, the railroad unionist who would soon become leader of the Socialist Party, emerged from jail to greet a throng of his supporters. "Manifestly the spirit of '76 still survives," he declared. "The fires of liberty and noble aspirations are not yet extinguished."[7]

Yet as the United States grappled with a flood of new immigrants and became an imperial power, the most aggressive promoters of Americanism were eager to prop up the established order, and they held political power. These figures were not necessarily conservative, as we now define the term. But Theodore Roosevelt's praise of the melting pot and of martial virtues stemmed from his fear that immigrants who retained even a shred of loyalty to their native countries weakened America's resolve in a dangerous world.

Inevitably, such fears intensified during World War I. All but ignoring the First Amendment, the federal government jailed radicals who opposed the war and looked the other way when vigilantes forced German Americans to prostrate themselves before the flag. The new American Legion crafted a "100 per cent Americanism" that stressed only the self-protective, coercive aspects of the creed.[8] In the 1920s, this defensive style of Americanism merged with the desire for cultural homogeneity to produce a spate of restrictive immigration laws. Throughout this period, racists found little difficulty rationalizing racial segregation as an essential component of the "American way of life."

Dissidents did not relinquish their claim to the great tradition, but they did have to defend their interpretations of it against official voices. Democrat William Jennings Bryan based his opposition to the U.S. conquest of the Philippines on the difference between imposing one's will on other peoples through force, as Great Britain had done, and persuading them with the example of altruism. "Anglo-Saxon civilization," Bryan declared in 1899, "has carried its flag to every clime and defended it with forts and garrisons. American civilization will imprint its flag upon the hearts of all who long for freedom."[9] But U.S. troops defeated the Philippine insurrection in a savage war. When the conflict ended in 1903, only a small minority of their fellow citizens seemed troubled that the same nation that cherished the Declaration of Independence now had an overseas empire of its own.

The armoring of Americanism at the turn of the twentieth century also produced unexpected consequences. Wartime service in uniform or in defense industries allowed immigrants to legitimize their struggles for justice by draping them in the mantle of Americanism. Those struggles were further validated during World War I as the government enticed ethnic workers with the promise of "industrial democracy" and the idea that, in America, "the People ARE the Government." Even the immigration restrictions of the 1920s, by weakening ties between immigrants and their countries of origin, fostered an Americanization from below that set the stage for a new regime of cultural pluralism that would soon make Americanism a more capacious ideal.

During the 1930s and World War II, New Deal liberals managed to daub the nationalist faith with a tolerant, populist hue. The federal government hired artists to paint historical murals in post offices that highlighted the heroism of farmers and workers. It also published guides to every big city and region that documented the riches of local histories and cultures. In the new National Archives building next to the National Mall, the founding documents of the United States were displayed as if they were the relics of secular saints. Meanwhile, filmmakers and wartime propagandists like Frank Capra depicted America as one big, friendly house for ordinary people of all religions and races (even if most politely kept to their own rooms).

Yet the left's attempt to marry class-consciousness to nationalism did not hold up well over time. During the Great Depression, CIO organizers described their nascent unions as expressions of "working-class American-ism," while pro-Soviet radicals portrayed Communism as "Twentieth Century Americanism."[10] But domestic opponents ridiculed these leftist twists on a common theme, and they all but vanished during the Cold War. That new global conflict recast Americanism as the antithesis of Communism and identified the national creed as the last best hope of a world threatened by totalitarianism and yearning for freedom.

The subsequent hunt for "un-American activities"—which stretched far beyond the House committee of that name—brought to a close the long period during which no single political faction controlled the meaning of the national canon. To be sure, the civil rights struggle of the late 1950s and early 1960s did briefly reinvigorate the dissident tradition. But, by the late 1960s, Americanism had become virtually the exclusive property of the cultural and political right.

The politics of the Vietnam War played a critical role in this change. In a decisive break with tradition, leading activists in the protest movements of the era took issue not just with government policies but with the ideals from which those policies were supposedly drawn. Young radicals did not seek to draw attention to the distance between America's promise and its reality as much as to debunk the national creed itself as inherently re-actionary and destructive. Many black, Native American, and Chicano militants viewed themselves as victims of Americanism, while white New Leftists dismissed appeals to patriotism as a smokescreen for imperialist war and the squelching of dissent.

That cynical view held firm among dissenters through the remainder of the twentieth century and beyond, despite a sprinkling of posters declaring that "peace is patriotic." In 2001, Noam Chomsky, one of the most popular writers on the left, dismissed patriotism as the governing elite's way of telling its subjects, "You shut up and be obedient, and I'll relentlessly advance my own interests."[11] Meanwhile, conservatives redoubled their efforts to claim Americanism as their cause. They successfully yoked to their larger purposes such rituals as saluting the flag, honoring the found-ing fathers, and singing patriotic songs—from "God Bless America" to

Lee Greenwood's "Proud to Be an American." But their victory occurred largely by default.

The passionate anti-Americanism that emerged in the Vietnam era raises the question: how did the ideals grow powerful and attractive enough to require a fury of debunking? In fact, scholars, journalists, and other commentators have been dissecting the living corpus of Americanism as long as there has been a United States.

Beginning with Alexis de Tocqueville in the 1830s, this literature focused on how the manners and mores of the natives enabled a rather unique form of democracy to flourish. Tocqueville, an aristocrat who spent just nine months in the United States, claimed that a rough "equality of conditions" both stabilized America and generated the tireless pursuit of self-interest that he regarded with fearful fascination. Six decades later, Frederick Jackson Turner—raised in Wisconsin—held that "the frontier is the line of most rapid Americanization." He argued that Americans' individualism, inventiveness, "restless, nervous energy," faith in progress, and hatred of pretense and big government all stemmed from the experience of living on the border between civilization and savagery. Despite or because of their many blind spots (racial, temporal, ideological), these two nineteenth-century interpretations became benchmarks for all future examinations of the subject.[12]

But most scholarly explorations of "the American character" that proliferated in the early to mid-twentieth century adopted a more critical or, at least, a more ironic view. The historian Charles Beard narrowed the interplay of conflict and motivation in America to their economic components. From the making of the Constitution to the onset of World War II, the drive to acquire wealth and defeat one's competitors became, for Beard, nearly the only factor propelling key events from one generation to the next. During the 1950s, the historian David Potter made plenty itself the key to Americanism. He claimed that everything from modes of toilet training to styles of advertising could be traced to the abundance of land, commodities, and leisure time. The political scientist Louis Hartz and the historian Richard Hofstadter argued that political debate and conflict in the United States revolved around a narrowly liberal, capitalist, rather anti-intellectual worldview. Americans—in their relentless, thoroughgoing modernity—had gained world power without wisdom and material progress without good taste.[13]

The 1960s assault on every kind of establishment quickly made this paradigm seem passé. Young scholars, most of whom leaned leftward, scorned the notion of a unitary "American character" as both condescending and simplistic. A few historians—Ernest Tuveson and William Appleman Williams, most notably—drew attention to the ideological roots of the aggressive foreign policy pursued by presidents from James K. Polk to Lyndon B. Johnson. Specialists in the late eighteenth and early nineteenth centuries debated whether "republicanism," the desire for a moral commonwealth, influenced more Americans at the founding than did the liberal demand for "rights." But most young historians rejected all attempts to view Americans as having one character, one set of ideals, or even the same history. The nation, they argued, was smaller than the sum of its diverse and constantly changing parts—immigrants, black people, workers of all skill levels, women from each of these groups, and more. Even if they did not accept Chomsky's view that Americanism was hardly more than a device to force millions of citizens to do the state's bidding, the social historians of the 1970s saw little value in identifying and exploring the uses of common national ideals. Their main concern was with the distinctive histories of their chosen groups.[14]

Such insular approaches could not long endure. In the 1980s, two changes—one in politics, the other in scholarship—began a modest revival in studies of Americanism, as culture and ideology. Ronald Reagan swept into the White House in 1981 at the head of a conservative mass movement. The right's defense of national virtue dovetailed with such events as the Iran hostage crisis, which began in 1979, and the victory of the U.S. hockey squad over its Soviet rival during the 1980 Winter Olympic Games. One could not dismiss the fact that millions of citizens responded to these events with flag-waving ardor. Scholars like Gary Gerstle and Cecelia O'Leary began to investigate, with a discerning empathy, how a variety of groups and thinkers used patriotic language in earlier eras for ends both self-interested and visionary.[15]

Meanwhile, such non-American scholars as Benedict Anderson, Eric Hobsbawm, and Linda Colley were taking a fresh, sophisticated look at nationalism—as an emotional phenomenon as well as a political reality. The modern nation might be an "imagined community," as Anderson dubbed it. But to imagine that one could explain the course of U.S. history without paying attention to the national faith began to seem like ignoring the obvious.[16]

Early in the twenty-first century, American scholars have renewed the debate about whether that faith is worth defending. One school of interpretation adds nuance and detail to the view of Americanism as form of manipulation, shaped by the changing attitudes of politicians and thinkers and the needs of business, the military, churches, and other powerful institutions. Thus literary scholar Amy Kaplan and historian Matthew Frye Jacobson view the national canon as thoroughly imperial, shot through with racial myopia and reinforced by messianic arrogance. According to Jacobson, America's "trumpeted greatness" in the period from Reconstruction to World War I was dependent on "the dollars, the labor, and, not least, the very *image*, of the many peoples with whom Americans increasingly came into contact and whom they blithely identified as inferiors." Kaplan argues that "the denial of empire" has structured "the discourse of American exceptionalism." In her view, American exceptionalism is largely an "argument for boundless expansion." It is not simply that these scholars warn against the dangers inherent in romanticizing the national faith. They suggest that the long history of Americanism has been a cruel and dangerous illusion.[17]

At the same time, another influential group of scholars has offered a measured defense of America's civic religion. In the past, argues historian James Kloppenberg, enlightened leaders and movements have employed the oft-cited principles of equality and pluralism to battle for just treatment for minorities and for just struggles against tyrants, both at home and abroad. The philosopher Richard Rorty echoes this "aspirational nationalism" when he challenges the left to reject the "cultural politics" of academia and to articulate instead a nonsectarian vision for a patriotic left. David Hollinger sees an emerging "postethnic ideal" in American culture, with its mosaic of new immigrants, that might transcend racial fears and defeat imperial overreach. Such works, in the pragmatic tradition, assume that Americanism, as resource rather than blind faith, can help forge a more humanitarian order.[18]

This debate suddenly seemed a great deal less academic after the terrorist attack of September 11, 2001. In their grief and shock, many Americans believed that the nation's ideals were also under siege. With or without the urging of the Bush administration, citizens began flying the flag and, as in World War II, made "God Bless America" the surrogate national anthem.

Neither the attacks of 9/11 nor the wars in Afghanistan and Iraq that followed in their wake really changed the terms on which historians and other commentators discussed the politics of Americanism. If anything, they hardened positions on each side. For critics in the United States and around the world, talk about defending American "values" was largely an excuse to promote the Christian right, enrich oil companies, and drive the nation into a war against Iraq that its architects hoped would remake the Middle East in America's image. "A Manichean discourse was promoted," writes Anatol Lieven, "which identified American values as the terrorists' target, with those values both absolutely good in themselves and identical with the good of the world." Liberal patriots tried to straddle the gulf between angry anti-imperialists on the left and the governing juggernaut on the right but found the task increasingly difficult once the Iraq war began. For their part, most conservatives backed President Bush's unilateralist foreign policy and applauded his claim that "the advance of human freedom—the great achievement of our time, and the great hope of every time—now depends on us. Our nation—this generation—will lift a dark threat of violence from our people and our future."[19]

The conflict of words and symbols drew new attention to an ongoing debate about the degree to which, in the context of world history, America is an "exceptional" nation. From Tocqueville to Hartz, leading interpreters, whether admirers or critics, focused on what seemed distinctive about the character and ideology of Americans and viewed the development of the nation as unique. The list of exceptional qualities is a lengthy one. It includes the primacy of individual identity over communal ties, belief in almost unlimited social mobility, absence of an established state church and the consequent flourishing of both diverse denominations and grassroots piety, and a potent tradition of antiauthoritarian and anticentralist politics. One should also add the remarkable self-confidence of most Americans, particularly white ones, that they live in a nation blessed by God that has a right, even a duty, to help other nations become more like the United States. Over the decades, the exceptionalist argument was repeated so often—by scholars, journalists, and politicians—that it hardened into cliché.[20]

But, since the 1960s, most American historians have come to reject the idea that every nation has unique, timeless qualities of its own. "Cultural essentialism," they argue, ignores the fact that powerful institutions invent and promote traditions. What is more, exceptionalist thinking can legitimize an aggressive foreign policy, causing grief to nations weaker and less fortunate than the United States. Cosmopolitan in their tastes and left-leaning in their politics, these scholars see more danger than insight in analyses that place the United States in a category different from all other countries.[21]

The growing field of world history has further marginalized exceptionalist thinking. American scholars increasingly want to decenter U.S. history, to see the country, in Thomas Bender's term, as merely one "province" in an interconnected world that European colonizers began to create during the fifteenth century. Thus such topics as the Atlantic trade in minerals, foodstuffs, and slaves and the international exchange of ideas and proposals about reforming industrial, capitalist societies take the place of a "default" narrative that, implicitly or explicitly, sees America as a distinct case. In 1998, Janice Radway gave a presidential address to the American Studies Association in which she criticized, in jargonized prose, the name of her own group. "A society that was not hemmed in by the need to peg cultural analysis of community and identity-formation to geography," she argued, "might better be able to attend to the full variety of cultural negotiations, negotiations that do not recognize national borders but flow across them to solicit the identifications of attentive and like-minded individuals." Dismissing the "notion of a bounded national territory and a concomitant national identity," Radway wondered whether it made sense to "perpetuate a specifically 'American' studies" at all. As David Hollinger writes, with tongue held firmly in cheek, "Historians have less use for the United States than they once did."[22]

Most non-American scholars, however, continue to view the history and the culture of the United States as, if not exceptional, at least distinct in significant ways from those of other powerful nations in Europe and Asia. They tend to assume the unity of something called "America," of a promised land or a hegemonic behemoth that bestrides the world—represented by powerful individuals, large and prosperous groups, and a national culture and state. This America is the apotheosis of one version of modernism: it subverts traditional cultures, destabilizes and sometimes overthrows indigenous rulers, and spreads its ideology, its effervescent popular culture, and even its form of government wherever and whenever it can. As Charles Bright and Michael Geyer observe, "Today people around the world think of America as the first democracy or, alternatively, as the land of McDonald's."[23] In the wake of the U.S. invasion of Iraq, many of these same people have also come to regard America as home to the world's most powerful and least restrained military apparatus.

Perhaps, some exceptionalisms, some nationalist ideologies, are more equal than others. For over two hundred years, the idea of America—as new Jerusalem or new Rome or something in between—has had a uniquely potent meaning for a broad variety of people outside the United States: from French aristocrats like Tocqueville to European Communists like

Antonio Gramsci to Saudi terrorists like Mohammed Atta to teenagers all over the world with Nikes on their feet and posters of Eminem, Britney Spears, and Michael Jordan on their walls. Recently, non-American scholars have joined U.S. historians in concentrating on the fragmented, disputatious nature of American society and the influence of those factors on the development of nationalist ideology. But there remains a persistent inclination among academics as well as ordinary citizens in other lands to view America as a whole—to examine how "it" uses and abuses its ideology both within the nation's borders and outside them.

What makes *Americanism* exceptional is thus its confluence with the realities of historical development itself. Ultimately, Americanism demands understanding on its own terms because of the unrivaled power for good or ill that the United States now wields in the world. As Hollinger wrote in 2002, the United States is "the most successful nationalist project in all of modern history. . . . Two-and-one-quarter centuries after its founding and 135 years after its Civil War, the United States is the most powerful nation-state in the world and the only twenty-first century power that operates under a constitution written in the eighteenth century. Its significance is measured by its sheer longevity, its influence in the world arena, and its absorption of a variety of peoples through immigration, conquest, and enslavement and emancipation."[24]

The success of the American nation has, in turn, bestowed tremendous power on the notion of Americanism, with all its contradictions and silences. It allows Mormons from Utah and Pentecostalists from Missouri to go into the world, converting people to a faith marked by the material success of its adherents as much as by the appeal of their doctrines and ceremonies. It has also given dissident groups in the United States the ability to inspire analogous movements in other parts of the globe. The U.S. movement for black freedom helped galvanize the antiapartheid struggle in South Africa, and the radical feminist movement (although indebted to texts by non-Americans like Juliet Mitchell and Simone de Beauvoir) helped spark like-minded insurgencies on every continent. The same is true of the gay and lesbian rights movement, spawned in the United States at the end of the 1960s.[25]

The recent rise of anti-Americanism notwithstanding, one cannot neglect the worldwide appeal of Americanist ideology in the laudable desire to internationalize the study and teaching of U.S. history. The very perception that a distinct set of American "values" exists was greatly boosted, particularly from World War II onward, by the unmatched power and allure of the United States itself. Of course, no "civilizing mission" proceeds by discourse alone. Yet without a well-developed, internally persuasive ideology, no national mission, whether humane or barbarous, ever gains much sway. Nor can one hope to advance a more benevolent Americanism without understanding the history of the nation's public ideology and learning how to speak effectively within its idioms. It is toward that end that we have organized this volume.

The original essays gathered here testify to the growing interest in Americanism among historically minded intellectuals. The dozen authors include both renowned scholars and younger ones who are gaining influence in the academic fields of history and American studies. They further an understanding of the concept in all its complexity—as an ideology, an articulation of America's rightful place in the world, a set of traditions, a political language, and a cultural style pregnant with political meaning. By illuminating some of the significant ways in which Americanism has been defined and contested over the past two centuries, they help us grasp the potential and limitations of the ideals it represents and of the term itself in our own time.

A central theme pursued in the essays is the inescapable conflict that Americanism provokes, within each articulator and interpreter of the national faith as well as between patriots and their critics. Nearly every significant naysayer also pays tribute to Americanism, in principle, while most tributes contain a degree of sadness that U.S. citizens are not living up to the high promise of their ideals. This internal tug-of-war provides tension and drama to the ideological history, while ensuring that the concept will never lose its significance, its freshness, and its power to inspire and provoke.

We have separated the essays into two sections: one concerns debates and narratives within the United States, and the other examines what people abroad have made of the Americanist mission. This division is, inevitably, somewhat arbitrary: several of the essays cross national boundaries or adopt a comparative perspective.

Each contribution in the first section—"Whose America?"—focuses on a particular group of citizens who sought to mold national ideals into a form that could further their interests and advance their beliefs.

Four essays span the period from the early republic to the beginning of World War II. Mia Bay describes how free black men and women interpreted the American Revolution as a set of promises only the abolitionist movement could fulfill. The founders' ideology both legitimized the struggle against slavery and gave activists a language with which to challenge their opponents, among whom was Thomas Jefferson himself. By examining the extraordinary diary of a Vermont farmer named Hiram Harwood, Robert Shalhope provides a fresh look at the long-running debate about whether republicanism or liberalism reigned in the new nation. Together with his relatives and neighbors, Harwood was alternately exhilarated at the egalitarian accomplishments of his society and fearful that new forms of hierarchy would destroy them. In the republicanism of this small producer, Shalhope finds a precursor to the Americanism that would emerge in the mid-nineteenth century. Jonathan Hansen analyzes the effort by a variety of Progressive intellectuals—from Jane Addams to W. E. B. Du Bois to Randolph Bourne—to define a strain of Americanism that would both celebrate ethnic and racial difference and nurture a unified civic culture. Stephen Whitfield offers a close, ironic reading of Henry Luce's famous 1941 editorial that heralded the start of an "American Century." Whitfield argues that the vision expressed in the publisher's manifesto was remarkably liberal in its time and has proved quite prescient in ours.

The next three essays examine vital topics in the making of Americanism during and just after the long Cold War. Mae Ngai explains how liberal scholars and policymakers, most of whom were the children of European immigrants, shaped the epochal 1965 reform of immigration law around a conception of "equal rights" derived from the black freedom movement. This ideological framework unintentionally helped establish regulations that encouraged illegal immigration and failed to consider the particular experiences of the Mexicans and East Asians who began to enter the United States in large numbers. Gary Gerstle analyzes how liberal filmmakers, historians, and politicians sought to reclaim the ideal of the citizen soldier during the post-Vietnam era, one dominated by conservatives. He shows how vital military service remains to the popular conception of what it means to be an American patriot. Finally, Alan Wolfe offers an appreciation of the significance and singularity of the diversity of faiths in the United States, grounded in a history of revivalist Protestantism. He reminds us that public religiosity has always been a central feature of Americanism and argues that its expression has become far more tolerant in recent years.

In the second section of the book—"Americanism in the World"—five scholars make sense of how the national creed and its critics have shaped diplomacy, war, and global culture in the twentieth century and the early years of the twenty-first. Alan McPherson examines the language of betrayed ideals used by American dissidents such as Mark Twain and James Weldon Johnson, who protested U.S. military intervention in East Asia and the Caribbean. McPherson demonstrates that foreign critics of American power did much to shape the course of homegrown dissent against war in the Philippines and Haiti. Jun Furuya charts the painful voyage of Japanese intellectuals who first sought to emulate American ideas and institutions but then made a sharp turn toward viewing them as the font of evil in the Western world. Their arguments anticipated those of a host of recent critics.

Next, Louis Menand and Rob Kroes examine the meaning and uses of Americanism in France, the one Western nation whose claim to the universality of its founding ideals rivals that of its more powerful ally across the Atlantic. Menand contributes a wide-ranging essay about the uses to which French thinkers like Sartre and Camus put *le style americain* that they distilled from the novels of Hemingway, Caldwell, and Faulkner and the crime movies known as *film noir*. His provocative narrative of intellectual history points to an aspect of American "character" that even firm critics of Americanism find seductive and worthy of imitation. Rob Kroes takes his fellow European intellectuals to task for evincing a distaste for products of U.S. mass culture, such as popular films and the Internet, that they refuse to live without. He argues that contemporary French writers who warn against the "American" forces that are threatening the artistic integrity of their nation and that of others fail to grasp how deeply Europeans themselves are implicated in the simultaneous fragmentation and flattening of culture in the postmodern world.

Melani McAlister concludes the second section with an interpretive narrative about one of the most provocative issues on the global battleground of gender politics. Her topic is the charged debate that took place in the 1970s and 1980s between American feminists and their Arab counterparts over the practice of clitoridectomy. McAlister illuminates how, in their sexual views, advocates of woman's liberation from the United States combined transnational humanitarian concerns with blinkered assumptions about other cultures.

This anthology sheds light on the ways in which scholars are coming to terms with one of the most controversial, as well as more contested, ideologies in the modern world. Too often, Americanism has been a battle cry, a smug assumption, a curse, or a cliché. These essays demonstrate how rich and conflictual its history has been. The authors offer a broad range of interpretations of the role Americanism has played in the history of the United States and in its dealings with other nations. As editors, we made no attempt to advance one point of view or to choose contributors with a uniform vision.

Yet we are not just scholars of a phenomenon that has attracted, repelled, and intrigued millions throughout its history. We are also citizens concerned about the future of our nation. We cannot, therefore, avoid taking a stand ourselves.[26]

In our opinion, the ideals of Americanism deserve not just to endure but to be revived and practiced as the foundation of a new kind of progressive politics. The quality of our democracy, the health of our pluralistic culture, and the role our nation plays in the world all hinge on our ability to recreate Americanism in the years ahead. The national ideology will continue to flourish, whether or not it is embraced by the left. But if progressives—as scholars and citizens—wish to play a significant role in shaping this nation's future, they must learn again how to speak in terms of ideals they share with other Americans.

When intellectuals on the left abandoned this project—believing it was an obstacle to achieving a humane, democratic society—they also lost the ability to speak convincingly to their fellow citizens and thus to pose convincing alternatives for the nation as a whole. Although these intellectuals can take credit for spearheading a multicultural, gender-aware revision of the humanities, their record outside the academy has been far less impressive. The right set the political agenda, in part because its partisans spoke forcefully in the name of American principles that knit together for mutual ends such disparate groups as anti-union businessmen, white evangelicals, Jewish neoconservatives, and traditionalist Catholics.

In the face of such evidence, many progressives would respond that civic idealism should not be confined within national borders. In a provocative 1994 essay, the philosopher Martha Nussbaum argued that patriotism is "morally dangerous" because it encourages Americans to focus on their own concerns and minimize or disregard those of people in other lands. "We should regard our deliberations," she wrote, "as, first and foremost, deliberations about human problems of people in particular concrete situations, not problems growing out of a national identity that is altogether unlike that of others."[27] Echoing her words, activists and intellectuals muse about challenging global exploitation with some form of global citizenship.

Nussbaum certainly stands on solid ethical ground. As we have seen in recent years, smug insularity is a grave danger, both to Americans and to the people of other lands. Americans ought to take a massacre in Africa as seriously as one that takes place in lower Manhattan—and demand that their government move rapidly to halt or help to prevent it. But Nussbaum offers no guidance for how global progressives can get the power to carry out their laudable objectives in a world in which political power still resides with nation-states and their governments. No planetary government is on the horizon. Nation-states—and therefore nationalism—will be with us for quite some time. Instead of raging against their persistence, we should view them empathetically, doing what we can to help realize the best rather than the worst possibilities of faith in a country and its people. That project is most pressing, it seems to us, in the world's most powerful nation-state.

Progressive intellectuals need not parrot the Pledge of Allegiance or affix flag pins to their lapels or handbags. But we must do more than rail against patriotic ideals and symbols. For to do so is to wage a losing battle—one that marginalizes us and sets us against the overwhelming majority of Americans for no worthwhile intellectual or political purpose. As Todd Gitlin wrote soon after the attacks of 9/11, "It's time for a patriotism of mutual aid, not just symbolic displays, not catechisms or self-congratulations. It's time to diminish the gap between the nation we love and the justice we also love. It's time for the real America to stand up."[28]

In this spirit, progressives should claim, without pretense or apology, an honorable place in the long line of those who have demanded that Americanism apply to all and have opposed the efforts of those who have tried to reserve its use for privileged groups and belligerent causes. This narrative includes visionary activists from Frederick Douglass to Eugene Debs to Martin Luther King Jr. During the height of the Vietnam War, the winner of the Nobel Peace Prize spoke in a way that can still inspire those who would nurture a progressive version of the national faith. "I oppose the war in Viet Nam because I love America," King said. His most "passionate desire," he declared, was "to see our beloved country stand as the moral example of the world."[29]

Today, it is difficult to strike such a balance between affirmation and self-criticism. Those who trumpet an Americanism of self-righteous expansion struggle against those who view anti-Americanism as the only virtuous posture. But two other national icons suggest how one might embrace Americanism with humility and mobilize behind patriotic ideals without succumbing to a martial spirit. In the fall of 1862, Abraham Lincoln told Congress why emancipation was in the American grain: "In *giving* freedom to the slave, we *assure* freedom to the *free*—honorable alike in what we give, and what we preserve." As historian Ronald C. White comments, "Lincoln shared with his contemporaries a belief in the special destiny of America." But "brooding over the honor and dishonor in his nation's actions, he was unwilling to reduce political rhetoric to national self-congratulation."[30]

Almost half a century later, William James took issue with a warrior's definition of Americanism. "The deadliest enemies of nations are not their foreign foes," he wrote, "and from these internal enemies civilization is always in need of being saved. The nation blest above all nations is she in whom the civic genius of the people does its saving day by day."[31] It is our hope that this volume will become both a useful resource and a point of departure for those who hope to revive that "civic genius," a generous Americanism free of the patriotic vanity that Lincoln rejected. Never has our nation or the world been in greater need of such a revival.

NOTES

1. Winthrop quoted in Sydney E. Ahlstrom, *A Religious History of the American People* (New Haven, Conn.: Yale University Press, 1972), 147; Adams quoted in Ernest Lee Tuveson, *Redeemer Nation: The Idea of America's Millennial Role* (Chicago: University of Chicago Press, 1968), 102.

2. Mark A. Noll, *A History of Christianity in the United States and Canada* (Grand Rapids, Mich.: Wm. B. Eerdmans, 1992), 166–70; Mark A. Noll, *America's God: From Jonathan Edward to Abraham Lincoln* (New York: Oxford University Press, 2002), 9–11; Nathan Hatch, *The Democratization of American Christianity* (New Haven, Conn.: Yale University Press, 1989).

3. William Leggett, a newspaper editor in New York City, quoted in Russell Hanson, *The Democratic Imagination in America: Conversations with Our Past* (Princeton, N.J.: Princeton University Press, 1985), 128.

4. *David Walker's Appeal, in Four Articles: Together with a Preamble to the Coloured Citizens of the World, but in Particular, and Very Expressly, to Those of the United States of America*, rev. ed. (New York: Hill and Wang, 1995), 75; Garrison quoted in *William Lloyd Garrison and the Fight against Slavery*, ed. William E. Cain (New York: Bedford Books of St. Martin's Press, 1995), 36; Frederick Douglass, "What to the Slave Is the Fourth of July?" (July 5, 1852), <http://douglassarchives.org/doug_a10.htm>.

5. Douglass, "What to the Slave . . ."

6. Schurz quoted in Willi Paul Adams, *The German Americans: An Ethnic Experience*, translated and adapted by LaVern J. Rippley and Eberhard Reichmann, <http://www.ulib.iupui.edu/kade/adams/cover.html>.

7. Michael Walzer, *What It Means to Be An American* (New York: Marsilio, 1992), 59; Cecilia Elizabeth O'Leary, *To Die For: The Paradox of American Patriotism* (Princeton, N.J.: Princeton University Press, 1999), 161 and passim; Nick Salvatore, *Eugene V. Debs: Citizen and Socialist* (Urbana: University of Illinois Press, 1982), 153.

8. See Gary Gerstle, *American Crucible: Race and Nation in the Twentieth Century* (Princeton, N.J.: Princeton University Press, 2001), 14–94; Stephen Vaughan, *Holding Fast the Inner Lines: Democracy, Nationalism, and the Committee on Public Information* (Chapel Hill: University of North Carolina Press, 1980), 63.

9. Bryan, "America's Mission," in *Speeches of William Jennings Bryan*, vol. 2 (New York: Funk and Wagnalls, 1909), 16.

10. Quoted in James G. Ryan, *Earl Browder: The Failure of American Communism* (Tuscaloosa: University of Alabama Press, 1997), 104.

11. "On Escalation of Violence in the Middle East: Noam Chomsky Interviewed by Toni Gabric," <http://www.chomsky.info/interviews/20020507.htm>.

12. Alexis de Tocqueville, *Democracy in America*, trans. Arthur Goldhammer (New York: Library of America, 2004); Frederick Jackson Turner, *The Frontier in American History* (New York: Holt, Rinehart and Winston, 1962).

13. On Beard, see the lengthy discussion in Richard Hofstadter, *The Progressive Historians: Turner, Beard, Parrington* (New York: Knopf, 1968). The relevant study by David M. Potter is *People of Plenty: Economic Abundance and the American Character* (Chicago: University of Chicago Press, 1954); for a critique of Potter's work, see David Stannard, "American Historians and the Idea of National Character: Some Problems and Prospects," *American Quarterly* 23 (May 1971): 202–20. The relevant books by Hofstadter and Hartz are Richard Hofstadter, *The American Political Tradition and the Men Who Made It* (New York: Knopf, 1948), and Louis Hartz, *The Liberal Tradition in America: An Interpretation of American Political Thought since the Revolution* (New York: Harcourt, Brace, 1955). For a pithy summary from a British perspective, see D. W. Brogan, *The American Character* (New York: Vintage, 1956). Among influential studies of this type, Daniel Boorstin's trilogy, *The Americans* (1958–73), is a rare celebration of its subject. For a witty contemporary perspective on some of these issues, see David Brooks, *On Paradise Drive: How We Live Now (and Always Have) in the Future Tense* (New York: Simon and Schuster, 2004).

14. Ernest Tuveson, *Redeemer Nation: The Idea of America's Millennial Role* (Chicago:

University of Chicago Press, 1968); William Appleman Williams, *The Tragedy of American Diplomacy* (New York: Dell, 1962). Also see Sacvan Bercovitch, *The American Jeremiad* (Madison: University of Wisconsin Press, 1978).

15. Gary Gerstle, *Working-Class Americanism: The Politics of Labor in a Textile City, 1914–1960* (Cambridge: Cambridge University Press, 1989); O'Leary, *To Die For.*

16. Benedict Anderson, *Imagined Communities: Reflections on the Origins and Spread of Nationalism*, rev. ed. (New York: Verso, 1991); E. J. Hobsbawm, *Nations and Nationalism since 1780: Programme, Myth, Reality* (Cambridge: Cambridge University Press, 1990); Linda Colley, *Britons: Forging the Nation, 1707–1837* (New Haven, Conn.: Yale University Press, 1992).

17. Matthew Frye Jacobson, *Barbarian Virtues: The U.S. Encounter with Foreign Peoples at Home and Abroad, 1876–1917* (New York: Hill and Wang, 2001), 5; Amy Kaplan, *The Anarchy of Empire in the Making of U.S. Culture* (Cambridge, Mass.: Harvard University Press, 2002), 17, 16.

18. James Kloppenberg, "Aspirational Nationalism in America," *Intellectual History Newsletter* 24 (2002): 60–71; Richard Rorty, *Achieving Our Country* (Cambridge, Mass.: Harvard University Press, 1998); David Hollinger, *Postethnic America: Beyond Multiculturalism*, rev. ed. (New York: Basic Books, 2000); Eric Foner, *The Story of American Freedom* (New York: Norton, 1998); Walzer, *What It Means to Be an American*; Alan Wolfe, *Return to Greatness* (Princeton, N.J.: Princeton University Press, 2005). William A. Galston, *The Practice of Liberal Pluralism* (Cambridge: Cambridge University Press, 2005). Also see Gerstle's *American Crucible*, which focuses on the enduring conflict between an inclusive "civic nationalism" and a more exclusive "racial" variety.

19. Anatol Lieven, *America Right or Wrong: An Anatomy of American Nationalism* (New York: Oxford University Press, 2004), 73. For a large sample of the popular response to 9/11, see the website developed by the Center for History and New Media, <http://911digitalarchive.org/>. President George W. Bush quoted from his address to a joint session of Congress, Sept. 20, 2001, <http://www.white house.gov/news/releases/2001/09/20010920-8.html.

20. For a recent summary, see Seymour Martin Lipset, *American Exceptionalism: A Double-Edged Sword* (New York: Norton, 1996).

21. See the critiques of Lipset's book and of the notion of exceptionalism more generally in *American Historical Review* 102 (June 1997). Major sources of this critique were Edward Said, *Orientalism* (New York: Pantheon, 1978), and *The Invention of Tradition*, ed. Eric Hobsbawm and Terence Ranger (New York: Cambridge University Press, 1983).

22. Bender's forthcoming book on this subject is tentatively titled *In the American Province*; Janice Radway, "What's in a Name? Presidential Address to the Ameri-

can Studies Association, 20 November, 1998," *American Quarterly* 51 (1999): 22, 16–17; David A. Hollinger, "The Historian's Use of the United States and Vice Versa," in *Rethinking American History in a Global Age*, ed. Thomas Bender (Berkeley: University of California Press, 2002), 381.

23. Charles Bright and Michael Geyer, "Where in the World Is America? The History of the United States in the Global Age," in *Rethinking American History in a Global Age*, ed. Bender, 72.

24. Hollinger, "Historian's Use of the United States," 382–83.

25. There are also influences that run in the other direction: Simone de Beauvoir's work was an important intellectual catalyst for American feminists, and anticolonial struggles in Africa helped inspire the U.S. civil rights movement.

26. Some sentences in the following paragraphs are adapted from Michael Kazin, "A Patriotic Left," *Dissent*, Fall 2002, 41–44.

27. Martha Nussbaum, "Patriotism and Cosmopolitanism," in *For Love of Country?* (Boston: Beacon Press, 1996), 7.

28. Todd Gitlin, "Varieties of Patriotic Experience," in *The Fight Is For Democracy*, ed. George Packer (New York: Perennial, 2003), 138.

29. Martin Luther King Jr., "The Casualties of the War in Viet Nam," speech given in Los Angeles, Calif., February 25, 1967, <http://www.stanford.edu/group/King/publications/speeches/unpub/670225-001_The_Casualties_of_the_War_in_Vietnam.htm>.

30. Abraham Lincoln, Second Annual Message to Congress, December 1, 1862; Ronald C. White Jr., *Lincoln's Greatest Speech: The Second Inaugural* (New York: Simon and Schuster, 2002), 159.

31. William James, "Robert Gould Shaw," in *Memories and Studies* (1912), quoted in Jonathan M. Hansen, *The Lost Promise of Patriotism: Debating American Identity, 1890–1920* (Chicago: University of Chicago Press, 2003), x.

I

Whose America?

★ ★ ★ ★

★ See Your Declaration Americans!!!

★ *Abolitionism, Americanism, and the Revolutionary*

★ *Tradition in Free Black Politics*

Sometime during the eventful year of 1776, a mulatto man named Lemuel Haynes sat down and composed his own addition to the Declaration of Independence: a manuscript entitled "Liberty Further Extended."[1] A Massachusetts resident and fervent patriot, the twenty-three-year-old Haynes might have also used the title to describe the course of his own life up to that point. Raised in indentured servitude, and released in 1774, Haynes had lent his own newly gained liberty to the defense of American freedom. He served as a minuteman that year and enlisted in the Continental army in 1776; when he contracted typhus, his military career came to an end. Haynes had no complaints about his military service but clearly thought the patriot cause was incomplete. Heading his manuscript with the preamble to the Declaration of Independence, which had been issued that summer, Haynes joined the founding fathers in condemning British "tyrony," but called for self-scrutiny as well: "While we are Engaged in the important struggle," he wrote, "it cannot Be tho't impertinent for us to turn an eye into our own Breast, for a little moment, and See, whether thro some inadvertency, or a self-contracted Spirit, we Do not find the monster Lurking in our own Bosom." At a time when his countrymen were "zelous to maintain and foster our own invaded rights," Haynes observed, a much "greater oppression" than "that which Englishmen seem so much to spurn at" existed among them: "the practice of *Slave-keeping*." The problem was as obvious as its remedy, Haynes contended, outlining his "main proposition: . . . That an *African* or, in other terms, *that a Negro may Justly Challenge, and has an undeniable right to his* ['free(dom)' is blotted out] Liberty: *Consequently, the practice of Slave-keeping is illegal.*"[2]

Lemuel Haynes was by no means alone in questioning the legitimacy of slavery in the new republic. From the dawn of the American colonists' conflict with Britain, both black and white Americans had difficulty reconciling natural rights ideology with servitude. "The Colonists are by the law of nature free born, as indeed all men are, white or black," pondered Massachusetts attorney James Otis in his widely circulated revolutionary manifesto, *The Rights of the British Colonies Asserted and Proved* (1764): "Does it follow that 'tis right to enslave a man because he is black?" Otis thought not, and named the slave trade as one of Britain's many crimes against liberty. "Nothing better can be said in favor of a trade that is the most shocking violation of the law of nature, has a direct tendency to diminish the idea of the inestimable value of liberty, and makes every dealer in it a tyrant, from the director of an African company to the petty chapman in needles and pins on the unhappy coast," he wrote. "It is a clear truth that those who every day barter away other men's liberty will soon care little for their own."[3]

Unlike Haynes, however, Otis and other white patriots did not see the abolition of slavery as a central goal of the new republic. Antislavery sentiment was widespread during the revolutionary era and generated considerable consensus against American participation in the African slave trade. But the importation of slaves was the only aspect of slavery as it was practiced in the United States that the white men who led the American Revolution even contemplated abolishing at the Constitutional Convention in 1787. And rather than requiring its abolition, the Constitution they wrote prohibited Congress from banning the slave trade before 1808, and did not require it to end thereafter—laying a very tentative sanction on a form of commerce already on its "last economic legs."[4] To be sure, antislavery activity was more vigorous on the state level, as well as among individual whites. The decades after the Revolution saw the passage of a series of gradual emancipation laws, which eventually ended slavery in the northern states. Likewise, these years witnessed a wave of manumissions undertaken by slaveholders in both the North and the upper South who were moved to renounce bondage by the liberating influences of the Revolution and/or the Great Awakening—which posed its own evangelical challenges to the sin of slavery. But despite slavery's uneasy relationship with both evangelical Christianity and republican ideology, white antislavery activists of the revolutionary era, as Patricia Bradley notes, "failed to make the issue central to national identity."[5]

The same, however, cannot be said of the nation's black population, for whom, as Benjamin Quarles has observed, the Revolution was "truly revolutionary."[6] Among the enslaved, the Revolution fostered what Gary Nash has called "the largest slave uprising in American history," inspiring tens of thousands of bondsmen and bondswomen to flee their masters for the British.[7] Moreover, it had an equally profound effect among the black

Americans who remained with the patriots. The American Revolution, as we see in the writings of Lemuel Haynes, offered African Americans new conceptions of liberty and natural rights, which informed and defended their attempts to liberate themselves as a people.

Long before 1776, as Peter Wood has noted, the experience of enslavement very likely ensured that "African-Americans thought longer and harder than any other sector of the population about the concept of liberty, both as an abstract ideal and as a tangible reality."[8] Not until the Revolution, however, did they acquire a powerful and commonly accepted lingua franca that could express their aspirations for liberty. Inextricably entwined with American nationality from the very start, black abolitionism took shape during the revolutionary era and encompassed not only challenges to the legality of slavery in the new republic, such as the one posed by Haynes, but also the long black struggle for freedom and civil rights in the new northern states. Looking back on that struggle in 1844, the ever-eloquent black abolitionist and physician James McCune Smith observed that "freedom . . . has bound us to American institutions with a tenacity that nothing but death can overcome."[9]

Black Americanism and black abolitionism, however, are rarely discussed in tandem in scholarship on African American thought or abolitionism.[10] The convergence between these two inextricably entwined elements of African American intellectual history is all too often lost in a historiography on black thought that assesses much of nineteenth-century black thought and politics in relationship to black rather than American nationalism and a historiography of abolitionism that typically begins with William Lloyd Garrison's conversion to a commitment to the immediate abolition of slavery in 1830s.[11] Unlike the history of white abolitionism, which usually starts with Garrison's rejection of gradual emancipation and schemes for the African colonization of American blacks, black abolitionism has no canonical story of its origins. Recent revisionist works on abolitionism have begun to stress the central role free blacks played in Garrison's conversion to immediatism, which, although acknowledged by Garrison, has not always been recognized by historians.[12] Still, the question of exactly where the African Americans who influenced Garrison got their ideas remains underexplored. Studies of black abolitionism such as Benjamin Quarles's *Black Abolitionists* (1969), Jane H. Pease and William H. Pease's *They Who Would Be Free: The Black Search for Freedom, 1830–1861* (1974), and Patrick Rael's *Black Identity and Protest in the Antebellum North* (2002) pick up in the antebellum era. Written over a span of more than thirty years, all three books locate the beginning of this movement in free black opposition to the American Colonization Society (ACS), a white organization founded in 1816 that was dedicated to sending free blacks to Africa.[13]

The story may well begin earlier, however. The black anticolonization movement that mobilized shortly after the ACS's inaugural meeting drew on antislavery conceptions of America that African Americans had championed since the very dawn of the revolutionary era. Forged in a crucible of slavery, servitude, and racial discrimination, African American ideas about liberty and the new nation were all the more powerful for being so difficult to realize and gave coherence and character to the long black struggle for abolition. This essay explores the foundations of black Americanism and abolitionism, tracing the multitude of links between the two.

The Same Principle Lives in Us:
The Impact of Revolutionary Ideology on American Blacks

The connections were obvious enough at the time. In the decades immediately preceding and following the Revolution, regardless of whether they fought in its battles, African Americans could not help but be aware of the emancipatory ideology that fueled American resistance to British rule. As Sylvia Frey comments, "Blacks, slave and free, urban and rural, artisan and field hand, were swept up by the force of the ideological energy."[14] Almost universally poor, and largely enslaved, black Americans had little direct interest in revenue stamps or sugar duties. But the idea of natural rights held an obvious appeal among the most unfree of Americans. As early as 1765, for example, the rhetoric of revolution sparked the imagination of a group of slaves in Charleston, South Carolina. Not long after watching a white mob protesting the Stamp Act with cries of "Liberty! Liberty and stamp'd paper," they adapted the slogan to their own situation, throwing whites into a panic with calls for "Liberty." South Carolina politician Henry Laurens, who recorded this incident, dismissed the slaves' chant as "a thoughtless imitation" of whites. But a rising tide of slave unrest in Charleston and beyond would prove him wrong. The year 1775 saw the Charleston militia mobilizing against not only the possibility of a British invasion but also "any hostile attempts that may be made by our domestics."[15]

Likewise, the small population of blacks in the North, who lived in close quarters with whites, proved equally receptive to discussions of revolutionary politics. Exposed to discussions of natural and inalienable rights among the whites with whom they lived, as well in the taverns, town halls, and marketplaces of the North, northern blacks embraced the principles of the Revolution as an expression of their own heartfelt political desires. "In every human Breast," the young black poet Phillis Wheatley wrote a long-time correspondent in 1774, "God has implanted a Principle, which we call Love of Freedom; it is impatient of Oppression, and pants for Deliverance; and by the Leave of our modern Egyptians I will assert, that the same Principle lives in us"—a sentiment borne out by the poetry she wrote as a slave. Moreover, Wheatley, along with many other revolutionary-era Americans, had no trouble spotting the contradictions between the colonists' demands for freedom from Britain and their determination to uphold slavery: "How well the Cry for Liberty, and the reverse Disposition for the exercise of oppressive Power over others agree,—I humbly think it does not require the Penetration of a Philosopher to determine," she observed.[16]

Emancipated by her owner in 1773, Phillis Wheatley critiqued this contradiction in a public letter; other blacks who remained enslaved felt compelled to challenge it still more directly. Starting in 1771, northern blacks began to petition their local legislatures for freedom, often making explicit reference to the political principles that animated American opposition to Britain.[17] "We expect great things from men who have made such a noble stand against the design of their *fellow-men* to enslave them," a group of blacks told the Boston legislature that year in a bid to be allowed to purchase their own freedom.[18] Black petitioners for "the Enjoyments of that which is the Natural Right of all men" grew more radical over time, warning that emancipation was required so that "the Inhabitance of this Stats No longer [be] chargeable with the inconsistency of acting themselves in the part which they condemn and oppose in others." They also dropped their offers to pay for their freedom: Connecticut blacks who petitioned in 1779 noted that "we ask for nothing; but what we are fully persuaded is ours to Claim."[19] Moreover, slave petitioners also took their claims to the enemy. Between 1773 and 1774, British general Thomas Gage received several petitions from "a grate number of blacks," all of whom promised to "fight for him providing he would arm them and engage to liberate them if he conquered"—an offer that Abigail Adams described to her husband John Adams as a "conspiracy of the Negroes."[20]

None of these petitions succeeded. Still, by June 1775, Thomas Gage had begun to advocate the British recruitment of blacks, and, five months later, John Murray, the earl of Dunmore and royal governor of Virginia, issued a proclamation offering freedom to slaves who supported the British cause—an offer that as many as one hundred thousand southern slaves would ultimately take up.[21]

Meanwhile, in the North, African American challenges to slavery also had far-reaching effects. In the decades following the Revolution, most northern states passed gradual emancipation laws—although Vermont abolished slavery by constitutional fiat in 1777, and slavery was declared illegal in Massachusetts and New Hampshire by way of a long and confusing series of court cases. In part, these laws reflected the antislavery sentiment of revolutionary-era white northerners. Yet the death of slavery in the North was by no means a purely legislative matter decided by whites. On the contrary, one of the most striking features of America's first emancipation was the central role that African Americans played in securing the abolition of slavery in the North. A practical fact during the revolutionary era, black abolitionism encompassed far more than the challenges to slavery seen in slave petitions and the writings of Lemuel Haynes. African American efforts to bring about the immediate end of slavery are also seen in the multitude of routes to freedom black Americans managed to forge during the revolutionary era—both legal and otherwise.

As we have seen, even before the American Revolution, slavery was under siege from within in both the North and South. Slave freedom suits and petitions for liberty proliferated during the 1770s and 1780s, as did slave runaways, all of which helped pave the way for passage of gradual emancipation laws in the North. Well before slavery was legally abolished in Massachusetts, as Joanne Melish notes, "antislavery petitions, suits, and litigation combined to undermine whites' confidence in their property rights" while also emboldening "enslaved persons of color to demand manumission or wage compensation from their owners—or to simply walk away from them." Indeed, according to Massachusetts resident John Adams, as early as 1768, slaves there had become "lazy, idle, proud, vicious and at length wholly useless to their masters, to such as degree that the abolition of slavery became a measure of economy."[22]

Adams's view of abolition as an economy measure, however, was far from universally shared. Although America's free black population increased dramatically during the revolutionary era, emancipation did not come easily to many who gained it. For all that slave manumissions increased dramatically in the North and upper South during this time, most of the African Americans who won their freedom during the revolutionary era did so at least partly by their own efforts.

By far the largest initial wave of emancipation was created by the slaves themselves. According to Thomas Jefferson, thirty thousand enslaved blacks sought liberty when British troops invaded Virginia in 1781—a figure that represented approximately half the new state's male slave population. And South Carolina saw similar losses during the British southern campaigns between 1779 and 1781.[23] Most southern slaves who joined the British did not end up in the North, however. Thousands died of "camp fever, malnutrition and battle wounds," while those who survived were evacuated along with other loyalists and resettled in British territories, such as Florida, Jamaica, and Nova Scotia.[24] However, the large numbers of northern slaves who were runaways neither joined the British nor left with them. For example, Crispus Attucks, whose death in the Boston Massacre of 1770 had made him legendary as the first casualty of the American Revolution, was an escapee—albeit not a recent runaway, having been a fugitive for some twenty years.[25] More to the point, many northern slave runaways stayed in place, assuming a freedom that was ultimately realized under law.

Meanwhile, many of the black northerners who did not run away or join the British achieved their freedom by fighting for the patriot cause. The exact number of blacks who served in the Continental army is unknown. Eighteenth-century muster rolls did not usually record race, and most black soldiers served in integrated units. But at least five thousand African Americans are estimated to have fought on the American side.[26] Among them were free blacks, such as the young Lemuel Haynes, but still more were slaves fighting on two fronts. Often enlisted as substitutes for their white owners, slaves typically received freedom in return for their service.

Many revolutionary leaders, including Virginia slaveholder George Washington, had profound reservations about the enlistment of blacks in general and slaves in particular. But as popular enthusiasm for the conflict faded after 1775, soldiers of any color were desperately needed, and slave enlistment came to seem a necessity. Washington's initial attempt to bar black enlistment when he assumed command of the American army in 1775 never took effect. Troops from Massachusetts, who fought many of the war's first battles, were integrated from the start, and after 1776 other states in both the North and South began to use slave soldiers to fill enlistment quotas. Only South Carolina and Georgia barred black enlistment, a policy that the Continental Congress made an unsuccessful attempt to alter in 1779 with a resolution requesting "three thousand able bodied negroes." Congress offered generous compensation to the "proprietor of such negroes"—up to $1,000 for each man who qualified for enlistment—while planning to reward the blacks themselves with emancipation and a less generous sum of $50, but the plan went nowhere.[27] Predicting "terrible consequences," the two states refused, and the following year the poorly fortified city of Charleston fell to the British—undefended by the black troops that Congress had sought to raise.[28]

Still, black soldiers were common enough elsewhere. Often enlisted for extended terms of service, they were so ubiquitous that many American commentators did not remark on their presence. But foreign observers often took note of their numbers. One Hessian mercenary who encountered them on the battlefield wrote, "The Negro can take the field instead of his master; therefore, no regiment is seen in which there are not negroes in abundance, and among them are able bodies, strong and brave fellows."[29]

Service in the Continental army brought African American soldiers not only freedom but also an enduring sense of entitlement to liberties for which the war had been fought. Even before the war was won, black veterans, such as Prince Whipple, joined other New Hampshire slaves in petitioning to demand black freedom "for the sake of justice, liberty, and the rights of mankind."[30] The African-born Whipple, who served with Washington, is now primarily known as the black soldier in the front of Emanuel Leutze's famous 1851 painting, *Washington Crossing the Delaware*, which commemorates the American victory in the 1776 battle of Trenton— although his actual presence there is now disputed.[31] But as of 1779, Whipple coupled his loyalty to the Revolution with other loyalties by signing a petition to the New Hampshire legislature that called for the extension of the Revolution's principles to all Americans. "Freedom is an inherent right of the human species," the New Hampshire petitioners wrote, "not to be surrendered, but by consent, for the sake of social life."[32]

Similar revolutionary principles and black claims to the revolutionary tradition provided the foundation for subsequent black activism, starting with the long struggle for freedom and civil rights in the new northern states. First came the battles to achieve gradual emancipation, which was not easily accomplished in states where slavery was a viable economic institution. As late as 1810, more than a quarter of blacks in the North remained enslaved; and, both before and after that, many African Americans had to fight to claim the eventual emancipation offered to them under northern state laws.[33] The gradual emancipation plans instituted in Pennsylvania, Connecticut, Rhode Island, New York, and New Jersey between 1780 and 1804 were all designed to minimize disruption to the labor force and compensate the slaveholders by granting them the right to the lifelong labor of slaves in their possession and the uncompensated labor of these slaves' children through adulthood. Such laws, as Ira Berlin notes, "assured that the demise of slavery would be a slow, torturous process."[34]

Blacks in these areas still did what they could to speed the process of emancipation through flight and negotiation. In New York, for example, despite the limitations of its 1799 gradual emancipation law—which freed only the children of slaves and required them to serve a lengthy indenture prior to emancipation—"slaves throughout [the] state saw the law as a sign that whites recognized black people's rights to freedom." Indeed, the 1799 law may have spurred slave escapes, historian Leslie Harris suggests, and also fostered successful negotiating on the part of adult slaves to limit the terms of their servitude by indenture or cash payment. "Although such practices depended on the flexibility of the slave owner," she notes, "they became more common after the passage of the 1799 law, hastening slavery's decline in the first decades of the nineteenth-century ahead of the schedule laid out in the law."[35]

When slave owners were uncooperative, or sought to bypass gradual emancipation altogether by way of a variety of schemes that included selling their slaves to southern slaveholders—an illegal but not uncommon practice—emancipation was even more hard won. Northern blacks protested and resisted these tactics. In addition to challenging their owners' actions in court, they sought support from early white antislavery societies such as the Pennsylvania Abolition Society (PAS) and the New York Society for Promoting the Manumission of Slaves, and Protecting Them as Have Been or May Be Liberated, founded in 1775 and 1784 respectively. Moderate organizations that discouraged or excluded black members—and in some cases welcomed slaveholding members—these organizations are not usually linked to black activism. But they did offer legal aid to blacks facing illegal enslavement, many of whom sought out their help.

Collaborations between white antislavery societies and black litigants protesting illegal enslavement may well constitute the earliest form of interracial abolitionism, and they provide important insights into the ways in which the black freedom struggle helped shape the activities of these white organizations. In a recent work on the origins of American abolitionism, Richard Newman writes that the PAS first established its legal aid system in response to "the explosion of black complaints following the American Revolution," and they became increasingly active in the courts thereafter as such complaints continued: "Throughout the 1790s and early 1800s, in fact,

PAS legal action paralleled black complaints in and out of the Quaker state. In the 1810s, for instance, as black concerns about kidnapping grew (due in part to the banning of the overseas trade) the PAS became much more active on the matter in state and federal courts. As fugitive slaves increasingly sought refuge in Pennsylvania during the 1820s and 1830s, Pennsylvania abolitionists devised new strategies to deal with them."[36]

Interracial cooperation, however, had distinct limits in the early national period. Blacks were almost wholly unsuccessful at securing white aid to gain, or even retain, other citizenship rights—an area in which they lost ground during this period. Indeed, as the North's free black population grew during the decades following the Revolution, white northerners mobilized a variety of proscriptive practices and discriminatory laws to contain a freed population increasingly regarded as inferior by nature. Free black suffrage, for example, contracted as the North's free black population grew. In the immediate aftermath of the Revolution, many northern state constitutions did not ban black voting—a right also granted to propertied free blacks in North Carolina, Maryland, and Tennessee. But African Americans lost the vote in New Jersey in 1807, in Connecticut in 1814, in Rhode Island in 1822, and in Pennsylvania in 1842. Meanwhile, New York retained forbiddingly high property requirements for black voters, even after abolishing all property requirements for white voters in 1821. Moreover, racial prejudice seemingly escalated over these years, which also saw the expulsion of blacks from white churches, the beginnings of segregation laws in many northern states, bans on black immigration to the Midwest, and the growing exclusion of black workers from skilled jobs of any kind.[37] Among other things, this web of discrimination was one of the powerful consequences of slavery's "slow demise." The gradual and contested process by which emancipation took place, according to Ira Berlin, "handicapped the efforts of black people to secure households of their own, to find independent employment, and to establish their own institutions. It gave former slaveholders time to construct new forms of subordination that prevented the integration of black people as equals."[38]

Still, as the foregoing discussion suggests, the lengthy and contested abolition of slavery in the North may have had other, less tragic implications, for the black community. Whatever its limitations, gradual emancipation fueled the growth of the northern free black community that took shape alongside the nation itself and would provide crucial manpower and leadership in the abolitionist crusade to come. Making up a population of 27,109 in 1790, the number of free blacks in the North would increase fourfold by 1830, reaching 137,529.[39] As American as it was African, this community was shaped by a history of bondage in America and an enduring commitment to the egalitarian principles to which the new nation was at least rhetorically committed. Such principles provided the foundation for the black struggle for emancipation in the post-Revolution North, and they remained enduringly relevant to black northerners thereafter.

To a far greater degree than is usually acknowledged, black struggles for liberty in the North formed a crucial context for the black anticolonization struggle that gave birth to the abolitionist movement of the antebellum era. By far the most important right fought for by black activists prior to the anticolonization movement was personal freedom, which was hard won. As we have seen, northern slavery did not simply expire: it was defeated through both legislative challenges and unending black opposition. And no one understood this better than early nineteenth-century blacks, for whom the victory was recent, triumphant, and long in coming. On the heels of this victory, free black opposition to colonization did not rouse a politically quiescent community but one that had just emerged from a long and formative struggle. Hindsight has sometimes fostered a view of the early nineteenth-century free black community as a powerless and poorly organized group buffeted by an increasingly large web of racial restrictions, who had little claim to American citizenship. But it is far from clear that African Americans ever viewed themselves in such terms. Northern black opposition to colonization was fueled by decades of active pursuit of American rights and freedoms on the part of free blacks.

Never Forgotten by Us:
The Legacy of the Revolution in the Antebellum Black Freedom Struggle

This experience came in handy after 1816, when free blacks mobilized to oppose the American Colonization Society. Often credited with having "originated abolitionism" by galvanizing black opposition to both colonization and slavery, the ACS was a white organization dedicated to sending blacks back to Africa, with the idea of someday ending slavery. Its reverse diaspora did not begin with the slaves, however. Instead, the ACS targeted only free blacks for immediate colonization, an agenda that inspired widespread suspicion and alarm among free blacks, along with questions about ACS's ostensibly emancipationist goals.[40] The ACS's role in galvanizing black opposition to slavery cannot be denied, but this opposition did not come out of nowhere. Rather, the black anticolonization movement took shape around the reiteration and amplification of long-standing African American claims to American ancestry, rights, and destiny—heartfelt claims that help explain northern free blacks' outraged response to the ACS. An Americanizing influence on northern blacks, the anticolonization movement both drew on and nourished antislavery conceptions of America that African Americans had championed since the very dawn of the revolutionary era.

Among other things, the very different reception of the ACS across the color line illustrates the gulf between white and black conceptions of American identity that had emerged in the aftermath of the Revolution. Abhorred from the start by free blacks, the ACS was popular and influential among a broad spectrum of whites, including some slaveholders—a fact that further confirmed free black suspicions about the organization. As conservative as it sounds today, the ACS was, in many respects, not that different from other early national white antislavery societies, such as the Pennsylvania Society for Promoting the Abolition of Slavery. Located mostly but not exclusively in the northern states, these societies coalesced around religious opposition to slavery as a sin for which "God would eventually exact retribution."[41] Most restricted their membership to whites and called for a gradual compensated emancipation, which would bring a peaceful end to slavery without compromising the property rights of slaveholders. Moderate, conciliatory, and increasing moribund as revolutionary antislavery sentiment faded among whites, most of these societies soon came to support the ACS, which, in promoting the colonization of free blacks, promised to rid America of both black people and slavery.

The ACS's vision of a white America cleansed of both slavery and black people met little support among free blacks, who suspected that the ACS's plans did not provide for the actual eradication of slavery. A dangerous shadow on their newfound, hard-fought, and insecure liberties, the Colonization Society's agenda seemed to threaten the wholesale deportation of the free black community. A meeting organized by Philadelphia black leaders to discuss the ACS's plans, held just weeks after the society first convened, attracted 3,000 people, of whom "not one sole [sic] . . . was in favor of going to Africa."[42]

In rejecting repatriation, free blacks expressed an American identity crafted through decades of struggle and made confident by the recent achievement of emancipation in the northern states. Participants in one of the early anticolonization meetings in Philadelphia denounced the ACS's plans as an anathema. Declaring their resolve not to cooperate, they noted that the "plan of colonizing the free people of color of the United States on the coast of Africa . . . [was] not asked for by us: nor will it be required by any circumstance, in our future or present condition, as long as we are permitted to share the excellent laws and just government which we now enjoy, in common with every individual in the community." Moreover, although they deplored the fact that many of their "brethren" remained enslaved, they expressed great optimism about the future of blacks in America. Despite their fears that colonization was a scheme to eliminate free blacks and make the bondage of the slaves perpetual, their own recent history assured them that the antislavery battle could be won. "The ultimate and final abolition of slavery in the United States, by the operation of various causes, is, under the guidance of a just God, progressing," they wrote. "Every year witnesses the release of numbers of the victims of oppression, and affords new and safe assurances that freedom of all will be in the end accomplished. . . . Every year, many of us of us have restored to us by the gradual, but certain march of the cause of abolition—parents, from whom we have long been separated—wives and children whom we had left in servitude—and brothers in blood as well as suffering, from whom we had long been parted."[43]

The anticolonizationist gatherings in Philadelphia marked the beginning of a sustained black protest movement that swept from Boston to Baltimore and ultimately encompassed far more than resistance to the ACS.[44] African American activists lambasted the ACS for casting an "unmerited stigma" on the free black population, which was indeed sometimes characterized as a "dangerous and useless part of the community" in ACS propaganda.[45] Perhaps because of such unflattering characterizations, northern free blacks as a group proved largely immune to the Colonization Society's more tactful overtures. Pioneering a celebration of the "African genius" and the ancient glories of the black race that would not be out of place in contemporary Afrocentric thought, the ACS's official organ, the *African Repository and Colonial Notes*, did its best to convince African Americans that they would be better off in the more hospitable climate of their native land, where "Princes shall soon come of Egypt and Ethiopia shall soon stretch her hands forth to God," as predicted in Psalm 68:31. Not even this vision of the African American redemption of black Africa, however, could lure very many northern blacks to the Liberian Colony that the ACS sought to populate. Of the 2,886 blacks the society managed to send to Africa between 1820 and 1833, only 169 came from the North.[46]

African Americans who rejected colonization stressed their enduring ties to "this Land of Liberty" as the source of their resolution to remain there. Typical was the response of James Forten, a wealthy black Philadelphia sailmaker, who became an early leader of the anticolonization movement. Not initially opposed to the idea of settlements in Africa per se, Forten had supported his friend Paul Cuffe, a black New England merchant and ship captain with whom Forten did business, in his 1815 attempt to establish an African American colony in Sierra Leone. Moreover, he shared Cuffe's early enthusiasm for the ACS, writing to him in January 1817 that black Philadelphians needed to consider colonization because "they will never become a people until they com[e] out from amongst the white people."[47] However, as the ACS gathered steam, Forten soon changed his views. By that summer, he led black Philadelphia's opposition to colonization. What clearly angered Forten most about the ACS's plans was the white colonizationists' assumption that free blacks had no place in America. "My great-grand-father was brought here a slave from Africa," he said in 1833, looking back on his response to the ACS's mandate:

My grandfather obtained his own freedom. My father never wore the yoke. He rendered valuable service to his country during the War of the Revolution; and I, though a boy, was a drummer in that war. . . . I have since lived and labored in a useful employment, have acquired property, and have paid taxes in the city . . . and have brought up and educated a family. . . . Yet some ingenious gentlemen have recently discovered that I am still African; that a continent, three thousand miles, and more, from the place where I was born, is my native country. And I am advised to go home.[48]

One can hardly be surprised by the reaction of this fourth-generation American and third-generation free black, whose closest African relatives were great-grandparents with histories largely unknown to him. More surprising, perhaps, is that Forten's sense of American identity was widely shared among free blacks, not all of whom were as distantly connected with Africa.[49] The three thousand blacks who gathered at the first anti-colonization meeting in Philadelphia condemned the ACS's objective as a measure designed "to exile us from the land of our nativity." Noting that "our ancestors (not of choice) were the first successful cultivators of the wilds of America," they claimed both American soil and American traditions as their own. "We, their descendants feel ourselves entitled to participate in the blessings of her luxuriant soil, which their blood and sweat manured," they maintained, adding that any of expulsion of free blacks "would not only be cruel but in direct violation of those principles, which have been the boast of this Republic."[50]

These black American claims to freedom embraced both a history of bondage in America and an enduring commitment on the part of African Americans to the egalitarian principles around which the United States had recently taken shape. Some early black anticolonizationists, such as James Forten, were not too old to remember the patriotic zeal expressed by black Americans during the American Revolution. Both a witness to and participant in the Revolution during his youth, Forten embodied James McCune Smith's claim that black Americans were bound to American institutions. A lifelong patriot, Forten would maintain that he loved America because he had "drawn the spirit of her free institutions from her mother's breast."[51] Exactly what he meant by this is unclear, but the sentiment is not surprising coming from a man who as a nine-year-old watched the Declaration of Independence being read to the public for the first time in Philadelphia's crowded State House yard.[52] At fourteen, he joined the navy as a powder-boy—his "young heart fired with enthusiasm . . . of the patriots and revolutionaries of that day." In service alongside numerous other black volunteers, Forten could hardly have failed to notice that the American Revolution was not won by whites alone, a fact that must have been underscored for him the following year when he witnessed the Continental army marching through Philadelphia. More than fifty years later, he recalled, "I well remember when the New England Regiments passed through this city to attack the English Army under the command of Lord Cornwallis, there was [sic] several Companies of Coloured People, as brave men as ever fought."[53]

By the 1840s, the story of black service to the patriot cause was all but forgotten among whites, who made no effort "to preserve a record," as one antebellum commentator noted.[54] However, memories such as Forten's remained vivid among African Americans, who handed them down from generation to generation, enshrining the unfulfilled promise of the Revolution as a long overdue legacy, still unattained. Too young to have served in the war, a number of black abolitionists of the antebellum era had fathers who did. One example is Jeremiah Asher, who looked back to the American Revolution as the inspiration for antebellum black struggles.[55] In his autobiography, Asher underscored that his father, Gad Asher, had been a combatant in both the American Revolution and the War of 1812. Of the Revolution he noted, "This eventful period will never be forgotten by us whose fathers fought for liberty not from the yoke of Britain, but from the yoke of American slavery." Black service in the two wars amounted to an unpaid debt, he maintained. "These periods, I say will never be forgotten by us, whose fathers fought, bled and died for the liberty neither they nor their children have received."[56]

The "Unfinished Work": Americanism in Black Thought

Inspired by such sentiments, free blacks in the early republic fought for both liberty and citizenship as rights they shared equally with other Americans. Black suffrage in Massachusetts was first achieved in 1781 after free blacks twice petitioned to either receive representation or be relieved from taxation—a familiar argument that Massachusetts legislators settled in favor of collecting taxes. In later years, however, similar arguments were less effective. Both Jeffersonian-Republicans and the Jacksonian Democrats who were the first heirs to the Jeffersonian political tradition supported increasingly expansive notions of democracy, but only for white males. Naturalization in the growing young nation was limited to white immigrants, who also found it relatively easy to gain the franchise thanks to the gradual abandonment of property requirements—a phenomenon that free blacks found galling. "Foreigners to the government and laws—strangers to our institutions are permitted to flock to this land, and in a few years are endowed with all the privileges of citizenship," the editor of the *Colored American* complained in 1837. "But we, native born Americans, the children of the soil, are most of shut out."[57] A litany of similar black complaints did not stay the rise of what some have called "the white republic."[58]

On the contrary, the antebellum era saw universal white manhood suffrage become the norm as black citizenship rights dwindled—a process culminating in the *Dred Scott* decision of 1857, in which the chief justice of the Supreme Court, Roger B. Taney, famously declared that blacks had "no rights which the white man was bound to respect." Taney believed that both the Constitution and the Declaration of Independence made no reference to African Americans. Of the latter, he concluded: "It is too clear for dispute, that the enslaved African race were not intended to be included, and formed no part of the people who framed and adopted this declaration."[59]

Less well known is the fact that this reading of America's revolutionary tradition was endlessly disputed by African Americans, who insisted that in all matters related to citizenship they were Americans. As we have seen, assertions of an explicitly American identity and a pursuit of American rights and freedoms formed the ideological core of black abolitionism, which began to mobilize during the Revolution itself. Moreover, these visions of America as the homeland in which African Americans were destined to claim liberty only multiplied as the anticolonization movement mobilized. In part, they took shape around colonizationists' assertions that the destiny of African Americans lay in Africa, which, ironically enough, encouraged African Americans to embrace an unequivocally American identity.

Indeed, there is considerable evidence that the colonizationist challenge to the American identity of blacks changed the very names by which African Americans chose to be known as a group. Popular at the start of the nineteenth century, the word "African" as a description for their group fell into disfavor among antebellum-era black northerners as they came to resent the ACS's insistence that they were the eternal "sons of Africa." By the late 1830s, many black northerners, who were largely American born, had begun to oppose any African modifier of their American status, preferring instead to be known by the appellation "colored Americans." The impact of such choices went beyond personal preference, influencing the terms by which the new organizations and newspapers that arose out of antebellum black activism were known. "In complexion, in blood and nativity, we are more exclusively 'American' than our white brethren," New York minister and newspaper editor Samuel Cornish wrote, explaining his decision to change the name of the abolitionist newspaper he began to edit in 1837 from the *Weekly Advocate* to the *Colored American*: "Hence the propriety of the name of our people, Colored Americans, and of the identifying the name with all our institutions, in spite of our enemies, who would rob of us our nationality and reproach as exotics."[60]

Patriotic, but in no way conformist, black claims to American nationality served a variety of subversive ends, as can be seen in David Walker's *Appeal* (1829). A fiery attack on colonization and slavery written by a black abolitionist in Boston, it was addressed to the "*Colored Citizens of the World, But in Particular, and very expressly those of the United States of America.*" In his *Appeal*, Walker laid claim to all American rights and institutions, including the right to revolt as described in the Declaration of Independence. "See your Declaration Americans!!!," he wrote, warning white Americans that a slave rebellion would be neither unmerited nor unprecedented, while also encouraging black Americans to revolt:

Do you understand your own language? Hear your language proclaimed to the world on July 4th, 1776—"We hold these truths to be self-evident— that ALL MEN ARE CREATED EQUAL!! That they *are endowed by their creator with certain inalienable rights*; that among these are life, *liberty*, and the pursuit of happiness!!" . . . Hear your language further! "But when a long train of abuses and usurpation, pursuing invariably the same object, evinces a design to reduce them under absolute despotism, it is their *right*, it is their *duty*, to throw off such government and provide new guards for their future security."[61]

Enlisted in support of both rights and rebellion, Americanism cuts through antebellum black literature and oratory, including seemingly unpatriotic black sources such as Frederick Douglass's famous jeremiad "What, to the Slave, Is the Fourth of July?" Delivered in the dark days after the Compromise of 1850, it reflected Douglass's despair over the apparently growing power of the slaveocracy and the steady erosion of black citizenship rights, as well as the perennial frustration that colored black American nationality in the white republic. "This Fourth of July is *yours*, not *mine*," Douglass mournfully told white Americans. Yet this complaint did not keep him from also laying claim to the legacy of the American Revolution—far from it. He closed by predicting that the Constitution would ultimately be found "entirely hostile to the existence of slavery."[62]

Indeed, even in the troubled political climate of the 1850s, Douglass's veneration of the American tradition only increased over time. In 1851, he parted ways with his longtime mentor, William Lloyd Garrison. Among other things, Douglass disagreed with Garrison that the Constitution was a "proslavery" document.[63] And shortly thereafter Douglass embraced not only the Constitution but also America's revolutionary tradition as the deciding evidence on black citizenship. In his 1853 "Address to the People of the United States" on behalf of the Colored National Convention, Douglass proclaimed: "By birth we are American Citizens; by the principles of the Declaration of Independence we are American citizens; within the meaning of the Constitution we are American citizens; by the hardships and trials endured; by the courage and fidelity displayed by our ancestors in defining the liberties and in achieving independence in our land, we are American citizens." African American citizenship was a legacy of the American Revolution, Douglass went on to argue, glossing over considerable evidence to the contrary. Far from being proslavery, the Constitution was the work of a better era and contained "nothing whatsoever of that watchful malignity which has manifested itself lately in the insertion of the word '*white*,' before the term '*citizen.*'" Indeed, "the word '*white*' was unknown to the framers of the Constitution of the United States in such connections—unknown to the signers of the Declaration of Independence—unknown to the brave men at *Bunker Hill, Ticonderoga, and at Red Bank*. It is a modern word, brought into use by modern legislators, despised in Revolutionary times."[64]

Admittedly, Douglass's review of American history in support of these claims was more strategic than sincere. He knew quite well that the founding fathers had not extended the same privileges and immunities to blacks and whites; he had informed a London audience a few years earlier "that the very men who drew up the Declaration of Independence 'were trafficking in the bodies and souls of their fellow men.'" However, the adamant faith that Douglass expressed in the founding fathers throughout the 1850s reflected his belief that the Constitution was a weapon that "could be wielded in behalf of emancipation," especially in areas where the federal government had exclusive jurisdiction.[65]

Such views went hand in hand with Douglass's advocacy of antislavery politics; a supporter of the Liberty Party as of 1851, and later a Republican, he hoped for legislative action against slavery.[66] Nonetheless, the increasing tendency of antebellum-era black thinkers to claim the American political tradition as a mandate for African American emancipation cannot be dismissed as party politics. For not only do such claims have a long tradition in African American thought—which predates the antislavery political parties of the 1840s and 1850s—they also cut across the work of black intellectuals who supported very different strategies for black emancipation. African American claims to American liberties informed not only the party politics of Frederick Douglass but also David Walker's calls for a slave revolt. Moreover, they are also oddly central to the separatist vision of the famous black nationalist Martin Robinson Delany.

A frequent critic of Frederick Douglass, Delany is best known today for his deep engagement with Africa and his advocacy of emigration in the 1850s—one of the subjects on which he and Douglass disagreed. However, this unlikely advocate of Americanism never let his enthusiasm for Africa and his qualms about the future of blacks in America entirely erode his vision of American citizenship as an African American entitlement. For all his advocacy of mass black emigration from the United States in *The Condition, Elevation, Emigration, and Destiny of the Colored People of United States* (1852), Delaney also insisted throughout that work that African Americans were deeply American. "Our common country is the United States," he wrote in a two-paragraph chapter titled "The United States is our Country. We are Americans, having a birthright citizenship—natural claims upon the country—claims in common with our fellow citizens—natural rights, which may by the virtue of unjust laws, be obstructed, but never annulled."[67] While seemingly at odds with his support elsewhere in the book for black emigration, Delaney's Americanism was central to his black nationalism. As John Ernest notes, "Delaney's argument for leaving the United States is not a denial of African American rights to citizenship but rather an assertion that the United States is not what it claims to be and therefore that the national ideals of political economy must be relocated both racially and geographically."[68]

Ernest's analysis is borne out by the fact that Delany never pursued any of his emigration schemes. Instead, he fought for the Union during the Civil War and pursued a political career in South Carolina during Reconstruction, where he worked to realize the American citizenship he saw as the birthright of the freedmen. Only in the late 1870s, as redeemer governments restored white supremacy across the South, did he again consider African colonization, and even then he did not go himself. A lifelong black nationalist, Delany had a vision that was always centered on America and took shape around the revolutionary ideals that his forebears had long fought to realize. "The world belongs to mankind," he wrote in 1850s, once again undercutting his own advocacy of emigration. "And our present warfare is not upon European rights, nor for European countries; but for the common rights of man, based on the great principles of humanity— taking our chance in the world of rights, and claiming to have originally more right to this continent, than the European race."[69]

Delany's black nationalist writings, along with the words and struggles of generations of African American activists who preceded him, bear out James McCune Smith's observation that freedom forged powerful ties between African Americans and American institutions. All the more powerful for being so difficult to achieve, African American claims to American ideals and institutions shaped both the rhetoric and the goals of black abolitionism. Moreover, thanks to the emergence of biracial support for abolitionism in the 1830s and 1840s, black conceptions of a more-inclusive Americanism ultimately crossed the color line and helped shape an antislavery Republicanism that would prove incompatible with slavery. Lincoln said nothing new to black Americans in his Gettysburg Address. His famous opening only underscored what African Americans had been arguing for almost half a century: the founding fathers' new nation had been "conceived in liberty, and dedicated to the proposition that all men are created equal." Likewise, African Americans had long seen the Revolution as "unfinished work" and wished for a "new birth of freedom"—a project that the Civil War would help begin to realize but remains unfinished to this day.[70]

NOTES

1. Lemuel Haynes, "Liberty Further Extended" (1776), reprinted in *Black Preacher to White America: The Collected Writings of Lemuel Haynes, 1774–1833*, ed. Richard Newman (Brooklyn: Carlson Publishing, 1990). Unpublished during Haynes's lifetime, "Liberty Further Extended" was printed for the first time in 1983 in an article by Ruth Bogin, who discovered the handwritten, undated manuscript in a Harvard University archive. Exactly when Haynes completed this manuscript is unknown. But the title page, which quotes the Declaration of Independence, points to 1776 "as the earliest possible year," while the fact that Haynes makes no reference "to Independence, or to the Americans, or to states," precludes the possibility that it was written much later. On the basis of such evidence, as well as biographical information on Haynes, Bogin is confident that "Liberty Further Extended" can be "assigned to 1776." Intriguingly, she also suggests that the text itself, as opposed to the title page, was "probably composed entirely before the news of the Declaration reached . . . [Haynes's] vicinity in 1776," as the document itself makes no reference to independence. If so, Haynes's manuscript is all the more remarkable, but, lacking real evidence on this point, I hesitate to follow this rather speculative dating of the manuscript and do not assume that the body of the text predates the first page. Ruth Bogin, "Liberty Further Extended: An Antislavery Manuscript by Lemuel Haynes," *William and Mary Quarterly* 40, no. 1 (January 1983): 90. On Haynes's life, see also John Saillant, *Black Puritan, Black Republican: The Life and Thought of Lemuel Haynes, 1753–1833* (New York: Oxford University Press, 2002).

2. Haynes, "Liberty Further Extended," 17, 19.

3. James Otis, *The Rights of the British Colonies Asserted and Proved* (1764), in *Pamphlets of the American Revolution*, ed. Bernard Bailyn (Cambridge, Mass.: Harvard University Press, 1965), 439–40.

4. Winthrop Jordan, *White Over Black: American Attitudes toward the Negro, 1550–1812* (Chapel Hill: University of North Carolina Press, 1968), 323.

5. Patricia Bradley, *Slavery, Propaganda, and the American Revolution* (Jackson: University of Mississippi Press, 1998), 82. A political hot potato among white patriots of all factions, antislavery was taken up primarily as a religious cause by whites in

the new nation. Bradley contends that the religious character of antislavery sentiment among revolutionary-era whites limited its power and influence. Not only did religious arguments against slavery construct bondage as a spiritual rather than a political issue—denouncing slaveholding as a sin rather than a crime—they were also far from ecumenical. "The most consistent lance carriers for antislavery during the revolutionary period," she writes, "were members of religious denominations—Quaker; the evangelical sides of Presbyterians, Methodists and Baptists; and a branch of Calvinism that was not even embraced by all of New England, New Divinity. Advocates from these denominations preached, wrote, and campaigned for antislavery political action, but in the end failed to provide antislavery with enough of a broad American persona to go beyond local venues" (83).

6. Benjamin Quarles, "The Revolutionary War as a Black Declaration of Independence," in *Slavery and Freedom in the Age of the American Revolution*, ed. Ira Berlin and Ronald Hoffman (Urbana: University of Illinois Press, 1986), 285.

7. Gary B. Nash, *Race and Revolution* (Madison, Wis.: Madison House, 1990), 57.

8. Peter Wood, "'Liberty Is Sweet': African-American Freedom Struggles in the Years Before White Independence," in *Beyond the American Revolution: Explorations in American Radicalism*, ed. Alfred F. Young (DeKalb: Northern University Press, 1993), 152.

9. James McCune Smith to Horace Greeley, 29 January 1844, in *The Black Abolitionist Papers*, 5 vols., ed. C. Peter Ripley (Chapel Hill: University of North Carolina Press, 1985–92), 3:433.

10. Notable exceptions include Quarles, "The Revolutionary War as a Black Declaration of Independence," and David Waldstreicher's brief but excellent discussion of early black nationalism in *In the Midst of Perpetual Fetes: The Making of American Nationalism* (Chapel Hill: University of North Carolina Press, 1997), chap. 6.

11. Many of the most influential studies of nineteenth-century black thought date back to the 1960s and 1970s, when scholars wrote African American history with an acute awareness of the tumultuous debates between integrationists and separatists that marked their own era. Scholars such as Sterling Stuckey sought to locate "the ideological origins of black nationalism"—although the latter two words were perhaps never used together by African Americans in the nineteenth-century United States—sometimes to the neglect of other sources of African American identity and political mobilization. See Sterling Stuckey, *Slave Culture: Nationalist Theory and Foundations of Black America* (New York: Oxford University Press, 1987), and the introduction to *The Ideological Origins of Black Nationalism*, ed. Sterling Stuckey (Boston: Beacon Press, 1972). A fine discussion of the impact of the politics of the black power era, which reviews the above-

mentioned scholarship at greater length and contends that this period saw "the invention of a black nationalist tradition," appears in Dean E. Robinson, *Black Nationalism in American Politics and Thought* (Cambridge: Cambridge University Press, 2001), 79.

12. See, for example, Paul Goodman, *Of One Blood: Abolitionism and the Origins of Racial Equality* (Berkeley: University of California Press, 1998).

13. Benjamin Quarles, *Black Abolitionists* (New York: Oxford University Press, 1969); Jane H. Pease and William H. Pease, *They Who Would Be Free: Blacks' Search for Freedom, 1830–1861* (Urbana: University of Illinois Press, 1974); Patrick Rael, *Black Identity and Protest in the Antebellum North* (Chapel Hill: University of North Carolina Press, 2002).

14. Sylvia Frey, *Water from a Rock: Black Resistance in a Revolutionary Age* (Princeton: Princeton University Press, 1999), 49.

15. Laurens is quoted by Frey; as is Josiah Smith, a Charleston merchant, who recorded the activities of his city's militia. Ibid., 15, 57.

16. Phillis Wheatley, "Letter to Samson Occum," *Connecticut Gazette*, March 11, 1774. On the influence of the American Revolution on the poet, see Betsy Erkkila, "Phillis Wheatley and the American Revolution," in *A Mixed Race: Ethnicity in Early America*, ed. Frank Shuffleton (New York: Oxford University Press, 1993), 225–40; Henry Louis Gates Jr., *The Trials of Phillis Wheatley: America's First Black Poet and Her Encounters with the Founding Fathers* (New York: Civitas Books, 2003).

17. Massachusetts Archives, "Revolutionary Resolves," quoted in Joanne Pope Melish, *Disowning Slavery: Gradual Emancipation and "Race" in New England, 1780–1860* (Ithaca, N.Y.: Cornell University Press, 1998), 65.

18. "Slave Petitions for Freedom during the Revolution, 1773–1779," in Herbert Aptheker, *A Documentary History of the Negro People in the United States* (New York: Citadel Press, 1951), 7.

19. Aptheker, *Documentary History*, 10, 11. On the increasing radicalism of these petitions, see also Thomas J. Davis, "Emancipation Rhetoric, Natural Rights, and Revolutionary New England: A Note on Four Black Petitions in New England," *New England Quarterly* 62, no. 2 (June 1989): 248–63.

20. Sidney Kaplan, "The Domestic Insurrections of the Declaration of Independence," *Journal of Negro History* 61 (July 1976): 249–50; Adams Family Correspondence cited in Bradley, *Slavery, Propaganda, and the American Revolution*, 132.

21. At this time, Gage resolved that "things are now come to that Crisis, that we must avail ourselves of every resource, even to raise the Negroes, in our cause." Quoted in Sidney Kaplan, *The Black Presence in the Era of the American Revolution* (Greenwich, Conn.: New York Graphic Society, 1973), 15.

22. Melish, *Disowning Slavery*, 65; John Adams quoted in John Wood Sweet, *Bodies Politic: Negotiating Race in the American North, 1730–1830* (Baltimore: Johns Hopkins University Press, 2003), 253.

23. Thomas Jefferson to William Gordon, July 16, 1788, cited in Nash, *Race and Revolution*, 60.

24. Nash, *Race and Revolution*, 61; on the impact of the Revolution on the black population, see also Frey, *Water from a Rock*, and Willie Lee Rose, "The Impact of the American Revolution on the Black Population," in *Slavery, Revolutionary America, and the New Nation*, ed. Paul Finkelman (New York: Garland Publishing, 1989), 411–26.

25. On Crispus Attucks, see Peter H. Wood, "Strange New Land, 1619–1776," in *To Make Our World Anew: A History of African Americans*, ed. Robin D. G. Kelley and Earl Lewis (New York: Oxford University Press, 2000), 97–98.

26. Lois E. Horton, "From Race to Class: Northern Post-Emancipation Reconstruction," in *Race and the Early Republic: Racial Consciousness and Nation-Building in the Early Republic*, ed. Michael A. Morrison and James Brewer Stewart (Lanham, Md.: Rowan and Littlefield, 2002), 60.

27. *Journals of the Continental Congress, 1773–1798*, quoted in Henry Wiencek, *An Imperfect God: George Washington, His Slaves, and the Creation of America* (New York: Farrar, Straus and Giroux, 2004), 232.

28. Wiencek argues that Charleston fell to the British, "as a direct result of the failure to form a black legion to defend South Carolina." Wiencek, *An Imperfect God*, 234.

29. Quoted in Sweet, *Bodies Politic*, 203.

30. This petition is reprinted in "Slavery in New Hampshire," *Magazine of American History with Notes and Queries* 21 (January–June 1889): 64.

31. Richard S. Walling, "Prince Whipple: Symbol of African Americans at the Battle of Trenton," <http://www.whipple.org/prince/princewhipple.html>.

32. "Slavery in New Hampshire," 63.

33. Ira Berlin, *Slaves without Masters: The Free Negro in the Antebellum South* (New York: Oxford University Press, 1974), 47.

34. Ira Berlin, *Generations of Captivity: A History of American Slaves* (Cambridge, Mass.: Harvard University Press, 2003), 104.

35. Leslie M. Harris, *In the Shadow of Slavery: African Americans in New York City, 1626–1863* (Chicago: University of Chicago Press, 2003), 73.

36. Richard Newman, *The Transformation of American Abolitionism: Fighting Slavery in the Early Republic* (Chapel Hill: University of North Carolina Press, 2002), 62.

37. On the rise in racial prejudice and discrimination during the early national

period, see the essays in Michael A. Morrison and James Brewer Stewart, eds., *Race and the Early Republic: Racial Consciousness and Nation-Building in the Early Republic* (Lanham, Md.: Rowman and Littlefield, 2002); on free black life during these years, see James Oliver Horton and Lois E. Horton, *In Hope of Liberty: Culture, Community, and Protest among Northern Free Blacks, 1700–1860* (New York: Oxford University Press, 1997), chaps. 3–7.

38. Berlin, *Generations of Captivity*, 105.

39. Berlin, *Slaves without Masters*, 46, 136.

40. P. J. Staudenraus's *The African Colonization Movement* (New York: Columbia University Press, 1961) remains the most detailed account of the history of the ACS in the United States. Since then, however, the goal and aims of the ACS have been reappraised by a variety of historians, including Laurence J. Friedman, "Purifying the White Man's Country: The American Colonization Society Reconsidered, 1816–1840," *Societas* 6 (Winter 1976): 1–25; David Brion Davis, "Reconsidering the Colonization Movement: Leonard Bacon and the Problem of Evil," and George Frederickson, "Comment on Davis, 'Reconsidering the Colonization Movement,'" *Intellectual History Newsletter* 14 (1992): 3–20; Amos J. Beyan, *The American Colonization Society and the Creation of the Liberian State* (New York: University Press of America, 1991); Bruce Dorsey, "A Gendered History of Colonization in the Antebellum United States," *Journal of Social History* 34, no. 1 (2000): 77–103; Claude Clegg III, *The Price of Liberty: African Americans and the Making of Liberia* (Chapel Hill: University of North Carolina Press, 2004); and David Kazanjian, *The Colonizing Trick: National Culture and Imperial Citizenship in Early America* (Minneapolis: University of Minnesota Press, 2003).

41. Quarles, *Black Abolitionists*, 9.

42. James Forten quoted in Julie Winch, *A Gentleman of Color: The Life of James Forten* (New York: Oxford University Press, 2002), 191.

43. "To the Humane and Benevolent Inhabitants of the City and County of Philadelphia" (August 10, 1817), reprinted in William Lloyd Garrison, *Thoughts on African Colonization* (1832; repr., New York: Arno Press, 1968), 10–11.

44. In addition to energizing black abolitionism, anticolonizationist sentiment also helped inspire the growth of an independent black press. Founded in 1827, *Freedom's Journal*, the nation's first black newspaper, coalesced at least partially around opposition to the ACS. Moreover, the need to refute colonizationist discussions of black people also fostered new discussions of the history and character of black people among black intellectuals. For two different perspectives on this, see Mia Bay, *The White Image in the Black Mind: African-American Ideas about White People, 1830–1925* (New York: Oxford University Press, 2000),

chap. 1; and Bruce Dain, *A Hideous Monster of the Mind: American Race Theory in the Early Republic* (Cambridge, Mass.: Harvard University Press, 2002.

45. "A Voice from Philadelphia" (1817), in Garrison, *Thoughts on African Colonization*, 9.

46. Dain, *Hideous Monster of the Mind*, 107; Pease and Pease, *They Who Would Be Free*, 22.

47. James Forten to Paul Cuffe, January 25, 1817, quoted in Winch, *Gentleman of Color*, 191.

48. James Forten quoted in Ray Allan Billington, "James Forten: Forgotten Abolitionist," in *Blacks in the Abolitionist Movement*, ed. John H. Bracey Jr., August Meier, and Elliott Rudwick (Belmont, Calif.: Wadsworth, 1971), 10.

49. According to Ira Berlin, the biggest wave of African arrivals in the North took place in the middle decades of the eighteenth century, when European wars limited the supply of indentured servants and frontier migration contracted the white labor market. At this time, the number of slaves imported directly from Africa increased dramatically, which reoriented African American culture in the direction of Africa. However, these imports ceased well before the Revolution, ensuring that by the early nineteenth century many Northern blacks were American born. Less certain, however, are the origins of many southern fugitives and revolutionary-era soldiers who swelled the North's free black population after the Revolution, some of whom may have had more recent African roots. Still, according to W. E. B. Du Bois's estimate, by the beginning of the nineteenth century only 15 percent of black Northerners were African born; Du Bois cited in Elizabeth Raul Bethel, *The Roots of African-American Identity* (New York: St. Martin's Press, 1997), 87. On slaves imported into the North in the eighteenth century, see Ira Berlin, "Time, Space, and the Evolution of Afro-American Society in British Mainland North America," *American Historical Review* 85, no. 1 (February 1980): 51–54; and Berlin, *Generations of Captivity*, chaps. 2 and 3.

50. "Voice from Philadelphia," 9.

51. Forten quoted in Winch, *Gentleman of Color*, 41.

52. Winch, *Gentleman of Color*, 30–31.

53. Forten quoted in Winch, *Gentleman of Color*, 38, 41; why he says he was drummer in the previous quote I am note sure. His biographer, Winch, makes no mention of his being a drummer during his service in the navy.

54. Antebellum-era poet John G. Whittier, speaking in 1847, quoted in William C. Nell, *Colored Patriots of the American Revolution* (1855; repr., New York: Arno Press, 1968), 9. One of the first works on African American history, *Colored Patriots* was written to "rescue from oblivion" (9) the black record in the War. On the political goals of this work as a black "site of memory," see John Ernest,

Liberation Historiography: African American Writers and the Challenge of History, 1794–1861 (Chapel Hill: University of North Carolina Press, 2004), 132–53.

55. Other examples include black abolitionist Hosea Easton, whose lineage is chronicled in *"To Heal the Scourge of Prejudice": The Life and Writings of Hosea Easton*, ed. George R. Price and James Brewer Stewart (Amherst: University of Massachusetts Press, 1999), and the black abolitionist brothers Lewis and Milton Clarke, discussed in Nell, *Colored Patriots*, 154–55.

56. Jeremiah Asher, *Incidents in the Life of Rev. J. Asher* (1850; repr., Freeport, N.Y.: Books for Libraries Press, 1971), 18.

57. Quoted in Lois Horton, "From Class to Race in Early America: Post-Emancipation Racial Reconstruction," in *Race and the Early Republic*, ed. Morrison and Stewart, 67.

58. The burgeoning new literature on the white republic is too extensive to cite detail here. Among the most relevant and influential historical works are David Roediger, *The Wages of Whiteness: Race and the Making of the American Working Class* (London: Verso, 1994); and Matthew Frye Jacobson, *Whiteness of a Different Color: European Immigrants and the Alchemy of Race* (Cambridge, Mass.: Harvard University Press, 1998). On black citizenship in the white republic, see also Rogers M. Smith, *Civic Ideals: Conflicting Visions of Citizenship in U.S. History* (New Haven: Yale University Press, 1997).

59. *Dred Scott v. Sanford* (1857), 60 U.S. 393.

60. *Colored American*, March 4, 1837. Cornish is quoted in a discussion of how anti-colonization sentiment influenced black naming practices in Leonard I. Sweet, *Black Images of America, 1784–1870* (New York: Norton, 1976), 53.

61. David Walker, *David Walker's Appeal* (1829; repr., New York: Hill and Wang, 1995), iii, 75.

62. Frederick Douglass, "What, to the Slave, Is the Fourth of July?" in *Lift Every Voice: African American Oratory, 1787–1900*, ed. Philip Foner and Robert James Branham (Tuscaloosa: University of Alabama Press, 1998), 255, 267.

63. On Garrison and Douglass's friendship and subsequent estrangement, see William S. McFeely, *Frederick Douglass* (New York: Norton, 1991).

64. Frederick Douglass, "Address to the People of the United States" (1853), in *Pamphlets of Protest: An Anthology of Early African-American Protest Literature, 1790–1860*, ed. Richard Newman, Patrick Rael, and Philip Lapansky (New York: Routledge, 2001), 218, 219.

65. Frederick Douglass, "Report of the Proceedings at the Soiree Given to Frederick Douglass, London Tavern, March 30, 1847," quoted in Benjamin Quarles, "Antebellum Free Blacks and the 'Spirit of '76,'" *Journal of Negro History* 61, no. 3 (July 1976): 230.

66. On Douglass's party politics, see John Stauffer, *The Black Hearts of Men: Radical Abolitionists and the Transformation of Race* (Cambridge, Mass.: Harvard University Press, 2002).

67. Martin Robinson Delany, *The Condition, Elevation, Emigration, and Destiny of the Colored People of the United States* (1852; repr., Salem, N.H.: Ayer, 1988), 48, 48–49.

68. Ernest, *Liberation Historiography*, 127.

69. Delany, *Condition, Elevation, Emigration, and Destiny*, 49.

70. Abraham Lincoln, "The Gettysburg Address," November 19, 1863, <http://www.law.ou.edu/hist/getty.html>.

ROBERT SHALHOPE

★ ★ ★ ★

★ Anticipating Americanism

★ *An Individual Perspective on Republicanism*

★ *in the Early Republic*

Throughout the late eighteenth and early nineteenth centuries, American citizens rarely employed the term "Americanism." It was, for the most part, nonexistent in both their private correspondence and their public pronouncements. On those rare occasions when individuals did employ the term, they meant to convey simply allegiance to the nation-state rather than a pervasive loyalty to a distinctive set of ideological principles.[1] This does not mean that Americans of this time lacked such a belief system; they most certainly did not. A deep-seated belief in republicanism permeated their culture and helped to shape both their thoughts and their actions.

Even though nearly a century separates them, it is instructive to elucidate the striking parallels that exist between two cultural systems—Americanism and republicanism—in order to understand better the ways in which Americanism may be viewed as the ideological descendant of republicanism. To accomplish this, we must first seek a deeper understanding of republicanism. Fortunately, we have reached a fruitful juncture in the historiography of this historical concept, one that allows us more easily to grasp similarities and connections between republicanism and Americanism than an earlier generation of scholarship may have allowed. Years of heated debate between the scholars who pioneered the republican synthesis and the critics who disputed this synthesis are now giving way to a more complex view of the history of republicanism itself. As a quick review of the history of this debate indicates, the upshot of recent scholarship has been to call greater attention to the protean nature of republicanism. This insight in turn helps us to better understand its parallels to Americanism.

This review is all the more necessary given the fact that subsequent to the publication of my essay "Toward a Republican Synthesis"[2] in 1972, republicanism as a historical concept experienced quite a checkered career. Although republicanism had become omnipresent in scholarly lit-

erature by the mid-1980s ("republican motherhood," "artisan republicanism," "free labor republicanism," "pastoral republicanism," "evangelical
republicanism"), there were a good many scholars, particularly social historians, who remained firmly convinced that the emphasis on republicanism obscured far more than it clarified about early American society. For
them the scholarly concentration on republicanism "squeezed out massive
domains of culture—religion, law, political economy, ideas of patriarchy,
family and gender, ideas of race and slavery, class and nationalism, nature
and reason—that everyone knew to be profoundly tangled in the revolutionary impulse."[3]

The greatest challenge to republicanism, however, came not from social
historians but from scholars wedded to the concept of liberalism. For these
individuals, Americans of the revolutionary era manifested aggressive individualism, optimistic materialism, and pragmatic interest-group politics.
In their minds John Locke's liberal concept of possessive individualism,
rather than Machiavelli's republican advocacy of civic humanism, best
explained American thought and behavior during the years after 1760.[4] The
intellectual conflict that emerged between advocates of republicanism and
those of liberalism ushered in a decade and a half of sterile debate. An
entirely unproductive "either/or" situation resulted: either scholars supported republicanism or they espoused liberalism.[5] Fortunately,in realizing
that "partisans of both the republican and the liberal interpretations have
identified strands of American political culture whose presence can no
longer be convincingly denied,"[6] a great many scholars have transcended
this tiresome dialogue. Replacing it with a "both/and" mode of analysis,
recent work dealing with the intellectual foundations of the early republic
reveals the manner in which republicanism, liberalism, and other traditions of social and political thought interpenetrated to create a distinctive and creative intellectual milieu. Over time a "paradigmatic pluralism"
emerged; scholars employing a "multiple traditions" approach drew fully
on concepts drawn from natural rights, British constitutionalism, English
opposition writers, contract theory, Protestant Christian morality, Lockean
liberalism, and republicanism.[7]

While the multiple traditions approach now pervades studies of the
early republic, it has not swept the field. There remain scholars who either
refuse to accept the presence of republicanism or greatly discount its contribution to early American thought. Historians who have taken the "cultural turn" recognize republicanism as one of a number of "competing
ideologies," but they consider its appeal limited to "the tiny minority of

white males who were trained in the classics in colonial colleges from Harvard to William and Mary and who formed America's intellectual elite."[8] A prominent American intellectual historian even questions the very existence of a tradition of republicanism; he considers the term itself to be "a name of art applied long after the fact."[9] To his way of thinking, republicanism was anything but a vital tradition present at the creation of the new republic.[10]

Political philosophers have worked most assiduously to exclude republicanism from consideration as a viable tradition on which the founders might have drawn in their efforts to create a viable new republic.[11] Focusing intently upon the thought of John Locke, they discuss republican ideas only to dismiss them out of hand. While contributing to the depth and sophistication of our understanding of Locke, their research deals in ideal types and abstract belief systems that have only the most problematic links to actual participants of the founding generation. Classic exemplars of text entirely devoid of context, these works represent political theory at its most elusive and ethereal. Consequently, it is difficult to imagine that the Lockean concepts portrayed by these scholars would have been recognizable even to such individuals as Thomas Jefferson, James Wilson, and James Madison—men whose use of Locke was far more casual and eclectic than that suggested by these modern political theorists.[12]

If scholars are to reconstruct the past in a manner that would be recognizable to the people of the time who actually experienced it, they must pay close attention to the context within which viable ideas circulated. To reveal a deep sense of process and culture, they must search for those times, places, and occasions in which traditional ideas interact with actual people. It is at such times that the "processes of persuasion and argument, the making and sustaining of collective identities and identifying rhetorics begin to come clear."[13]

One way to discover the manner in which ideas interacted with the lives of actual people is to focus on the life of a single individual living during the years of the early republic. With this in mind, let us turn to the life of a common farmer living in Bennington, Vermont, during the late eighteenth and early nineteenth centuries. What is extraordinary about this man, Hiram Harwood (1788–1839), is the diary he left behind. Over 4,000 pages in length, it is replete with deeply introspective insights into the life and thought of an ordinary individual, his family, his neighbors, and his community. In the pages of this diary, we gain access to actual times, places, and occasions in which traditional ideas interacted with real people; we gain access as well to the cultural process within which this interaction took place.[14] Harwood's story refutes those intellectual historians and political philosophers who have questioned the importance of the concept of republicanism to early Americans. Harwood was both a participant in a vibrant republican political culture and an eloquent and explicit exponent of the republican tradition in his own humble way. Yet his story provides insight not only into the vitality of republican thought in the early nineteenth century but also into the contested and shifting nature of republicanism. Seen in light of the "multiple traditions approach" that has come to the fore in the recent literature, Harwood is particularly important because his life suggests the intricate ways in which the seemingly conflicting worldviews of republicanism and liberalism intersected in the thoughts and practices of early Americans. By illuminating this complex interplay, Harwood's life in turn helps us to understand how republicanism could ultimately give way to Americanism, the protean concept that animated American political life by the early twentieth century as powerfully as republicanism had animated it a century earlier.

To glean such insights from the life of Hiram Harwood, it is necessary first to understand the world into which he was born. His grandfather was among the hardy band of Strict Congregationalists (New Light Separatists) that originally settled Bennington township in 1762. Bred to traditions of intense localism, extreme egalitarianism, and the Calvinist rule of equity and charity, the Harwoods supported Ethan Allen and his Green Mountain Boys in their struggle to defend the small farmers of the New Hampshire Grants against the manor lords of New York. This same struggle between "power" and "liberty" emerged within the Bennington community following the Revolution and the entrance of Vermont into the Union. Factions developed between those espousing a simple, egalitarian communalism and those committed to a more cosmopolitan, hierarchical perception of society. The Harwoods remained staunchly loyal to the former in their opposition to the emergence of Federalist leaders in Bennington. "A Farmer" articulated their feelings perfectly when he warned the people of Bennington of the appearance of an "aristocratical party"; in fact, he claimed that the "republican spirit" of the town was in danger of being eclipsed by a "patrician order." If allowed to succeed, Federalists would live in "idleness" while "the poor peasant and his family" toiled away in poverty to support the "splendor and luxury" created by a government of "energy and power." Devotion to "liberty, equality, and the rights of man" demanded that aristocratic politicians be brought down "on an average" with ordinary citizens. Equality, not hierarchy, must remain the rule in Bennington.[15]

During Hiram Harwood's formative years, two local institutions—the church and the common school—reinforced this sense of the worth of the common man and the dangers emanating from aristocratic tyranny. Daniel Marsh, pastor of First Church in Bennington, had been trained by Ebenezer Bradford—characterized by the orthodox clergy of Massachusetts as a "vandal" and an "insurgent."[16] Bradford, a fervent New Light, advocate of emotional preaching, ardent democrat, and enthusiastic supporter of Thomas Paine, even went so far as to preach that Paine's political sentiments were perfectly "consonant to the nature, end and genius of all republican government, and not at all inconsistent with the great principles of Revelation."[17] Daniel Marsh brought these same beliefs, as well as an ardent loyalty to the Jeffersonian-Republican Party, to the pulpit of First Church. He constantly preached the simple love and equality of the Lord while simultaneously exalting the virtues of the common man. In a sermon commemorating the American victory at the battle of Bennington, Marsh celebrated the "wonders" of ordinary American militiamen in their struggle against the professional troops of the British army. No matter what the "skill of the enemy in military tactics, their experience in the arts of war, their former successes, and their great bravery in facing danger" might have been, none of these apparent advantages enabled them to overcome the natural strength of "the yeomanry of America."[18]

In his local school, Hiram learned many of the same lessons. A reverence for the ideals of the Revolution permeated his studies. Even in later years he gained immense satisfaction from reading the orations of Dr. Joseph Warren and John Hancock found in "Webster's old Third Part."[19] Hiram remained particularly fond of this "old book, which I hold in great reverence on account of its being a celebrated school book in my youthful days."[20] The orations of Warren and Hancock spoke eloquently to the manner in which "Liberty" opposed the "slavery" of "tyrants."[21] Another of Hiram's favorites—an oration that Thomas Dawes delivered on July 4, 1787, in Boston—declared that is was "easy to see that our agrarian law and the law of education were calculated to make republicans; to make *men*."[22]

Further evidence of a struggle between the forces of liberty and those of power became evident to the Harwoods when their good friend Anthony Haswell, the editor of the local newspaper, spoke out repeatedly in the most strident terms against Federalist leaders in Bennington. When these men crowed that the bulk of a Jeffersonian-Republican celebration of the Fourth of July consisted of "boys and negroes," Haswell responded that the Federalist parade included primarily "old tories who opposed our Revolution," "professed opposers of republicanism on the avowed principle that no people has virtue enough to support such a form of government," and men "who have sworn out of gaol to defraud their creditors." On the other hand, "real republicans, substantial farmers, veterans of our Revolution and youth who have embibed their sentiments" made up the Jeffersonian procession.[23]

By the fall of 1799, Federalist authorities had had enough. On October 8 two deputy marshals arrested Haswell and escorted him to Rutland, where he faced indictments on two counts of violating the Sedition Law. The following May a jury selected from Federalist strongholds in the eastern part of the state found Haswell guilty on both counts, and he was fined and sentenced to two months in prison. Knowing their champion would be released on July 9, Jeffersonian supporters in the Bennington area postponed their Fourth of July celebration until that day. The moment Haswell left the Bennington jail a free man, celebrants fired a salute with the old cannon on the parade ground. Several thousand strong, they escorted him through town to the tune of "Yankee Doodle." When they reached the States Arms Tavern, they began singing patriotic songs that Haswell had composed for the occasion. Before the day was over, more people had flocked onto the parade ground to celebrate the release of this martyr to liberty than had ever previously assembled in Bennington.[24]

This gathering to celebrate Haswell's freedom represents a classic example of what Rhys Isaacs refers to as a *tableau vivant*—a highly charged form of patterned action that communicates far more than words are able to while engendering "a collective consciousness of belonging to a virtuous community, unanimously roused in support of its dearest rights." Such gatherings play an essential role in the "oral-dramaturgical processes through which emotions [are] communicated, intensified by sharing, and channelled into social action."[25]

Similar *tableaux vivants* played out repeatedly during Hiram's formative years. His father, a zealous Jeffersonian-Republican, took his son with him to a great many local celebrations. On these days Hiram never failed to witness scenes that reinforced the belief that he and his father were republicans and that they and their neighbors honored the precepts of republicanism. Fourth of July celebrations became particularly fertile opportunities to express such loyalty. On these occasions local notables from the

Jeffersonian-Republican Party arose to fete the heroes of America in a manner that affirmed their cause and their virtues while simultaneously equating them with those of the people gathered to celebrate them.

The dramaturgical possibilities of celebrations of the battle of Bennington exceeded even those of the Fourth of July. On one such occasion, Hiram accompanied his father to the annual Jeffersonian celebration of the battle. Since the Republicans who gathered far outnumbered the Federalists assembled at another tavern, Hiram's father exulted at being "among the enemies of aristocracy and monarchy—and the friends of the rights of man." Then, when his close friend Anthony Haswell read a letter from John Stark, commander of the American forces during the battle of Bennington, he praised its sentiments as "rousing to every republican who breathes american air."[26] The fact that Hiram, serving as his father's scribe, was responsible for recording these sentiments in the family diary helped to inculcate them in his own mind. Far more important, though, was the fact that he himself was present to hear Stark's very words. For his part, Stark recalled that he had commanded "American troops" at the battle, men who had neither learned the "ART OF SUBMISSION" nor had been trained in the "ART OF WAR." His incredible success taught all "enemies of liberty" that "UNDISCIPLINED FREEMEN" were in all ways superior to "veteran slaves." Stark wanted the citizens of Bennington to understand that he remained as always the stalwart friend of "the equal rights of men, of representative democracy, of republicanism, and the declaration of independence."[27]

When Stark valued the ordinary qualities of the yeoman over the sophistication and cosmopolitanism of the British, he articulated a theme that Haswell had been pressing for some time in the pages of his newspaper. "Franklin," for example, observed that students came out of college "with no other direction and no other object in view than to rise on the necks of the people." In addition, "these young nobles are manufactured into priests and lawyers with astonishing facility, and *clod hopper* and *geese* are their usual phrases when speaking of the people."[28] By the time this statement appeared, Hiram had become one of Haswell's most ardent supporters and an avid reader of his newspaper. Whether drawing his sentiments from the *Gazette* or from his own family heritage, Hiram heartily agreed with the egalitarian attitudes being expressed toward college-educated individuals. When a struggle between Bennington's opposing political leaders broke out over whether a new building being erected by the town should become a common school or a private academy, Hiram exclaimed: "I think myself that colleges & academies are nurseries of monarchy & aristocracy—that the money laid out for education there might do much greater service to the public to be put into a vast fund for the support of our common schools—I would not throw them *all* away, however, I would take care not to increase their numbers."[29]

Hiram's basic egalitarianism and his sensitivity to the power of wealth and status permeated his thought and behavior in local Bennington politics as well. When his friend and political mentor O. C. Merrill won a seat on the state council in September 1825, Hiram expressed his "thanks to the God of elections [that] Mr. M., although poor, obtains his seat at the Council board this year, in spite of every effort of his enemies who assailed with all the weapons they could invent of the low & meaner kind." He then exclaimed, "Let not the glare of riches and the popularity usually attached thereto always triumph, but let the men of worth when in low circumstances *sometimes* have his place."[30] Two years later, when his close friend Hiland Hall lost an election to the state assembly to Charles Hammond, proprietor of the Bennington Furnace Company, Hiram objected strenuously because "it looked too much like paying adoration to property."[31] The following year Hiram received additional support relative to his opinion of Hammond when a prominent Democratic leader visited with him about an upcoming election and "argued against Mr. Hammond." Such sentiments were superfluous since Hiram "disapproved of him [Hammond] enough before—we were against supporting these great capitalists for office."[32]

By the time of the new state assembly election, Hiram had been reading widely in a great variety of books and newspapers. Whenever he was not studying the *Gazette*, Hiram spent time with the *Philadelphia Aurora* and the *National Intelligencer*—the two most ardently Jeffersonian papers in the nation. Hiram was so taken with the *Aurora* that he declared he would not trade its editor, William Duane, "for all the federal and many of the democratic editors on this Continent."[33] Although he became increasingly well read, Hiram's favorite author remained Thomas Paine. Whenever possible, he would pick up *The American Crisis* or *Common Sense*, or he would peruse portions of the *Rights of Man*. Indeed, he considered these "all very fine Republican works which ought to be read by every friend of freedom in this & in all enlightened countries."[34]

At the time Hiram made these comments regarding Paine, his republican beliefs—fostered by his family, his church, his school, his reading, and the multiplicity of *tableaux vivants* he had witnessed over the years—had become thoroughly embedded within his consciousness. His republican beliefs had formed a layer of culture: a multiplicity of sentiments had been transformed into symbols; a great many ideas had become habits.[35] It was not just that certain concepts—such as slavery, tyranny, liberty, conspiracy, power, equality, and the sovereignty of the common people—emanated from or mirrored Hiram's perception of his community, his state, or his nation; they had actually become an integral part of that reality and taken on public meaning. Over the years republicanism had become encoded into the institutional fabric of Hiram's life, not as explicit axioms of conventional dogma, but rather as unreflective thought and behavior. Republican ideas had become a visceral part of Hiram's very being.

Republicanism had become so embedded within Hiram's consciousness that it became a standard by which he, self-consciously or not, evaluated the beliefs, actions, and ideas of others with whom he came into contact. On one occasion, while discussing the Hartford Convention with a neighbor, Hiram learned that the man "would fight against it sooner than almost anything." Much relieved, Hiram declared that the man's "republicanism was good."[36] Another time, local Federalists gained control of a town meeting and promptly began to misuse their authority. To Hiram's great chagrin, the Federalists, "not even having republicanism enough to consent to the question's being tried," overwhelmed a Democrat's desperate call for adjournment.[37] Similarly, whenever Hiram managed to find a family that would discuss hiring out one if its daughters to the Harwoods as a dairy girl, he invariably described "the Republican relation in which we hold such ladies," portrayed his "republican notions respecting hired girls," or explained "the respect in which we always held girls of proper character at our house."[38]

The culture of republicanism became even more central to Hiram when the Jeffersonian-Republican Party began to fragment following the War of 1812. By the time Andrew Jackson entered the presidential fray, the old party in Bennington was near total collapse. As a result, the certitude that had always characterized Hiram's reaction to national events in an earlier era was now missing; in its place, ambiguity and uncertainty troubled his mind. Unable to interpret the national scene with anything like the previous confidence he gained from his association with Bennington's Jeffersonian-Republican leadership, Hiram fell back on old republican principles as his only means of making sense of what he read in the newspapers. All too often, though, this resulted in further contradictions and ambiguities. Thus when "the papers of the day were filled with the speeches of Webster, Hayne & others on the Public Lands," Hiram, struggling to force current issues into an older, more familiar frame of reference, could only see them all "calling up Old Embargo, War and Hartford Convention times." Although he disapproved of Robert Hayne's stance on tariffs and internal improvements, Hiram considered the South Carolina senator's response to Daniel Webster "ably performed—too much truth in it for old Federalism, [which it] went hard against." Two weeks later, though, he read Daniel Webster's "last and very able speech" in response to Hayne. The very next night a friend read Webster's speech aloud to the Harwoods "in fine style." Jackson's use of republican rhetoric in his veto of the Maysville Road had much the same effect on Hiram. After reading the president's message, he "could not see but that [Jackson] reasoned fairly & correctly."[39]

With the passage of time, Hiram's ambivalence regarding national politics continued unabated. When he examined the "doings" of a "National Convention" in New York,[40] he "liked them well." Shortly thereafter he heard Colonel Merrill "talking of the justice & fairness of the Jackson administration." Barely a week after that, he "heard President's message read through by O. C. Merrill" and "did not see why it was not a very good one." Then, on reading the speeches of Daniel Webster and others in opposition to the appointment of Martin Van Buren as minister to Great Britain, Hiram approved of their actions. He considered Van Buren's rejection by the Senate "a just act" and thought it best to "keep our party quarrel at home." When he read Henry Clay's "last great speech in support of the American System," Hiram and his family "all thought [it] very fair and reasonable." However, when the matter of the National Bank arose, Hiram "liked well the remarks of R. M. Johnson of Kentucky"—one of Jackson's staunchest supporters. Perhaps as a consequence of his ambivalence, Hiram did not attend the meeting of either party when each held a caucus in town to nominate candidates for Congress.[41]

Early in June 1832 Hiram made an agreement with a neighbor to split a subscription to the *New York Spectator*. As a result of this bargain, Hiram and his family now read the *Vermont Gazette*, which had become the leading Jacksonian paper in the state, and the *Spectator*, a virulently anti-Jacksonian paper. When Andrew Jackson vetoed legislation to renew the charter of the Bank of the United States, the *Gazette* and the *Spectator* filled their pages with opposing viewpoints. Hiram did his best to absorb the material from both papers. By October, though, he was beginning to form a definite opinion regarding the matter. On reading Daniel Webster's speech of July 11 in opposition to the veto, he considered it "very able, and much to the point." Indeed, he believed it "left the Message [Jackson's veto] in a mangled state—we must support the U.S.B. [United States Bank] & the Constitution."[42]

Gradually, but nonetheless steadily, Hiram began to draw his political opinions almost exclusively from material published in the *Spectator*. As a result, when Hiram visited old friends, neighbors, and longtime Federalists, they "talked about Masonry, Anti-Masonry, Jacksonianism, etc.—in which [they] perfectly agreed." So, too, when a neighbor—and prominent leader of the old Federalist Party—visited and "gave his opinion freely on politics," Hiram confirmed that their views "of course coincided."[43] This could no longer be said of his old Democratic associates. Consequently, Hiram viewed the November 1832 elections with mixed emotions. Jackson's reelection disappointed him, but the fact that Hiland Hall won a seat in Congress pleased him no end. Not only had a like-minded individual been sent to Congress, but Hiram could now carry on a regular correspondence with his old friend that would enable him to gain personal insights into a process that had always seemed distant and a bit mysterious.

Nullification—the first issue to occupy Hiram's mind following the presidential election—elicited mixed reactions from him. On first glancing at the proceedings of the South Carolina nullification convention, Hiram "became highly incensed against them." He believed that "if their case is bad, the remedy is violent & uncalled for, but of a piece with Southern Impudence & folly." Then, emphatically in support of the president, he declared, "Let Jackson put them down if he can." The next day, however, after carefully reading the South Carolina convention report, he believed that there "appeared to be much good reasoning—but not enough to bear them out in all their doings." Here again, the presence of old republican themes—the tyranny of power and its threat to liberty, states' rights, fear of coercive central power—appealed to Hiram. This was particularly true for him when he noted the many references made to Thomas Jefferson as the "fair authority for the support of Nullification." When considering the threat South Carolinians posed to the Union, he "viewed Mr. Calhoun & his friends to be altogether lost in unprofitable theories—[their] brains turned," but when he read Calhoun's defense of nullification "though on the wrong side—yet it would entertain—many parts were grand & sublime."[44] Its "republicanism was good."

At nearly this same time, another divisive issue—the National Bank—arose. With the papers "full of Bank-Bank-Bank," Hiram, like so many of his fellow citizens, became intently involved in trying to come to grips with the issues of the Bank War.[45] In this effort, however, he found that the "great Bank Documents were so monstrously prolix" that he had difficulty reading through them. Consequently, he wrote Hiland Hall and asked him to discuss the matter "compressed in as few words as possible." Hiram also took this occasion to request that Hall send him a "description of leaders of parties—likewise of those who were most modest, unassuming, pleas't companions—not disposed to stir the waters of strife."[46]

Henceforth Hiram depended on correspondence with Hall, who by this time had become the preeminent Whig leader in the state, and the speeches of members of Congress published in the *Spectator* to shape his feelings on the Bank. Here again, though, the influence of old republican principles deeply affected his perceptions. He greatly admired the speeches of men such as George McDuffie in the House and John C. Calhoun in the Senate even though both men remained ardent nullifiers. He considered McDuffie's observations regarding Jackson and the removal of Bank deposits to be "very powerful."[47] He firmly believed that Jackson had unconstitutionally assumed far too much power for the executive branch. Likewise, he was enthralled when McDuffie warned that Jackson's removal of deposits from the Bank and subsequent placing of this money with selected state banks would lead to "the sacrifice of the honest and the industrious, to make princes of brokers, speculators, and stock-jobbers." A system of state banks tied to the federal government and associated with the political purposes of that government would create, the South Carolinian declared, a well-nigh unbreakable tyranny: "No human power can rescue us from the hand that wields the whole. The man who controls a bank, controls all who are indebted to that bank; and thus by sanctioning the meretricious union of money with power, you deliver up your country into chains which nothing but a Divine interposition can ever break or dissolve."[48]

When he read Calhoun's speech regarding the Bank deposits, Hiram believed the South Carolinian "used up Taney & Dr. Jackson." Indeed, Calhoun's observations so impressed Hiram that he "considered him able, even beautiful."[49] In his speech Calhoun had warned that the country was "in the midst of a revolution." The very existence of free government rested on the proper distribution of power. "To destroy this distribution and thereby concentrate power is to effect a revolution."[50] Observations made by Henry Clay, Daniel Webster, William J. Duane, and other prominent political figures elicited Hiram's enthusiastic approbation as well. They, too, warned against executive usurpation and decried the economic ruin that would befall the nation as a result of Jackson's actions.[51] When Jackson defended himself against his political opponents, Hiram delivered his most telling critique: the president's arguments were "far enough from being Republican."[52]

Hiram's conclusion received ample support from Hiland Hall. For his part, Hall believed that the most difficult issues he faced in his first sessions of Congress were related to Andrew Jackson's attack on the Bank, the president's insistence on a specie currency, and his disdain for those who lived on credit. As a result, Hall rose in the House of Representatives on May 5, 1834, to support a resolution to the effect that "the declaration of the President, that 'any man ought to break who trades on borrowed capital,' is a foolish and wicked assertion."[53] Warming to his subject, Hall defended the citizens of Vermont for being "as purely republican in their habits and notions" as any people in the country. In their minds, as well as his own, a reliance on credit was clearly "in accordance with their republican principles." Indeed, it was credit that "enabled the poor but enterprising citizen, who has established a character for integrity and skill, to commence life with some prospect of raising himself to the level of his neighbor who derives his capital from the gains of his ancestor." Credit placed "worth on something like an equality with wealth," enabling "honest poverty to outstrip and conquer riches on the fair field of honorable competition."[54]

Hall expressed only disdain for the remedy that Jackson recommended for the nation's economic troubles: hard money. In his opinion, "Congress might as well undertake to carry the people of this country back from the canal to the forest horse-path, from the steamboat to the scow with its setting poles, from the railroad car to the handbarrow, as to expect to legislate them back to a 'hard-money system.' "[55] Instead of the backward economy fostered by Andrew Jackson, Hall championed a progressive, democratic form of capitalism in which government—local, state, and national—fostered economic opportunity for all citizens by supporting institutions such as banks and factories. In essence, there could have been no stronger exponent of the Whigs' American System than Hiland Hall.

Hall could not have expressed Hiram's views with more precision. Indeed, by articulating the demands of his constituents, he provided meaning and coherence to Hiram's inchoate political beliefs. The Harwoods had long relied on credit. This was true from the time their efforts imperceptibly combined production for subsistence and production for exchange. Their dependence on credit became particularly acute, however, when Hiram initiated a commercial dairy operation in 1823. After that time he became deeply enmeshed in the burgeoning market economy that revolved around the production and sale of cheese. The entire venture rested squarely on Hiram's ability to purchase on credit the animals and other necessities required for a successful operation. In Hiram's mind the family's very existence depended on his own personal character and integrity; without these he could not gain the credit necessary to maintain the farm and the family's independence. Nothing could be more republican. At the same time, Hiram shared Hall's vision of progress. Bennington should not remain a sleepy village with business linked only to court days; instead, it should become a dynamic and prosperous town where all men were free to prosper through hard work. Hall's words resonated perfectly with Hiram's views on life and politics; they melded his devotion to republican independence with his desire for commercial success.

In many ways, then, Hiram Harwood's life may be representative of great numbers of nineteenth-century Americans. Republicanism—a familiar ideology permeating all walks of his life—shaped his thought; it provided him with meaning in his life and a sense of identity. But liberalism—an unarticulated behavioral pattern more than a sharply delineated mode of thought—unconsciously shaped his daily life. Consequently, he clung to a harmonious communal view of his society even while behaving in a materialistic, competitive manner. He quite unself-consciously blended the beliefs of the "venturesome conservative" described by Marvin Meyers with those of the Whig devoted to character building and self-improvement, whom Daniel Howe believes was most clearly epitomized by Abraham Lincoln.[56]

All Hiram's intellectual and visceral feelings for what his country was and represented were bound up in his perception of republicanism. At the same time, though, it must be recognized that republicanism remained a contested issue throughout the early nineteenth century. This became abundantly clear during the crisis over nullification—a time when Hiram's confusion and ambivalence regarding the views of John C. Calhoun, Daniel Webster, Andrew Jackson, and a great many other key political figures of the time became manifest. As David Waldstreicher has pointed out, American nationalism was real enough in the nineteenth century, but it was not an explicit quality of which one was either possessed or deficient; instead it was "a set of practices that empowered Americans to fight over the legacy of their national Revolution, and to protest their exclusion from that Revolution's fruits."[57] Thus celebrations of the Fourth of July could take place simultaneously in Bennington, Vermont, and Charleston, South Carolina. The participants in each, although acting on different agendas and identities, expressed themselves vehemently in banners, songs, parades, and toasts, which pledged their fundamental loyalty to the nation and to republican values of social and political unity. Such patriotic celebrations were actually carefully crafted expressions of particular versions of nationalism. Their particularities remained obscured, however, by the use of similar "national" symbols and identical republican rhetoric. Consequently, symbolic consensus allowed social and ideological conflict to proceed apace entirely undetected—that is, until issues like nullification arose. Hiram Harwood's loyalty to republicanism, like that of so many others both North and South, was quite unself-consciously embedded within him as a regional or sectional allegiance rather than a national one. Republicanism, like Waldstreicher's nationalism, had become a contested term that obscured its own internal divisions from view. When these divisions could no longer be obscured, competing versions of the concept led to civil war.

Contested or not, republicanism—far from being "a name of art applied long after the fact"—permeated the literature Hiram Harwood read and the orations he heard. Indeed, it formed the central core of his political culture. Nevertheless, Harwood stands as a classic exemplar of the multiple traditions understanding of early American culture. He remained wedded to republicanism throughout his life—this is what gave his life meaning and identity. Simultaneously, however, the day-to-day life of a man who never read a word of John Locke exemplified liberal tendencies—the aggressive, materialistic pursuit of individual gain. Woven into these two traditions was another of equal importance to Hiram: a strong strain of Protestant morality with its emphasis on equity and charity. Within this triad it is clear that republicanism, if no longer considered *the* key to understanding the early republic, remains *a* vital concept for those attempting to re-create the political culture of those years.

Even scholars who fully accept the critical role played by republicanism during these years understand yet another important aspect of the concept; it gradually, but nonetheless surely, faded from the American vernacular. At midcentury the term rarely appeared; by the end of the century, it had all but vanished. In its place increasing numbers of individuals and groups spoke of "Americanism" with the same reverence previously reserved for republicanism. Within a matter of decades, then, a term that never appeared in Hiram Harwood's diary assumed tremendous power and influence within American culture.[58] At the close of the nineteenth century, republicanism's emphasis on power, liberty, and equality had been transmuted into Americanism's fervent belief in nationalism, individualism, and free enterprise. Yet unmistakable parallels linked the two belief systems: the protean nature of the republicanism lived and experienced by Hiram Harwood bore a striking resemblance to the equally mutable Americanism so fervently espoused by subsequent generations of his countrymen. Both became encoded into the institutional fabric of the daily lives of vast numbers of citizens. A visceral part of the very being of these individuals, each served as an unreflective guide to thought and action—a vital standard by which citizens judged both the principles and the behavior of competing individuals and groups within their own society as well as those of other nations.

Another, and perhaps more important, parallel exists between republicanism and Americanism. This involves the highly contested nature of each concept and the meaning scholars may draw from those times in which this contentiousness becomes particularly acute. When the meaning of familiar words suddenly starts to shift, when a significant portion of the population abruptly begins to perceive the prevailing and long-accepted figures of political speech in radically new and different ways, when the self-evident truths that have traditionally supported the accepted structures of power become contested, something crucial indeed is taking place within American society.[59] Just as republicanism was most highly contested at critical periods in our nation's history, so, too, has Americanism displayed this characteristic. As scholars start to understand these vigorously debated periods as special windows into the culture that bred republicanism and then Americanism, they will gain a greater appreciation of the affinities between the two concepts. Such an appreciation, which strongly suggests the many ways that Americanism may be seen as the ideological descendant of republicanism, might therefore provide provocative new ways of viewing contemporary American culture.

NOTES

1. See, for example, Thomas Jefferson to Edward Rutledge, June 24, 1797, in *The Papers of Thomas Jefferson* (Princeton, N.J.: Princeton University Press, 2002), ed. Barbara Oberg, 29, 455–57, and John Adams to Benjamin Rush, July 7, 1805, in *The Spur of Fame: Dialogues of John Adams and Benjamin Rush, 1805–1813* ed. John Schutz and Douglass Adair, (Indianapolis: Liberty Fund, 2000), 29–31.

2. Robert E. Shalhope, "Toward a Republican Synthesis: The Emergence of an Understanding of Republicanism in American Historiography," *William and Mary Quarterly*, 3rd ser., 29 (1972): 49–80.

3. Daniel T. Rodgers, "Republicanism: The Career of a Concept," *Journal of American History* 79 (June 1992): 11–38 (quotation on 17.)

4. Representatives of this approach include Joyce Appleby, *Capitalism and a New Social Order: The Republican Vision of the 1790s* (New York: New York University Press, 1984); Isaac Kramnick, *Republicanism and Bourgeois Radicalism: Political Ideology in Late Eighteenth-Century England and America* (Ithaca, N.Y.: Cornell University Press, 1990); John Diggins, *The Lost Soul of American Politics: Virtue, Self-Interest, and the Foundations of Liberalism* (New York: Basic Books, 1984); and Thomas Pangle, *The Spirit of Modern Republicanism: The Moral Vision of the American Founders and the Philosophy of John Locke* (Chicago: University of Chicago Press, 1988).

5. For a particularly astute analysis of this debate, see Alan Gibson, "Ancients, Moderns and Americans: The Republicanism-Liberalism Debate Revisited," *History of Political Thought* 21 (2000): 261–307.

6. James Kloppenberg, "The Virtues of Liberalism: Christianity, Republicanism, and Ethics in Early American Political Discourse," *Journal of American History* 74 (1987): 9–33 (quotation appears on 11).

7. "Paradigmatic pluralism" is Isaac Kramnick's term in "The 'Great National Discussion': The Discourse of Politics in 1787," *William and Mary Quarterly*, 3rd ser., 45 (1988): 3–32 (the term appears on 32). For insight into the idea of "multiple traditions," see Rogers M. Smith, "Beyond Tocqueville, Myrdal, and Hartz: The Multiple Traditions in America," *American Political Science Review* 87 (1993): 549–66. In "Ancients, Moderns and Americans," Alan Gibson provides an outstanding analysis of the manner in which the multiple traditions approach transcended the liberalism-republicanism dialogue.

8. Eve Kornfield, *Creating an American Culture, 1775–1800* (Boston: Bedford/St. Martin's, 2001), 7.

9. Rodgers, "Career of a Concept," 37.

10. Daniel T. Rodgers, "Republicanism," in *A Companion to American Thought*, ed. Richard W. Fox and James T. Kloppenberg (Cambridge, Mass.: Blackwell, 1995), 584–87 (quotation on 584).

11. Most prominent among these scholars are Thomas Pangle, *The Spirit of Modern Republicanism: The Moral Vision of the American Founders and the Philosophy of John Locke* (Chicago: University of Chicago Press, 1988); Steven M. Dworetz, *The Unvarnished Doctrine: Locke, Liberalism, and the American Revolution* (Durham, N.C.: Duke University Press, 1990); Richard Sinopoli, *The Foundations of American Citizenship: Liberalism, the Constitution, and Civic Virtue* (New York: Oxford University Press, 1992); Jerome Huyler, *Locke in America: The Moral Philosophy of the Founding Era* (Lawrence: University of Kansas Press, 1995).

12. The work of Joshua Foa Dienstag stands as a signal exception to such criticism. His essays contribute greatly to our understanding of Locke's thought and the

manner in which Thomas Jefferson and John Adams incorporated his philosophy into their own. See especially "Serving God and Mammon: The Lockean Sympathy in Early American Political Thought," *American Political Science Review* 90 (1996): 497–511; and "Between History and Nature: Social Contract Theory in Locke and the Founders," *Journal of Politics* 58 (1996): 985–1009.

13. Rodgers, "Career of a Concept," 38.

14. Drawing on Joyce Appleby, I employ the concept of culture as "the hidden but shared matrix of attitudes, injunctions, and affirmations that guide social behavior." Appleby, "Value and Society," in *Colonial British America: Essays in the New History of the Early Modern Era*, ed. Jack P. Greene and J. R. Pole (Baltimore: Johns Hopkins University Press, 1984), 290–316 (quotation on 295).

15. *Vermont Gazette*, August 30, 1793, supplement.

16. Richard Harrison, *Princetonians, 1769–1775: A Biographical Dictionary* (Princeton, N.J.: Princeton University Press, 1980), 275.

17. Ebenezer Bradford, *Mr. Thomas Paine's Trial* (Boston: Thomas and Andrews, 1795), 12.

18. Daniel Marsh, *A Sermon Delivered on the 16th of August, 1809, in Commemoration of Bennington Battle* (Bennington: A. Haswell, 1809), 12.

19. Hiram's reference here is to the third part of Noah Webster's *Grammatical Institute of the English Language*, 3rd ed. (Philadelphia: Young and M'Cullough, 1787).

20. Harwood Diary, Bennington Museum, Bennington, Vermont, March 2, 1822. Hereafter cited as HD.

21. The orations of Warren and Hancock appear on 227–41 of Webster's *Grammatical Institute*. Jean Baker contends that the very structure and behavioral fabric of the common school—student monitors, the barring-out ceremony, spelling bees, the boarding around of the school master—inculcated republican principles into the students. Jean Baker, "From Belief into Culture: Republicanism in the Antebellum North," *American Quarterly* 37 (1985): 532–50.

22. Noah Webster, *An American Selection of Lessons in Reading and Speaking Calculated to Improve the Minds and Refine the Taste of Youth* (Salem: Cushing and Appleton, 1805), 160.

23. *Vermont Gazette*, August 15, 1799.

24. John Spargo, *Anthony Haswell, Printer-Patriot-Ballader* (Rutland, Vt.: Tuttle, 1925), 86–87.

25. Rhys Isaac, "Dramatizing the Ideology of the Revolution: Popular Mobilization in Virginia, 1774 to 1776," *William and Mary Quarterly*, 3rd ser., 33 (1976): 357–85. The quotations appear respectively at 378–79 and 362.

26. HD, August 16, 1809.

27. (Bennington) *Green Mountain Farmer*, August 21, 1809.

28. *Vermont Gazette*, March 17, 1809.

29. HD, January 7, 1823.

30. HD, September 21, 1825.

31. HD, September 5, 1826.

32. HD, September 4, 1827.

33. HD, November 29, 1810. See Jeffrey L. Pasley, *"The Tyranny of Printers": Newspaper Politics in the Early American Republic* (Charlottesville: University Press of Virginia, 2001), 176–95, for an excellent analysis of James Duane's republicanism. For the radical republicanism of the *Aurora*, see Richard N. Rosenfeld, *American Aurora: A Democratic-Republican Returns: The Suppressed History of Our Nation's Beginnings and the Heroic Newspaper That Tried to Report It* (New York: St. Martin's Press, 1997).

34. HD, August 27, 1834.

35. I am indebted to Jean Baker's "From Belief into Culture" for the following discussion of tradition and culture.

36. HD, October 25, 1814.

37. HD, June 23, 1816.

38. HD, February 13, 1829; July 8, 1832; June 2, 1835.

39. HD, February 24, March 8, 9, July 25, 1830.

40. The opposition to Andrew Jackson assumed the title National Republicans, or "Nationals," while Jackson's party took the name Democratic-Republicans.

41. HD, November 20, December 2, 9, 1831; February 13, March 6, 18, May 27, June 16, 1832.

42. HD, July 14, 19, October 6, 7, 12, 1832.

43. HD, October 21, 24, November 4, 10, 26, 1832.

44. HD, December 13, 14, 15, 1832; January 29, March 26, 1833.

45. For insight into the Bank War, see Charles Sellers, *The Market Revolution: Jacksonian America, 1815–1846* (New York: Oxford University Press, 1991), 321–26; Robert Remini, *Andrew Jackson and the Bank War: A Study in the Growth of Presidential Power* (New York: Norton, 1967); Bray Hammond, *Banks and Politics in America, from the Revolution to the Civil War* (Princeton, N.J.: Princeton University Press, 1957).

46. HD, December 26, 1833; January 6, 10, 1834.

47. HD, January 11, 1834.

48. *Spectator*, December 30, 1833.

49. HD, January 31, February 2, 1834.

50. *Spectator*, January 31, 1834.

51. For these observations, see the *Spectator*, December 1833, January, February, March, April 1834.

52. HD, January 11, April 28, 1834.

53. *Register of Debates in Congress*, 23rd Cong., 1st sess., 1834, 10, pt. 3, 3944.

54. Ibid., 3944–45.

55. Ibid., 3945–46.

56. Marvin Meyers, *The Jacksonian Persuasion: Politics and Belief* (Palo Alto: Stanford University Press, 1957), 33–56; Daniel W. Howe, *The Political Culture of the American Whigs* (Chicago: University of Chicago Press, 1979), 263–98.

57. David Waldstreicher, *In the Midst of Perpetual Fetes: The Making of American Nationalism, 1776–1820* (Chapel Hill: University of North Carolina Press, 1997), 3.

58. For amplification of this power and influence, see the succeeding essays in this volume.

59. This observation rests on the insights of Daniel Rodgers, *Contested Truths: Keywords in American Politics since Independence* (New York: Basic Books, 1987).

JONATHAN HANSEN

★ ★ ★ ★

★ True Americanism

★ *Progressive Era Intellectuals and*

★ *the Problem of Liberal Nationalism*

In the spring of 1894, Theodore Roosevelt surveyed the United States from Washington, D.C., and concluded that the nation lacked the spirit of "true Americanism." Absent that spirit, the U.S. Civil Service commissioner warned, American democracy would succumb to social disintegration. A critic might protest that social disintegration is typically a byproduct of structural maladjustment; Roosevelt simply insisted that all could be made well if citizens did as their forefathers had done, namely, think, work, conquer, live, and die "purely as Americans."

Ostensibly, the *purity* Roosevelt invoked pertained less to cultural homogeneity than to political and economic commitment. In Roosevelt's civic ideal, ethnically diverse, morally autonomous individuals pursued private ends within the constraints of a liberal political economy. But Roosevelt's vision was not culturally neutral. Anybody could participate in this national enterprise so long as he or she valued what Roosevelt valued—above all, the self-interested individualism at the core of Anglo-American liberal thought. Glorious opportunities awaited all who "cease to be Europeans, and become Americans like the rest of us," Roosevelt exclaimed. If "anarchists," "laborers who tend to depress the labor market," and assimilation-resistant "races" were disqualified out of hand, the rest had only to forsake old loves and loyalties—"to talk and think and be United States"—to qualify as *true* Americans.[1]

Two decades later, on Independence Day, 1915, Louis D. Brandeis, soon to be elevated to the U.S. Supreme Court, propounded his own vision of "true Americanism" at Boston's Faneuil Hall. Amid mounting agitation over the war in Europe, President Wilson had urged his fellow citizens to make the Fourth of July "Americanization Day." Brandeis was only too happy to go along with the idea. "What is Americanization?" he demanded. Superficially, Americanization entailed immigrants' adopting American clothes and customs; significantly, it meant immigrants' learning and using English "as the common medium of speech." Yet language was nothing compared to the more fundamental shift of allegiance that Americanization implied. "Immigrants must be brought into complete harmony with our ideals and aspirations and cooperate with us for their attainment," Brandeis declared. Only then could they be said to "possess the national consciousness of an American."

Thus far little distinguished Brandeis's ideal of "true Americanism" from Roosevelt's. But Brandeis acknowledged something Roosevelt did not: despite their strange customs and lack of English, many immigrants arrived in the new world "already truly American"—that is, already in harmony with American ideals. If their allegiance eroded on their arrival, the fault lay not with the newcomers but with the hosts' failure to extend liberal democratic rights and privileges to strangers. Prejudice and industrial dependence, not cultural diversity, threatened American democracy. It was the duty of all true Americans to safeguard equal opportunity and fair play.[2]

This essay describes the attempt of several prominent Progressive Era intellectuals to dislodge liberal democracy from its mooring in Anglo-American culture and history and to reestablish it on a civic foundation consistent with cultural pluralism. These thinkers all assumed that effective government requires a sense of community, or "peoplehood." They all recognized that political communities, like cultural communities, are constituted by boundaries and exclusions. The nation's urgent challenge, as they saw it, was to articulate an ideal of American national identity capable of balancing the principles of individuality and cultural inclusiveness with a sense of civic solidarity.[3]

Civic solidarity seemed in short supply at the turn of the twentieth century thanks to a series of political, social, and demographic developments.[4] The influx of southern and eastern European immigrants at the end of the nineteenth century; the migration of African Americans northward and of farmers to the cities; innovations in finance, production, communications, and retail that thrust individuals into a national marketplace; labor, women's suffrage, and African American civil rights agitation—these and other events combined to unsettle the Anglo-Saxon foundation of American citizenship and breed anxiety about the dissolution of an "American" consensus. Domestic cultural anxiety was complicated by America's triumphant emergence onto the international stage. The so-called closing of the American frontier augured the projection of American political and economic power around the world. The Spanish-American and World

Wars revealed a nation struggling to come to grips with the moral and political responsibility such power entails.

The developments that eroded the old Anglo-American cultural boundaries inspired an intellectual effervescence from which new ideas emerged and old concepts were given new meaning. These ideas were not solely, or even largely, liberating. For every Eugene Debs decrying the nation's yawning social disparity, there was a Henry Cabot Lodge erecting a model of national loyalty designed to quash dissent and bolster the faltering Anglo-American order. Women, African Americans, Asians, Jews, and southern and eastern Europeans suffered the brunt of this reaction; hitherto assumed to be inferior to white Anglo-Saxon men—and therefore unequipped to participate in republican government—they were allegedly proved so by the "scientific" practitioners of phrenology and eugenics.

The dubiousness of these ideas and the bigotry of their authors inspired a reaction among a group of liberal intellectuals and social scientists. Such figures as W. E. B. Du Bois, Horace Kallen, Randolph Bourne, and John Dewey shared Brandeis's conviction that cultural diversity and legal equality for women must be the test of American liberalism: a liberal democracy that denied citizenship to people on the basis of ethnicity, race, or gender, they argued, was unworthy of the name. These thinkers repudiated two fundamental tenets of classical liberalism: first, that ethnic, or cultural, allegiance was anathema to individual autonomy; second, that liberty was reducible to laissez-faire economics.

The two objections were related. They stemmed from skepticism about the presuppositions of liberal political economy. Individuals do not emerge independent and autonomous from the womb, as liberal theory suggests; rather, they develop these virtues in communities. Gross economic and political disparity can impede this process; hence government has a role to play in promoting both individual autonomy and healthy communities, and in ensuring the existence of a level playing field. As nativists campaigned relentlessly and successfully to restrict immigration, Du Bois, Kallen, Bourne, Dewey, and Brandeis attempted, under the banner of what Brandeis called "true Americanism"—and I will call "cosmopolitan patriotism"—to galvanize the nation in defense of cultural diversity and social justice.

I label these thinkers "cosmopolitan" to distinguish them from other liberals of their day. Most Progressive intellectuals can be divided into two camps regarding the role of national and ethnic affiliation in people's lives.

"Universalists" like Theodore Roosevelt viewed national and ethnoracial allegiances as parochial and divisive, the source of untold misery around the world; "cultural pluralists" led by Horace Kallen celebrated national and ethnoracial allegiances as wholesome and inviolable. The "cosmopolitan patriots" recognized partial truth in both accounts. They shared the universalists' commitment to individual self-realization but insisted that individuals realize themselves in specific communities. They acknowledged that communities and nations historically inhibited individuality, but they argued that this need not be so. A nation genuinely committed to individual freedom, they maintained, would view affiliation as a product of choice rather than as inborn and unchangeable.[5]

In recent years, intellectuals on the broad left have begun to appreciate the progressive potential of what some have called "liberal nationalism."[6] Those inclined to try to redeem nationalism from prejudice and jingoism might begin by revisiting the arguments of their Progressive Era predecessors, whose speeches, articles, and essays suggest how the goal of national solidarity may be harmonized with the principles of individuality, cultural diversity, and social and political justice. But readers with more modest aims may find this history compelling too: it is intended for all who are interested in the moral and political dilemmas inherent in identity politics, whereby every "we" begets a "they."

In the winter of 1915, the philosopher Horace Kallen published a two-part essay in the *Nation* entitled "Democracy *versus* the Melting Pot," which served as a wake-up call for democrats who had been slow to respond to a mounting wave of nativism. Kallen advanced an ideal of cultural pluralism, discarding the metaphor of America as a melting pot in favor of the symbol of orchestral harmony. The timing of his essay had much to do with its reception. The carnage of war in Europe had alerted American intellectuals to the toxicity of national identities based on geography, language, and ancestry. Was it possible, many wondered, to cultivate the communal aspects of nationalism without promoting the chauvinism that often accompanied them? Kallen—along with Du Bois, Bourne, Dewey, and Brandeis— argued that the same principle of self-interest that regulated individual behavior in a democracy might also safeguard the integrity of groups. In a heterogeneous nation and an increasingly interconnected world, the best way to protect the interests of one's own community was to defend the community rights of all.

Not all American intellectuals needed Kallen to alert them to the rise of cultural bigotry. In *The Souls of Black Folk*, published in 1903, Du Bois argued that releasing 4 million slaves into a competitive marketplace— "alone and unguided, without capital, without land, without skill, without economic organization, without even the bald protection of law, order, and decency"—had been irresponsible and foolish. For the members of historically oppressed groups and classes, freedom required more than the mere loosening of bonds; it demanded positive action on behalf of the victims. American racism belied the neutrality and universalism of liberal theory. A truly universal order required both a just distribution of resources— intellectual as well as material—and the respect of individuals and cultures for one another. Such respect, Du Bois insisted, would be granted only to those with self-respect, a quality he believed had been beaten out of African Americans by centuries of servitude.

Du Bois first expressed his own ideal of cultural pluralism in "The Conservation of Races," an address he delivered in 1897 at the inaugural meeting of the American Negro Academy, in Washington, D.C. The academy was the inspiration of the critic Alexander Crummell, who, like Du Bois, repudiated Booker T. Washington's policy of subordinating higher education and civil rights to industrial training. If African Americans were ever to take their place among the world's great races, Crummell and Du Bois vowed, they would have to develop minds as well as muscles, cultivate racial consciousness, and stand up unabashedly for their legal rights. "The Conservation of Races" assumed that the prospect for genuine social exchange between the races was dwindling. The founding of the American Negro Academy coincided with a mounting epidemic of lynching and the near-total disenfranchisement of southern black men, and it came just one year after the Supreme Court ruling in *Plessy v. Ferguson* that affirmed the constitutionality of racial segregation. In the face of this onslaught, it was natural for African Americans to want to downplay racial distinctions. But to do so, Du Bois insisted, defied the laws of nature and history and only invited further scorn and oppression.[7]

Du Bois's advocacy of "racial conservation" was based on a political rather than a biological argument. "What, then, is a race?" he asked. "It is a vast family of human beings, *generally* of common blood and language, *always* of common history, traditions and impulses, who are voluntarily or involuntarily striving together for the accomplishment of certain more or less vividly conceived ideals of life" (italics mine). Du Bois identified eight such races extant in the world whose "spiritual, psychical, differences" were "more important" than "common blood" in determining their "cohesiveness and continuity."[8] The cultural distinctiveness of these races sharpened as their physical differences blurred. The nineteenth-century nation-state had emerged as the repository for and guarantor of each race's unique ideals. England, Germany, and France had come to represent the zenith of Western civilization. Meanwhile, Du Bois observed, every other race was "striving, each in its own way, to develop for civilization its particular message, its particular ideal, which shall help to guide the world nearer and nearer that perfection of human life for which we all long."[9]

"The Conservation of Races" seems to advance a theory of cultural identity consistent with Kallen's pluralism. Du Bois's argument that each race had a particular contribution to offer might have come from Kallen himself. But by emphasizing the role of *history* in this process, Du Bois allowed for greater individual agency. Kallen expected individuals to perpetuate rather than shape a given culture. Du Bois expected them to participate in revitalizing individual and group life in America. He insisted that a people of mixed blood could develop its own identity. Indeed, he believed that a healthy racial identity depended on contact and comparison with others. Once a people had secured its place in history, it had to act the part of the talented tenth among races elsewhere, promoting self-expression and democracy throughout the world.[10]

For Du Bois, racial consciousness was perfectly compatible with American citizenship. In "The Conservation of Races," he underscored African Americans' overlapping affiliations: "We are Americans not only by birth and by citizenship," he maintained, "but by our political ideals, our language, our religion. Farther than that, our Americanism does not go. At that point, we are Negroes, members of a vast historic race that from the very dawn of creation has slept, but [is] half awakening in the dark forests of its African fatherland." Surely this was *far enough*. A still-fettered African American culture had lent the nation "its only touch of pathos and humor amid its mad money-getting plutocracy"; a freer one not only could "soften the whiteness of the Teutonic to-day" but also would promote "that broader humanity which freely recognizes differences in men, but sternly deprecates inequality in their opportunities of development."[11]

Du Bois's emphasis on the public and political benefits of cultural diversity allied him intellectually with the cultural critic Randolph Bourne, a contemporary of Kallen who is often credited with anticipating multiculturalism. In the summer of 1916, Bourne published an essay in the *Atlantic Monthly* entitled "Trans-national America," which claimed that all political communities inevitably excluded outsiders.[12] Bourne's "trans-nationalism" owed a great debt to Kallen. Like Kallen, Bourne marveled at the irony of "hyphenated English-Americans" lamenting the provincialism of America's immigrant groups. Far from encouraging immigrants to assimilate to a single cultural norm, chauvinistic Anglo-Americans encouraged ethnic bonding, which Bourne viewed not as a failure of American democracy but as a sign of its enduring strength. This unintended consequence of nativist fervor brought Bourne to contemplate "what Americanism may rightly mean." Here was a chance "to ask ourselves whether our ideal has been broad or narrow—whether perhaps the time has not come to assert a higher ideal than the 'melting pot.'"[13]

Amid the turmoil of the world war, Bourne regarded nationalism as, potentially, a saving grace. Liberals should not cede love of country to conservatives but redefine and redeem it. All U.S. citizens had foreign-born roots; all (except African slaves) had arrived seeking liberty and opportunity; all were initially reluctant to surrender their Old World traditions. To insist, as had imperialists during the Philippine-American War, that Anglo-Saxons possessed a unique genius for democracy and freedom was to misinterpret both the nature of mankind and the significance of the saga unfolding on the American frontier.[14]

For it was the frontier, in Bourne's view, not the Anglo-Saxon political inheritance, that rendered America exceptional. It produced "a democratic cooperation in determining ideals and purposes and industrial and social conditions." Skeptics need only compare the "the great 'alien' states of Wisconsin and Minnesota" to the American South—that most Anglo-Saxon of regions—to comprehend the frontier's transforming force. Would Anglo-Americans "really like to see the foreign hordes Americanized" along southern lines? Which American states produced "more wisdom, intelligence, industry and social leadership," he demanded, the so-called alien states of the Midwest or "the truly American" states of the South? Exposing Anglo-Americans' own parochialism, Bourne determined to demolish the "chief obstacle to the nation's social advance."[15]

Like Kallen and Du Bois, Bourne hoped America might become "a real nation, with a tenacious, richly woven fabric of native culture"; like them, Bourne recognized that achieving that goal would require replacing the prevailing laissez-faire conception of freedom with a more demanding ideal. "If freedom means the right to do pretty much as one pleases, so long as one does not interfere with others, the immigrant has found freedom, and the ruling element has been singularly liberal in its treatment of the invading hordes," Bourne observed. "But if freedom means a democratic cooperation in determining the ideals and purposes and industrial and social institutions of a country, then the immigrant has not been free, and the Anglo-Saxon element is guilty of just what every dominant race is guilty of in every European country: the imposition of its own culture upon the minority peoples."[16]

At this point Bourne diverged from Kallen, who called on the state to maintain group integrity and mediate group interaction. Bourne expected cultural exchange to promote social integration. Like Du Bois, Bourne viewed contact as the principal requisite of democracy and the means to both cultural development and national solidarity. America, he marveled, was the arena of a "thrilling and bloodless battle of Kulturs." In states like Wisconsin and Minnesota, Scandinavian, Polish, and German culture had found hospitable soil. The result was a liberating "cross-fertilization" in which politics and society had attained "new potency." Far from succumbing to a numbing assimilation, these communities "remained distinct but cooperating to the greater glory and benefit, not only of themselves but of all the native 'Americanism' around them." Indeed, quite by accident, America had developed into "a cosmopolitan federation of national colonies" living peaceably side by side. If citizens would cultivate this "world-federation in miniature," Bourne suggested, America might lead the way out of the world's devastating cycle of nationalist wars. This meant elevating America's inchoate cosmopolitanism to full national consciousness, no mean feat in a "loose, free country" in which "no constraining national purpose, no tenacious folk-tradition and folk-style hold the people to a line."[17]

While nobly conceived, Bourne's transnational ideal was less inclusive than it appears. He excluded from his cultural project millions of Americans who did not conform to his conception of virtue. For Bourne, only distinct ethnic groups could generate a vital national culture. He wanted to protect these rich cultures from Anglo-American intolerance. But his denigration of "cultural half-breeds" exposed the limits of his self-described "cosmopolitanism."[18] Bourne imagined himself to be an advocate for dispossessed Americans, but he wrote condescendingly about "hordes of men and women without a spiritual country, cultural outlaws, without taste, without standards but those of the mob. The influences at the fringe . . . ," he wrote, "are centrifugal, anarchical. . . . They become the flotsam and jetsam of American life, the downward undertow of our civilization with its leering cheapness and falseness of taste and spiritual outlook, the absence of mind and sincere feeling which we see in our slovenly towns, our vapid motion pictures, our popular novels, and in the vacuous faces of the crowds on the city street."[19] One wonders whether Bourne's half-breeds appeared so derelict and, by contrast, his cultural clashes so bloodless because he restricted his gaze to philosophical rivalries played out amid the open air of midwestern pastures and the nation's universities. Bourne did not explain how his "intellectual internationalism" would influence social relations in urban cauldrons like New York City, where Bourne himself resided and which would could not help but be the final test of his ideal.[20]

Lapsed Bohemians, Germans, and Jews were not the only people whom Bourne excluded from his imagined cosmopolitan community. In his enthusiasm for America's westward expansion, he also ignored the injustice to Indians and Chinese laborers that was perpetrated on the American frontier.[21] Unlike the philosopher William James, who had cautioned Americans against judging foreign cultures on the basis of local norms, Bourne believed his transnational ideal would uplift "the laggard peoples" of southeastern Europe.[22] Bourne assured Anglo-Americans that their fears about the loyalty of immigrants were groundless. Although they often took their earnings back to the old country, they inevitably returned to the Old World with a critical appreciation of "the superiority of American organization to the primitive living around them." James, who died in 1910, would have thought it ironic that Bourne defended cultural pluralism at home while he simultaneously celebrated a process by which Europe was becoming more like America.[23]

Like Bourne and Kallen, John Dewey entered the debate about American identity not to refute the arguments of fellow liberals, but to challenge the coercive drive for Americanization that Theodore Roosevelt and other Republicans were promoting during World War I. Dewey, the great educator, opposed the introduction of military drill in public schools as a means to inculcate national loyalty.[24] Yet, at the same time, he welcomed America's "awakening to the presence in our country of large immigrant masses who may remain as much aliens as if they never entered our gateways."[25] In a series of essays published between 1916 and 1918, Dewey tried to reconcile his enthusiasm for cultural diversity with the imperative of national cohesion.

For Dewey, economic life was the arena where Americans could renew their cultural vitality. This was his particular contribution to the debate about civic identity: "Any democracy which is more than an imitation of some archaic republican government must issue from the womb of our chaotic industrialism," he wrote. With a mature industrial base, a diverse citizenry, and a constitution that separated nationality from citizenship, America had the potential to blossom as a "community of directed thought and emotion." Dewey was not naive about the odds for success. The American political economy was fraught with conflict and inequality. But better to meet them head-on than to ignore them.[26]

Dewey emphatically shared Kallen's aversion to laissez-faire economics and the political passivity it bred. But he disagreed about the goal ethnic diversity should serve. Their difference stemmed from contrasting views of culture itself. In "Democracy *versus* the Melting Pot," Kallen endorsed the ideal of diversity as a means of safeguarding private life. Dewey viewed cultural differences as a source not only of public enrichment but also of the civic solidarity required of industrial and political reform. Kallen aimed to protect the cultural integrity of oppressed ethnic groups. Dewey expected ethnic and racial diversity to enrich a shared civic culture. "I never did care for the melting pot metaphor," he wrote to Kallen, "but genuine assimilation *to one another*—not to Anglo-Saxondom—seems to be essential to an America. That each cultural section should maintain its distinctive literary and artistic traditions seems to me most desirable, but in order that it might have the more to contribute to others."[27] By emphasizing self-preservation, cultural revivals could spawn the sort of self-serving, invidious cultural comparisons that had inspired Kallen's essay in the first place.[28]

In 1919, Kallen was moved to clarify his own thoughts on the relationship of pluralism to nationalism when the philosopher Morris Cohen attacked Zionism in the pages of the *New Republic*. Cohen accused Zionists of sacrificing Enlightenment rationality to group loyalty. Rooted in "nationalist philosophy," he contended, Zionism constituted an implacable "challenge to all those who still believe in liberalism." Zionists, in his view, were trying to evade the principal challenge of the early twentieth century: how different cultures could dwell harmoniously in a shrinking world.[29] Kallen's response to this critique suggests that his ideal of cultural pluralism was consistent with a cosmopolitan future. At the heart of his rebuttal lay the premise that nationalism and liberalism, far from being anathema, were both crucial components of a modern Enlightenment. Witness the great liberal, Giuseppe Mazzini, leader of the Italian risorgimento.[30]

Kallen was determined to retrieve nationalism from the historical wasteland to which Cohen had consigned it. Far from atavistic, nationalism, argued Kallen, was a natural and enduring sentiment no less universal than the individual's vaunted capacity for reason. Particularly strong among oppressed peoples, it revealed "a state of mind and feeling basic to established as well as aspiring nationalities." Of course, nationalism, "like other philosophies[,] . . . can be used to establish conclusions that are paranoia and fantasy," Kallen conceded. But the same was true of liberalism. Zionism rested on the "normal nationalist philosophy" common to Poles, Greeks, and Italians. Far from contradicting liberalism, as Cohen had suggested, Zionism extended the tenets of liberalism "from the individual to the group." Moreover, to decry Zionism for being anti-assimilationist in the face of the ongoing persecution of Jews was to side with the historical Inquisition. Genuine democracy was itself anti-assimilationist. "It stands for the acknowledgment, the harmony and organization of group diversities in cooperative expansion of the common life." It was just this ideal that had always been denied to Jews.[31]

A Jewish homeland would also resolve the problem of Jewish ambiguity. Kallen agreed with Cohen that any contribution American Jews made to civilization they would make *as Americans*. But Kallen was not satisfied with that. He found it "a curious sort of liberalism" that would celebrate the cultural distinctiveness of, say, the Spanish and French while denying such distinctiveness to Jews. America "must not only give to the immigrant the best we have, but must preserve for America the good that is in the immigrant," Brandeis observed in his "True Americanism." Kallen insisted that this vision depended on Jewish Americans having a homeland—that is, a source of constant cultural renewal. Only then could they make a significant and sustained contribution to American civic life. Kallen's America would absorb and assimilate aspects of other cultures and shape these cultures into a distinctive community of flesh and spirit. Here was a vision of America synonymous with the Enlightenment, "a democratic cooperative organization of nationalities, no less than of other forms of the association of men, in the endeavor after life, liberty and happiness."[32]

Liberal theory expects individuals, once freed from artificial fetters, to make their happy way in the world. Du Bois, Dewey, Kallen, and Brandeis recognized that the egalitarian marketplace assumed by liberal theory did not exist in early twentieth-century America. It was therefore up to the state to restore open competition and promote civic virtue—the better, in Brandeis's words, "to fit its rulers for their task." Like the Socialist leader Eugene V. Debs, the subjects of this essay regarded state coercion not as proof of the state's innate evil but as evidence that an ideally public institution had been overrun by private interests. If the state waxed monstrous at the turn of the twentieth century, that was because of its hijacking by a corporate elite and the failure of most Americans to turn back a serious threat to the national welfare. In "True Americanism," Brandeis argued that a state less obsessed with sorting, sifting, and fumigating immigrants at Ellis Island (as Henry James had put it) and more committed to ensuring the viability of "the American standard of living" would have no reason to fear for the loyalty of its citizens. By curbing "capitalistic combination," upholding the workers' right to organize, and introducing "some system of social insurance," the state could secure workers' health, education, and leisure—minimal requirements of an independent, and loyal, citizenry.[33]

Kallen and Cohen continued to debate the meaning of true American-ism into 1919. But the entry of the United States into the World War in April 1917 swamped cosmopolitan patriotism in a wave of jingoism. The civic loyalty that Brandeis and Dewey had hoped to cultivate via economic and political reforms and social insurance was created artificially by court order, nationalist propaganda, and loyalty oaths. The nation that emerged from war in 1919 was arguably less tolerant of ethnic and racial minorities than at any time in its history. The urgent necessity expressed by govern-ment officials and other shapers of public opinion was not to achieve a viable cultural pluralism but to stamp out communism, anarchism, and other movements for social equality. The ensuing Red Scare spawned con-ditions favorable to the passage of the Johnson-Reed Act in 1924, which, by establishing immigrant quotas based on national origin, effectively si-lenced the idea that cultural diversity was America's greatest asset. Plural-ist arguments would emerge episodically among American intellectuals over the next fifty years, but not until the 1960s and 1970s would Ameri-cans take up the problem of cultural diversity in significant numbers.[34]

But undue focus on the cosmopolitan patriots' defeat in World War I overlooks the cogency of their larger critique. The cosmopolitan patriots wanted Americans to act like democrats—to stand on moral principle, to mix freely with those above and below them regardless of their origin, to view an attack on others' liberty as an assault on themselves. If at times their civic vision appeared foreshortened (how could a champion of cul-tural diversity and integrity like Brandeis turn a blind eye to the plight of Palestinians, never mind that of African Americans and American Indi-ans?), it is because, like most American intellectuals of their era, they took Europe as their reference point. By contrast to the nationalist hostility that consumed the Old World during the Great War, America's record appeared noteworthy. Of course, such explanations only confirm the fact that national identity is constructed and relational, as we say in postmodern parlance.

But should we stop there? The cosmopolitan patriots took that premise as their starting point. They did not see America's jingoism and racism as a reason to give up on the idea of the nation itself. They recognized that all communities are, by definition, bounded—that all identities exclude and/or subordinate. Long before Benedict Anderson described nations as "imagined communities," the cosmopolitan patriots acknowledged that nations are "fictions," as William James put it; hence they set out to make the fiction of America as generous as possible.[35] The alternative to liberal nationalism, from their perspective, was not local (ethnic, racial, religious) affiliation or world citizenship—though if chosen these could be consistent with liberal nationalism—but illiberal nationalism. In a world in which political rights and legal protections are tied to national membership, their experience suggests, individuals who simply disdain nationalism of any sort commit their fate to the political right.

But cosmopolitan patriotism teaches us more than the mere fact of nationalism's inescapability. It offers us a model of social affiliation and political and moral engagement equal to the complexity of the contemporary world. In the Progressive Era, when most Americans regarded identity in ethnic, racial, and religious terms and defined u.s. interests in opposition to the outside world, the cosmopolitan patriots insisted that affiliations and interests change with context—that the unvarnished claims of cultural pluralism, nationalism, or universalism are plausible only in a political or moral vacuum. In real life, individuals maintain overlapping, often competing allegiances—as Eugene Debs learned when canvassing locally for international socialism or as Jane Addams discovered when getting to know and defend her neighbors in immigrant Chicago.

Cosmopolitan patriotism also reminds us that patriotism has not always been the province of the state. The subjects of this essay did not subordinate liberal democratic principles to state interests. From their perspective, critical engagement with one's country constituted the highest form of love. They rejected the notion that patriotism entailed uncritical loyalty to the government in wartime and that patriotism and internationalism were incompatible. They were not blind to the magnanimity of soldiers who sacrificed their lives on the battlefield; many endorsed America's entry into World War I in 1917. But they all insisted that love of country, like sacrifice itself, could take many forms. At the end of the nineteenth century, they launched a vigorous cultural and political campaign on behalf of equal opportunity and equality before the law. Critical vigilance was the keystone of their patriotism. Loving their country, they vowed to extend its privileges and immunities to all Americans regardless of gender, class, ethnicity, or (in Du Bois's and Dewey's cases) race. At the very least, their ideal of patriotism should provoke, if not inform, the contemporary left.

NOTES

For help with this essay I would like to thank Robert Chodat, Michael Kazin, Matthew Lindsay, and Joseph McCartin.

1. Theodore Roosevelt, "True Americanism," *Forum*, April 1894, in*Theodore Roosevelt: An American Mind*, ed. Mario R. DiNunzio (New York: Penguin Books, 1994), 166–72.

2. Louis D. Brandeis, "True Americanism," in *Brandeis on Zionism: A Collection of Addresses and Statements by Louis D. Brandeis* (Westport, Conn.: Hyperion Press, 1942), 4–5.

3. Rogers Smith poses this problem elegantly in the introduction to *Civic Ideals: Conflicting Visions of Citizenship in U.S. History* (New Haven, Conn.: Yale University Press, 1997), 1–12.

4. The sense of rupture and fragmentation is commonplace in Progressive Era cultural criticism. Henry James, *The American Scene* (1907; repr., New York: Penguin, 1994), chap. 3, is illuminating on the subject.

5. Jonathan M. Hansen, *The Lost Promise of Patriotism: Debating American Identity, 1890–1920* (Chicago: University of Chicago Press, 2003), introduction. Cf. David A. Hollinger, "Not Universalists, Not Pluralists: The New Cosmopolitans Find Their Way," *Constellations* 8 (2001): 236–48, and the postscript to the 2000 edition of Hollinger, *Postethnic America: Beyond Multiculturalism* (New York: Basic Books, 2000).

6. See, for example, Michael Lind, *The Next American Nation* (New York: Free Press, 1995); Yaël Tamir, *Liberal Nationalism* (Princeton, N.J.: Princeton University Press, 1993); David Miller, *On Nationality* (Oxford: Clarendon Press, 1997); Michael Ignatieff, *Blood and Belonging: Journeys into the New Nationalism* (New York: Farrar, Straus, and Giroux, 1993); Will Kymlicka, *Multicultural Citizenship: A Liberal Theory for Minority Rights* (New York: Clarendon Press, 1996); Richard Rorty, *Achieving Our Country: Leftist Thought in Twentieth-Century America* (Cambridge, Mass.: Harvard University Press, 1998); Tom Nairn, *Faces of Nationalism: Janus Revisited* (New York: Verso, 1998); and Hollinger, *Postethnic America*. For a skeptical perspective on liberal nationalism, see Joan Cocks, *Passion and Paradox: In-*

tellectuals Confront the National Question (Princeton, N.J.: Princeton University Press, 2002).

7. W. E. B. Du Bois, *The Conservation of Races* (Washington: Baptists Magazine Print, 1897), 2–15.

8. To quote Du Bois, they are "the Slavs of eastern Europe, the Teutons of middle Europe, the English of Great Britain and America, the Romance nations of Southern and Western Europe, the Negroes of Africa and America, the Semitic people of Western Asia and Northern Africa, the Hindoos of Central Asia and the Mongolians of Eastern Asia." Ibid., 9.

9. Ibid., 7–9.

10. In "Strivings of the Negro People," *Atlantic Monthly*, August 1897, 195—the fraternal twin of his "Conservation" address—Du Bois emphasized the importance of cultural contact between the races, stating that it was the "end of [Negro] striving . . . to be a co-worker in the kingdom of culture, to escape both death and isolation, and to husband and use his best powers." John Higham cogently captured the distinction between Du Bois and Kallen in "Ethnic Pluralism in Modern American Thought," in *Send These to Me: Jews and Other Immigrants in Urban America* (New York: Atheneum, 1975), 209–11.

11. Du Bois, *Conservation of Races*, 11–12. Du Bois reiterated this sentiment in "Strivings of the Negro People," 194–98.

12. Randolph Bourne, "Trans-national America," *Atlantic Monthly*, July 1916, in Randolph Bourne, *The Radical Will, Selected Essays, 1911–1918*, ed. Olaf Hansen (Berkeley: University of California Press, 1977).

13. Bourne, "Trans-national America," 248–51.

14. Woodrow Wilson, "The Ideals of America," *Atlantic Monthly*, December 1901; Hansen, *Lost Promise of Patriotism*, chap. 1.

15. Bourne, "Trans-national America," 250.

16. Ibid., 252.

17. Ibid., 253–58.

18. Ibid., 254.

19. Ibid., 254–55. Scathing indictments of mass culture would become a staple of twentieth-century left cultural criticism. It took books like Janice A. Radway, *Reading the Romance: Women, Patriarchy, and Popular Literature* (Chapel Hill: University of North Carolina Press, 1984), to awaken scholars to the amplitude of popular culture. See also Richard Wightman Fox and T. J. Jackson Lears, eds., *The Culture of Consumption: Critical Essays in American History* (Chicago: University of Chicago Press, 1993), especially the introduction. Jane Addams knew that screeds like Bourne's were as often as not the product of ignorance. "We hasten

to give the franchise to the immigrant," Addams wrote, "from a sense of justice, from a tradition that he ought to have it, while we dub him with epithets deriding his past life or present occupation, and feel no duty to invite him to our houses." Addams, "The Subjective Necessity for Social Settlements," in *The Social Thought of Jane Addams*, ed. Christopher Lasch (1965; repr., New York: Irvington, 1982), 32.

20. Bourne, "Trans-national America," 259. Bourne more readily admits the potential for cultural conflict in a pluralist state in his companion essay, "The Jew and Trans-national America," *Menorah Journal*, December 1916: 277–84.

21. Cf. Bourne's essay "The State," in *War and the Intellectuals: Essays by R. S. Bourne*, ed. Carl Resek (New York: Harper and Row, 1965), which is imbued with frontier mythology.

22. Bourne, "Trans-national America," 256. William James, "On a Certain Blindness in Human Beings," in *Talks to Teachers on Psychology: and to Students on Some of Life's Ideals* (1899; repr., New York: Norton, 1958).

23. Bourne, "Trans-national America," 262. On James's cosmopolitanism, see Hansen, *Lost Promise of Patriotism*, chap. 1. Historian Ian Tyrell shares my sense that Bourne's cosmopolitanism is, finally, parochial. See Tyrell, "American Exceptionalism in an Age of International History," *American Historical Review* 96, no. 4 (October 1991): 1052–53.

24. John Dewey, "Universal Service as Education," *New Republic*, April 22, 1916, in Dewey, *The Middle Works, 1899–1924*, ed. Jo Ann Boydston, vol. 10 (Carbondale: Southern Illinois University Press, 1985), 186.

25. Ibid., 183.

26. John Dewey, "American Education and Culture," *New Republic*, July 1, 1916, in *Middle Works*, 10:198.

27. John Dewey to Horace Kallen, March 31, 1915, in *Correspondence of John Dewey*, ed. Larry A. Hackman (Charlottesville, Va.: InteLex Corp., 1999).

28. John Dewey, "Nationalizing Education," *Journal of Education* 84 (1916): 425–28, in *Middle Works*, 10:205.

29. Morris R. Cohen, "Zionism: Tribalism or Liberalism," *New Republic*, March 8, 1919, 182.

30. Horace Kallen, "Zionism: Democracy or Prussianism," *New Republic*, April 5, 1919, 311–13.

31. Ibid., 311. It is interesting to note here that Kallen sees creed and nationality, not blood, as the basis for Jews' historical persecution, confirming the accounts of historians who traced the etymology of the concept of race and were careful to discern when the word "race" became associated with blood. See Michael Banton, *The Idea of Race* (Boulder, Colo.: Westview, 1978) and *Racial Theories* (Cam-

bridge: Cambridge University Press, 1987); and Ivan Hannaford, *Race: The History of an Idea in the West* (Washington: Woodrow Wilson Center Press, 1996).

32. Kallen, "Zionism," 312–13.

33. Brandeis, "True Americanism," 5–7.

34. See John Higham, "The Redefinition of America in the Twentieth Century," in *German and American Nationalism: A Comparative Perspective* (Oxford: Berg, 1999), ed. Hartmut Lehman and Hermann Wellenreuther; Higham, "Ethnic Pluralism in Modern American Thought"; and Werner Sollors, "E Pluribus Unum; or, Matthew Arnold Meets George Orwell in the 'Multiculturalism Debate,'" Freie Universität Berlin, John-F.-Kennedy-Institut für Noradamerikastudien, working paper no. 53/1992.

35. Benedict Anderson, *Imagined Communities: Reflections on the Origin and Spread of Nationalism* (New York: Verso, 1991); *The Correspondence of William James*, vol. 3, *William and Henry, 1897–1910*, ed. Ignas K. Skrupskelis and Elizabeth M. Berkeley (Charlottesville: University Press of Virginia, 1994), 63.

STEPHEN J. WHITFIELD

★   ★   ★   ★

★ The American Century of Henry R. Luce

In the course of the last century, was there a defining moment of patriotic expression and reflection? I move the nomination of 1941. The Four Freedoms were enunciated on January 6 of that year, and the next month an influential media magnate published "The American Century." As a characteristic of the American mind, the editorial that Henry R. Luce published in the February 17 issue of *Life* is the subject of this essay. But in envisioning the hegemony of the United States, Luce was not acting in a vacuum. Insisting that the United States would soon be fighting in World War II, he invoked the extension of American influence, inspired by democratic ideals and the promise of prosperity. Composed and published amid a period of crisis, "The American Century" had to reckon with the shock of economic devastation at home and with military peril from abroad. By formulating a definition of national purpose, the editorial exemplified the wider struggle to celebrate the nation's virtues and to reclaim its past. Luce offered, in effect, an account of Why We Fight (for he argued that "we are *in* the war").[1] The essay was therefore a milestone in the effort to distill the meaning of Americanism.

A decade earlier, the historian James Truslow Adams had advanced a pioneering formulation of the "American Dream," which he defined as "not a dream of motor cars and high wages merely, but a dream of social order in which each man and each woman shall be able to attain to the fullest stature of which they are innately capable." The title of the book was to be *The American Dream*. But the publisher doubted that so ethereal a claim would attract readers battered by the Great Depression; and therefore it was as *The Epic of America* that Adams found himself the author of a best seller, with a new edition released in the year of Luce's editorial. The Depression decade also made the "American Way of Life" a commonplace phrase.[2]

Perhaps the most famous formal effort to define the "American creed" came in 1944, when Gunnar Myrdal sought to codify the radiant democratic ideals that collided with the realities of racism. The popular arts also reinforced the gusts of patriotic feeling. Irving Berlin reached into his trunk and pulled out, for an Armistice Day broadcast in 1938, "God Bless

America"; and within two years it was sung to delegates at both the Republican and Democratic national conventions. In November 1939, the "Ballad for Americans" leaped to the top of the charts, with Paul Robeson singing: "Our Country's strong, our Country's young / And her greatest songs are still unsung." "Ballad for Americans" opened the GOP nominating convention the following summer (though without Robeson). In conveying what Americans could be grateful for, no visual art was more iconic or inspired than Norman Rockwell's *The Four Freedoms* (1942). When the oil paintings were exhibited in sixteen cities, well over a million visitors showed up; and nearly $133 million in war bonds were sold.[3]

This enlivened appreciation for "Americanism" sprang from the realization that the national experience diverged from the fanatical tyrannies that were devastating the Old World. The Atlantic Charter of August 1941 had forged ideological links between the United States and the former mother country. But American exceptionalism also made headway. The 1922 edition of Carl L. Becker's *The Declaration of Independence* was reprinted two decades later; the new introduction, written in September 1941, noted that "when political freedom, already lost in many countries, is everywhere threatened," the framers' ideals could be seen to stand out in relief, as worth fighting to preserve.[4] Two years later, the memorial to Jefferson himself was dedicated in Washington. Nationalist sentiments were also activated with the publication of Carl Sandburg's adulatory *Abraham Lincoln* in 1939 and with the premiere of Aaron Copland's *A Lincoln Portrait* two years thereafter. Jefferson and Lincoln joined George Washington and Theodore Roosevelt on Mount Rushmore by the time the sculptor Gutzon Borglum died, in 1941, on the eve of the country's entry into the war.

This was the zeitgeist of Luce's "American Century." His editorial had been distilled from three speeches road-tested in 1940 from Pasadena through Tulsa and then Pittsburgh. Luce had come to realize the necessity of military involvement, but he did not want to provoke a confrontation with the Axis powers. An emphatic advocacy of war would have been both lonely and risky. He did not need a weatherman to know which way the wind was blowing, but the case against isolationism had to be made compelling. So he adopted the argument that the United States was *already* at war—a datum of which Adolf Hitler was presumably aware, even if most of Luce's own compatriots were not.[5] In the summer of 1940, he also supplied a foreword to John F. Kennedy's *Why England Slept*. Its best-selling status defied the Do Not Disturb signs posted at the nation's twelve-mile limits. Because Luce's name was familiar to only 27 percent of those Americans who were polled, the interventionist pitch he made had to tap into reservoirs of faith in the power and attractiveness of a redemptive mission.[6]

By early February, *Life* picture editor Daniel Longwell was urging his boss to write "modern Federalist papers for this world A.D. 1941." Luce needed to be convinced no further. His intended title was "We Americans," for which either managing editor John Shaw Billings or senior editor John K. Jessup suggested a substitute: "The American Century."[7] Whoever provided his boss with it certainly deserved the rest of the afternoon off. Of course, the end of isolationism came nearly nine months after the editorial appeared with the attack on Pearl Harbor.

The United States was not ready for global responsibilities—or for global war. In August 1940 the army had conducted the largest peacetime maneuvers in its history. But trucks had to serve as "tanks," broomsticks as "machine guns," and beer cans as "ammunition." The half-million men under arms included the National Guard, making the U.S. military roughly equal in size to the Bulgarian armed services. Only about one in five Americans expressed themselves in favor of intervention.[8] Yet "The American Century" does not propose a "large peacetime army and navy—or even a declaration of war against the Axis powers," as one historian has noted. The editorial makes almost no reference to armaments at all, does not imagine the military-industrial complex that would take form so conspicuously after 1945, and does not anticipate that the projection of American power might be the correlate of force. There is simply no textual warrant for the charge of Luce's Pulitzer Prize–winning biographer, W. A. Swanberg, that "the American Century was . . . a militarist century."[9]

But was it to be an imperialist one? The historian John Morton Blum certainly thought so, claiming that Luce "contemplated a political, economic, and religious imperialism indistinguishable, except by nationality, from the doctrines of Kipling and Churchill."[10] Yet such a reading of the editorial is also unjustified. American internationalists and expansionists typically sought customers, not conquered peoples. American businessmen wanted new markets and investments, in contrast to Luce's own father and other missionaries, who wanted converts.

But unless one equates the expansion of influence with an imperium, Luce's editorial has to be seen as a document of exceptionalism rather than of domination. The United States had something to share, not something to impose. Luce wanted expertise to be put in the service of development— what liberal Democrats would champion in programs like Truman's Point Four and in best-selling novels like *The Ugly American* (1958). When Luce called for the United States to be "the principal guarantor of the freedom of the seas," he was echoing one of Woodrow Wilson's Fourteen Points.

"The American Century" also projected "the vision of America as the dynamic leader of world trade"; Luce could not fathom any economic basis for national leadership besides "free enterprise." More than *Time* or *Life*, *Fortune* was Luce's singular achievement, and its charter was to report on "American business . . . as the dynamic agency that was tearing up small-town life and catapulting the u.s. into world economic dominance," according to Daniel Bell; business "was doing so within the language and the cover of the Protestant Ethic." In 1938 the United States was responsible for 28.7 percent of world's manufacturing output; the comparable percentages for Germany and Japan were 13.2 percent and 3.8 percent, respectively.[11] Perhaps because the u.s. proportion of the world's productivity was so large, Luce's editorial does not allude to the Great Depression at all; he wrote as though the crisis of capitalism that began a dozen years earlier did not have to be considered.

Harrowing as the Depression was, Luce was surely right to focus on the magnitude of what the American economy could promise and achieve—and exceed. He did not believe in capitalism in one country. But his vision of a redeemer nation was less easily mocked than the pledge that future Nebraska senator Kenneth Wherry made in 1940: "With God's help, we will lift Shanghai up and up, ever up, until it is just like Kansas City."[12]

The nation that would pose the most serious immediate obstacle to Luce's vision after 1945 is not mentioned in his essay. "The American Century" is not prophetic enough to address itself to the challenge of the ussr. Early 1941 was too soon to predict the geopolitical conflict that would utterly rearrange the alliance system of World War II. "An editor's job is to stay ahead of his readers by three weeks, not ten years," Luce once averred;[13] and for three more years he did not envision the prospect of conflict with the Soviet Union.[14]

"The American Century" is thus not a playbook for postwar strategy. Still to come was that notorious special issue of *Life*, in which the NKVD was depicted as "a national police similar to the FBI," protecting the Russians, who were "one hell of a people," and therefore much like Americans themselves.[15] Having welcomed the publication of Walter Lippmann's *U.S. Foreign Policy: Shield of the Republic* in 1943, Luce considered serializing the sequel in *Life* the following year. But when he read the description in *U.S. War Aims* of our major ally as a totalitarian power, he refused to exercise the option: "It's too anti-Russian," the publisher complained to Lippmann.[16]

Luce did not expect the tyrannies on the planet to evaporate, nor did he believe that facsimiles of American democracy could be easily established elsewhere. But "The American Century" can be read as a complement to the Four Freedoms. In fact, all four of them (Freedom of Expression, Freedom of Worship, Freedom from Want, and Freedom from Fear) are addressed in the editorial.

It opens with an acknowledgement that "there is no peace in our hearts"; the anxiety and "gloom" could be dispelled by the decisiveness that would achieve Freedom from Fear. Far from exulting in an uncritical celebration of the American way of life, Luce acknowledged the tremulous state of public opinion—and he offered an antidote to irresolution. Freedom from Fear meant not merely from the danger of foreign attack (which Luce erroneously discounted). "Can we avoid a post-armament depression?" was also a question posed to members of the American Economic Association; 80 percent of those who answered said no, according to a report published in the spring of 1941.[17] Luce saw the American century as the alternative to doom, and he argued that "there is no possibility of the survival of American civilization except as it survives as a world power."[18]

The rest of the editorial establishes the twin themes of what America could offer the world by a decision to intervene: Freedom of Speech and of Worship and an end to poverty and misery. Soviet sympathizers often saw a tradeoff between political freedom and material security and defended the denial of the former as essential for the pursuit of the latter. Luce detected no either/or and did not even envision national sacrifice or heavy civic demands as the price of the Four Freedoms. Unlike Churchill's offer of "blood, toil, tears and sweat" as the way to national survival, Luce could not get beyond the pleasure principle.

In defining the American dream as liberation from want, as a dream that all of humanity could share, Luce's editorial deserves to be compared to a speech that drew only cheers from the left. On May 8, 1942, Henry A. Wallace's address "The Price of Free World Victory" was seen at the time as a rebuttal to Luce's editorial. Indeed the vice president remarked: "Some have spoken of the 'American Century.' I say that the century on which we are entering—the century which will come out of this war—can be and must be the century of the common man.'" Instead of the hegemony of one nation, Wallace recommended a "people's revolution."[19]

Wallace's speech also elicited great praise from the pundit Walter Lippmann, whose writings had helped shape Luce's own thinking.[20] He told the vice president that "The Price of Free World Victory" was "the most moving and effective thing produced by us during the war. In fact, I thought it perfect, and you need have no qualms about letting it be circulated not only all over the country but all over the world." Such praise and the implied contrast with "The American Century" irritated Luce, who wrote Wallace: "I should not like to think that anything of substance in [my] essay . . . is inconsistent with your hopes and promises for the increasing freedom and welfare of 'the common man.' "[21] Wallace conceded the point in a reply to Luce: "I do not happen to remember anything that you have written descriptive of your concepts of 'The American Century' of which I disapprove."[22] Wallace nevertheless "detested the confident chauvinism" of Luce's editorial, according to his biographer.[23]

In retrospect, Wallace looks more like Luce's body double; the dividing line was a matter of tone and nuance rather than ideological friction. After all, the *Life* editorial demanded that the United States "feed all the people of the world" who "are hungry and destitute." Yet when the vice president advocated something similar in May 1942, he was ridiculed for being so bubbleheaded a New Dealer as to favor passing out milk to all the Hottentots (a people presumably too unworthy of the dignity of decent nourishment). Such idealism was precisely what Luce's wife, Clare Boothe Luce, a Republican elected to Congress from Connecticut in November 1942, would famously scorn as "globaloney."[24] Although Luce's views have often been interpreted as Christian in origin, the language of the editorial betrays no hint of piety, other than one passing reference to the Psalms. There is no mention of God.

Wallace would become the darling of the Communists and their sympathizers in his presidential campaign on the Progressive ticket in 1948. But six years earlier he had expressed confidence in the victory of the "people's revolution" because "the devil and all his angels cannot prevail against it. They cannot prevail, for on the side of the people is the Lord." The vice president insisted that "no compromise with Satan is possible. . . . Strong in the strength of the Lord, we who fight in the people's cause will never stop until the cause is won."[25] For the Marxist mantra of historical inevitability, he had substituted a destiny that was divinely ordained. Yet Luce, the missionaries' son, is easily patronized as sanctimonious, while liberal and leftist historians have given a pass to Wallace—who after all became secretary of commerce. Either Luce was not as far to the right as he is often depicted, or Wallace was not as far to the left as is sometimes believed. And Wallace never figured out how the expansionist capitalism that he promoted could be harnessed to the worldwide social revolution with which he sympathized.[26]

In fact, Luce was more coherent—and more prescient—in imagining that the business civilization he favored would vindicate democratic hopes for human betterment. The imperative of a "people's revolution" offered a smaller chance of satisfying rising expectations than did Luce's American-ism, and the countries that became the most prosperous and productive are readily classified as capitalist.

In the decade following the end of World War II, two books pivotal to American historiography focused on the aims that Luce had formulated. For Louis Hartz, what distinguished American politics was a single tradi-tion: the ideology of liberalism. For David Potter, what Americans took for granted was what made them unique: an economy of abundance. These two phenomena that Luce highlighted were also mentioned in 1959 by Whittaker Chambers, his most famous former editor, who realized that "the West, I am more and more convinced, has two main goods to offer mankind: freedom and abundance. They interact, of course." And they were most conspicuously encountered, if not in America, then at least in the *idea* of America. In 1990, when the historian Eric Foner returned from a stint of teaching at Moscow State University, he noted that the younger Soviet academics whom he met considered the United States to be "the land of liberty and prosperity of our own imagination."[27]

Thus was Luce vindicated. If the opposite of liberty is submission (for which the Arabic word is "Islam"), and if no part of the planet is more generally cursed by poverty than in Muslim lands that lack oil reserves, then the lethal hatred animating Al Qaeda also measures what Luce had cherished in his own country.

In formulating a mission statement for modern America, Luce could not have selected a better forum than the magazine he happened to own. Founded in 1936, *Life* was soon achieving a sales record of 2.1 million copies per week, in an era when magazine sales above a million were extremely rare. The response to the publisher's 1941 editorial was strong: 4,541 letters came in, nearly all of them favorable. Time Inc. boosted—or responded to—popular interest by offering copies of "The American Century" free of charge. The *Washington Post* reprinted it, as did the *Reader's Digest*. Later in 1941 the publishing house Farrar and Rinehart stretched the editorial into a tiny book, with critiques by six commentators; and the essay was assigned in many high schools, colleges, and universities.[28]

Much of its impact was due to the democratic nationalism that had been building momentum for a decade. But "The American Century" also advanced a case for internationalism, for placing the Republic in a world that was commonly described as "shrinking." One commentator who shared billing with Luce when the essay appeared in book form was the syndicated columnist and foreign correspondent Dorothy Thompson. She endorsed the extension of American influence, not only because it would enable foreign peoples to enjoy freedom and prosperity, but also because "to Americanize enough of the world" was necessary to "have a climate and environment favorable to our growth. . . . This will either be an American century or it will be the beginning of the decline and fall of the American dream." Further confirmation of the Marxist theory that capitalism *required* expansion came from within the Roosevelt administration itself. Stanley K. Hornbeck, the Department of State political adviser whose jurisdiction was the Far East, cited the editorial in a memorandum sent to the under secretary of state, Sumner Welles. The assistant secretary of the navy believed that the *Life* editorial offered the most astute postwar vision. "We cannot avoid our world responsibilities," James V. Forrestal, a former Wall Street investment banker, concluded.[29]

But so hegemonic an ambition is precisely what troubled Senator Robert A. Taft, the isolationist Republican from Ohio. He doubted that Americans could successfully extend their system to the rest of the world: "Other people simply do not like to be dominated." The effort to impose ourselves on others, Taft correctly predicted, would require an enormous military establishment in peacetime. Nor could Herbert Hoover envision the United States serving as global policeman. Having seen much of the world as a mining engineer and as director of food relief after World War I, the former president warned: "America cannot impose its freedoms and ideals upon the twenty-six races of Europe or the world."[30] Taft and Hoover belonged to the wing of the Republican Party that the editorial explicitly repudiated.

The left turned the editorial into a piñata. Perhaps liberals and progressives simply could not get past Luce's status as a wealthy publisher, or his sweet tooth for the GOP, or his advocacy of an internationalism that might have exploitation as its downside. But the virulence of the left went well beyond a fair reading of the text. While acknowledging that Luce's vision as "magnanimous and benevolent . . . large and awe-inspiring," Freda Kirchwey, the editor and publisher of the *Nation*, also called it "smug, self-righteous, superior, and fatuously lacking in a decent regard for the susceptibilities of the rest of mankind. These particular qualities are the typical stigmata of the Anglo-Saxon in his role as imperialist." Indeed she discovered analogies in Hitler's *Neue Ordnung* and *Lebensraum*, and damned "The American Century" as "so toxic" that the Federal Trade Commission should be alerted to protect the public from it.[31]

A former editor of the *Nation*, Oswald Garrison Villard, did not demur, asserting that "The American Century" was a dangerous mixture of imperialism and aggression, roughly the counterpart to *Mein Kampf* in announcing a pursuit of "world domination," making his country as ominous a threat to humanity as the Third Reich or Soviet Russia or Japan. Socialist Party leader Norman Thomas also denounced Luce's "nakedness of imperial ambition" and the proposal to have "the English-speaking nations . . . police in God's name such places as we think necessary for our advantage."[32] Yet Luce thought of himself as a foe of British colonial rule, and he especially resented the imputation of an imperialist agenda: "You can't extract imperialism from 'The American Century.' "[33] Indeed the *Nation* had done so, not by reading a text but by reading *into* a text what was not there.

Unlike Villard and Thomas, liberal columnist Max Lerner was an interventionist, and he offered a progressive alternative to Luce's vision. A "People's Century" would mean that "we are leaders among equals, with their consent," rather than an "American-dominated world capitalism." Peoples under the boot of fascism could fight for "their own freedom and equality in an international community, or the privilege of sharing in an American Century" that smacked too much of narrow power politics.[34] There was something insufficiently humble in the language and spirit of Luce's editorial that caused discomfort to New Dealers like Vice President Wallace, who wrote Luce: "The phrase 'American Century' did rub citizens of a number of our sister United Nations the wrong way."[35]

Yet Luce saw no contradiction between asserting American leadership and extending the Four Freedoms. Indeed he believed the two aims to be inextricable. But they had to be uncoupled, his liberal critics believed, though the effect was a bit mushy. An example is Laura Z. Hobson's bestselling novel *Gentleman's Agreement*, published in 1947, when the Cold War had already begun. Hobson was a universalist whose protagonist ruminates that if injustice could be defeated, then "it might not be the American Century after all, or the Russian Century. . . . Perhaps it would be the century that broadened and implemented the idea of freedom, all the freedoms. Of all men."[36]

"The American Century" was a major event in the formulation of the U.S. role in world affairs and a source of heated public debate in 1941, and it has certainly endured as a phrase. But as a document the editorial has barely remained worthy of attention. Indeed it is not even easily accessible in print. "The American Century" is absent from the widely used anthologies of primary sources that two Columbia University historians compiled: Henry Steele Commager's *Living Ideas in America* (1951) and Richard Hofstadter's *Great Issues in American History* (1958). Excerpted in Warren I. Susman's *Culture and Commitment, 1929–1945* (1973), the editorial is praised as "a cultural statement of profound meaning as Americans sought to define their culture and define their commitments."[37] Yet Susman's volume is also out of print; and Luce's editorial is no longer a document to be reckoned with, an essay that is safe from oblivion.

The recent work of historians confirms such an impression. Olivier Zunz's book *Why the American Century?* makes only passing reference to the editorial that inspired his title, and the medievalist Norman F. Cantor's overview of the culture of the twentieth century, *The American Century* (1997), evinces even more indifference. The diplomatic historian Walter LaFeber claimed that Luce, in his essay, "rightly assumed" that the United States was "already deeply involved on the side of the British and the Russians." For all his prescience, Luce could hardly have envisaged involvement on the side of the Russians, who were then, of course, allied not with the British but with Nazi Germany.[38]

The phrase has been more bandied about than the editorial itself has been read, as though "the American Century" simply belonged to the patrimony of indispensable phrases whose original auspices merit little curiosity. Consider the special case of Walter Lippmann, whose biographer inserted "the American Century" in the title of his study. Ronald Steel makes only one direct, brief reference to the editorial, quoting Luce's argument for assuming "the leadership of the world"; thus was "inaugurate[d] what he modestly labeled 'the American Century.'" Steel categorizes the twentieth century as when "the American empire was born, matured, and began to founder, a time some have called, first boastfully, then wistfully, the American Century." The reluctance in this passage to credit Luce even for so indispensable a coinage is especially striking because Lippmann's own enunciation of "the American Destiny," in an essay by that title, was a source of Luce's editorial.

One of Lippmann's main functions as a pundit was to stuff ideas into other people's heads. During World War II, he opposed the messianic streak in the legacy of Wilsonian diplomacy, suspected the bona fides of the crusade on behalf of democracy and capitalism, and underscored the constraints on the application of American power.[39] Such positions were antithetical to Luce's. But the two journalists shared an opposition to pacifism and to isolationism, and Lippmann's claim in "The American Destiny" that national anxiety stemmed from the popular "refusal to accept the large responsibilities" of a new hegemon was transferred into Luce's account of malaise that opens "The American Century."[40]

As a plea for international involvement, "The American Century" was spurred by immediate circumstances. As a formulation of national purpose, the editorial exemplified a messianic idea that could be traced to the Puritan origins of the nation and had shown historical resilience. But the two features of Luce's essay were inseparable and bore a very personal imprint.

Born in Tengchow (P'eng-lai) in 1898, he spent his childhood almost entirely in China, within a walled compound where missionary families lived. There he grew up with what historian Alan Brinkley calls an "unquestioned belief in the moral superiority of Christianity and the cultural superiority of America." What Luce had cherished as a child was an idealized "image of America that . . . his father and other missionaries created to justify their work," Brinkley added. "It was an image Luce never wholly abandoned. Luce emerged from his youth with a deep sense of moral certainty."[41]

The national confidence that permeates "The American Century" can be traced to the Presbyterian missionary family into which Luce was born. This is why he took such offense at accusations of imperialism. He did not want his countrymen to be conquerors or occupiers or exploiters but rather to be the "Good Samaritan of the entire world."[42] Delivering the senior class oration at Yale in 1920, Luce had expected "American interests" and "American business ideals" to animate a foreign policy that should make the United States "the comrade of all nations that struggle to rise to higher planes of social and political organization."[43] Two decades later, such nationalism was ready for resurrection, and he could confidently advocate an American vocation to benefit a humanity afflicted with despotism and destitution.

Such a plea was not merely a delusion. Without referring to Luce's editorial, the British historian Eric Hobsbawm, in his recent memoir, is ungrudging in his claim that, "internationally speaking, the U.S.A. was by any standards the success story among 20th-century states." He explains:

Its economy became the world's largest, both pace- and pattern-setting; its capacity for technological achievement was unique; its research in both natural and social sciences, even its philosophers, became increasingly dominant; and its hegemony in global consumer civilization seemed beyond challenge. It ended the century as the only surviving global power and empire. If opinion is measured not by pollsters but by migrants, almost certainly America would be the preferred destination of most human beings who must, or decide to, move to a country other than their own, certainly of those who know some English.[44]

Coming from a historian long committed to Communism in politics and to cosmopolitanism in perspective, such a summation suggests that "The American Century" was not an exaggeration (much less a delusion) and cannot be put down as a gesture of national amour propre.

Yet Hobsbawm strikes a discordant note in adding that "America is less of a coherent and therefore exportable social and political model of a capitalist liberal democracy, based on the universal principles of individual freedom, than its patriotic ideology and Constitution suggest. So, far from being a clear example that the rest of the world can imitate, the U.S.A., however powerful and influential, remains an unending process, distorted by big money and public emotion. . . . It simply does not lend itself to copying."[45]

That relentless process has no foreseeable end, but neither can the beginnings be specified. In 1902 the English journalist William T. Stead took note of what he labeled in the title of a book "the Americanisation of the world," by which he meant not only the triumph of the machine but also the extension of mass culture. A year later, as though on cue, the Ford Motor Company was founded and soon became an eponym for mass-production efficiency, technical sophistication, and the deft satisfaction of a mass market of consumers. Writing in an Italian Fascist prison in 1934, the maverick Marxist Antonio Gramsci explicitly linked "Americanism and Fordism" and put the flair for industrial advancement within a cultural context that encouraged the cultivation of talent—in contrast to Europe, where the prevalence of "parasites" retarded such development. Gramsci's insight was eerily consistent with the definition of the American Dream that James Truslow Adams had proposed three years earlier—"opportunity for each according to his ability or achievement." Exactly a century after its birth, the Ford Motor Company was surpassed as the second biggest automobile manufacturer on the planet by Toyota; and though blue jeans remain the preeminent sartorial symbol of the United States, it has ceased to be the home of any more Levi Strauss factories.[46] No wonder that MIT's Robert M. Solow, a Nobel laureate in economics, has discounted "the notion that God intended for Americans to be permanently wealthier than the rest of the world. That gets less and less likely as time goes on."[47]

But if not the American Century, then whose? The twenty-first century may be the Chinese Century. A population of 1.2 billion people constitutes a far larger market than the United States can offer salesmen and investors. Indeed, by 2002 China had already surpassed the United States as the favorite recipient of foreign investment in the world.[48] Since 1991 the Chinese share of the world's output of goods and services has nearly doubled, to 12.7 percent. The European Union is still ahead (at 15.7 percent), but barely. The proportion enjoyed by India, with its population of over a billion, is 4.8 percent. The u.s. share of 21 percent has remained steady since 1980.[49]

The prospect of a Chinese Century might well have pleased the anti-isolationist whose birthplace had helped render him a socially insecure outsider whom his fellow Yalies nicknamed "Chink." Luce, after all, was the publisher who had put Generalissimo and Madame Chiang Kai-shek on the cover of *Time*, together or separately, a whopping eleven times; in 1938 they were "Man and Wife of the Year." (Soong Mei-ling, who had married the generalissimo in 1927, died in her Manhattan apartment in 2003 at the age of 105. She had lived in three different centuries—not just during the American Century.)

Luce could not have been expected to predict how long an American Century would last, whether it would stretch into a *longue durée*. His editorial is frustratingly oblivious to such challenges as bracketing the dates of the American Century. Perhaps understandably, it downplays the most conspicuous failures of the society that he asked to accept the responsibilities of world leadership. "I am biased in favor of God, the Republican party, and free enterprise," Luce once announced;[50] and such a credo could not be expected to stimulate an adversarial relation to his country.

Though Luce was a liberal on civil rights (and his magazines would be increasingly critical of the practices of white supremacy), his editorial ignores the various forms of bigotry that were then mostly taken for granted, including nativism. When "The American Century" was published, the immigration quota from Asia was a nice round number: zero. Not until 1943 was the Chinese Exclusion Act scrapped (and the annual quota set at 105). The bitter labor conflict that marked the Depression decade is also unmentioned in the editorial. (To be fair to Luce, though his politics were Republican, he was more decent than his overseas favorites. In 1943, when FDR casually asked the elegant Madame Chiang how she would deal with the pesky president of the United Mine Workers, John L. Lewis, "she drew her hand across her throat," a reporter noted.)[51]

Nor is any idea in "The American Century" original; so high a test the editorial could not be expected to pass. Luce invented neither democratic nationalism nor liberal internationalism, and he did not bother to fine-tune the distinction. Because his argument lacks internal tension, or any sense of values that are in conflict and probably cannot be reconciled, the essay is not intellectually stimulating.

But just because it lacks snap does not mean that it is wrong. From the perspective of the twenty-first century, the exercise of American power is too evident even to generate the animus that Luce's domestic critics registered over six decades ago. That such dominance has been misused is hardly disputed, but what vexed many of Luce's readers is that he favored using it at all.

That debate is long over. Luce's faith has become fact. No one proclaimed more effectively how the succeeding decades would play out within the framework of unprecedented American impact, facilitated by astounding affluence and economic growth and justified by the redemptive ideal of a distinctively democratic mission. His editorial managed the feat, as Alan Brinkley has observed, of combining a vigorous nationalism with reassuringly moralistic affirmations. Luce anticipated his compatriots' yearning to "spread the American model to other nations, at times through relatively benign encouragement, at other times through pressure and coercion, but almost always with a fervent and active intent."[52] Rarely has so compact an editorial statement exerted so consequential an import. The weight that the United States would throw around has become an inescapable feature of international relations. Luce—more than anyone else—made the case for that influence persuasive, at least to his fellow citizens.[53]

NOTES

The author is grateful to Alan Brinkley, James L. Baughman, Jason Bernard, Justus D. Doenecke, Jonathan M. Hansen, and the coeditors of this volume for their assistance, suggestions, and criticism.

1. Henry R. Luce, "The American Century," *Life*, February 17, 1941, 61, reprinted in *The American Century*, with comments by Dorothy Thompson et al. (New York: Farrar and Rinehart, 1941), 8.

2. James Truslow Adams, *The Epic of America* (Boston: Little, Brown, 1931), 415; Allan Nevins, *James Truslow Adams: Historian of the American Dream* (Urbana: University of Illinois Press, 1968), 68n; Warren I. Susman, *Culture as History: The Transformation of American Society in the Twentieth Century* (New York: Pantheon, 1984), 154, 157–58.

3. Martin Bauml Duberman, *Paul Robeson* (New York: Alfred A. Knopf, 1988), 236–37; Rob Kroes, *If You've Seen One, You've Seen the Mall: Europeans and American Mass Culture* (Urbana: University of Illinois Press, 1996), 113–14.

4. Carl L. Becker, *The Declaration of Independence: A Study in the History of Political Ideas* (New York: Alfred A. Knopf, 1942), xvi.

5. Mark Lincoln Chadwin, *The Hawks of World War II* (Chapel Hill: University of North Carolina Press, 1968), 63, 76; Robert T. Elson, *Time Inc.: The Intimate History of a Publishing Enterprise, 1923–1941* (New York: Atheneum, 1968), 460–61.

6. Robert E. Herzstein, *Henry R. Luce: A Political Portrait of the Man Who Created the American Century* (New York: Charles Scribner's Sons, 1994), 179.

7. Ibid.; Daniel Bell, "Henry Luce's Half-Century," *New Leader*, December 11, 1972, 14.

8. William E. Leuchtenburg, *Franklin D. Roosevelt and the New Deal, 1932–1940* (New York: Harper and Row, 1963), 306–7.

9. James L. Baughman, *Henry R. Luce and the Rise of the American News Media* (Baltimore: Johns Hopkins University Press, 2001), 131; W. A. Swanberg, *Luce and His Empire* (New York: Charles Scribner's Sons, 1972), 182.

10. John Morton Blum, *V Was for Victory: Politics and American Culture During World War II* (New York: Harcourt Brace Jovanovich, 1976), 284–85.

11. Luce, *American Century*, 36; Baughman, *Henry R. Luce*, 131; Bell, "Henry Luce's Half-Century," 13; William L. O'Neill, *A Democracy at War: America's Fight at Home and Abroad in World War II* (New York: Free Press, 1993), 9.

12. Quoted in Eric F. Goldman, *The Crucial Decade—and After: America, 1945–1960* (New York: Vintage Books, 1960), 116.

13. Quoted in Baughman, *Henry R. Luce*, 146.

14. Baughman, *Henry R. Luce*, 143–44.

15. "The Peoples of the U.S.S.R." and "Lavrentii R. Beria," in *Life*, March 29, 1943, 23, 40.

16. Ronald Steel, *Walter Lippmann and the American Century* (Boston: Little, Brown, 1980), 410.

17. Luce, *American Century*, 6; Lloyd Gardner, *Architects of Illusion: Men and Ideas in American Foreign Policy, 1941–1949* (Chicago: Quadrangle, 1970), 22.

18. Quoted in Herzstein, *Henry R. Luce*, 177.

19. Henry A. Wallace, "The Price of Free World Victory" (1942), in *The Price of Vision: The Diary of Henry A. Wallace, 1942–1946*, ed. John Morton Blum (Boston: Houghton Mifflin, 1973), 638.

20. Baughman, *Henry R. Luce*, 132.

21. John Morton Blum, ed., *Public Philosopher: Selected Letters of Walter Lippmann* (New York: Ticknor and Fields, 1985), 431n; Steel, *Walter Lippmann*, 404; Walter Lippmann to Henry A. Wallace, November 26, 1942, in Blum, *Public Philosopher*, 431; Elson, *Time Inc.*, 463.

22. Quoted in Elson, *Time Inc.*, 464.

23. Blum, *Price of Vision*, 25.

24. Luce, *American Century*, 37–38; Blum, *V Was for Victory*, 285 ("globaloney"); Blum, *Price of Victory*, 122n.

25. Quoted in Blum, *V Was for Victory*, 285, and in Alan Brinkley, "To See and to Know Everything," *Time*, March 9, 1998, 108.

26. Stephen J. Whitfield, *A Critical American: The Politics of Dwight Macdonald* (Hamden, Conn.: Archon Books, 1984), 38–39; Dwight Macdonald, "The (American) People's Century," *Partisan Review*, July–August 1942, 297–98, 304–5, 308.

27. Louis Hartz, *The Liberal Tradition in America: An Interpretation of American Political Thought since the Revolution* (New York: Harcourt, Brace, 1955); David M. Potter, *People of Plenty: Economic Abundance and the American Character* (Chicago: University of Chicago Press, 1954); Whittaker Chambers to William F. Buckley Jr., April 28?, 1959, in Chambers, *Odyssey of a Friend: Letters to William F. Buckley, Jr., 1954–1961* (New York: G. Putnam's Sons, 1969), 244; Eric Foner, *Who Owns History? Rethinking the Past in a Changing World* (New York: Hill and Wang, 2002), 80.

28. Terry A. Cooney, *Balancing Acts: American Thought and Culture in the 1930s* (New York: Twayne, 1995), 174; Brinkley, "To See and to Know Everything," 52–53; Elson, *Time Inc.*, 463; Herzstein, *Henry R. Luce*, 180–81.

29. Dorothy Thompson in Luce, *American Century*, 50–51; Herzstein, *Henry R. Luce*, 180–81, 232.

30. Quoted in Baughman, *Henry R. Luce*, 132–33, 135.

31. Freda Kirchwey, "Luce Thinking," *Nation*, March 1, 1941, 229–30; Swanberg, *Luce and His Empire*, 182.

32. Quoted in Swanberg, *Luce and His Empire*, 182.

33. Quoted in Elson, *Time Inc.*, 463.

34. Max Lerner, *Ideas for the Ice Age* (New York: Viking Press, 1941), 53–57.

35. Quoted in Elson, *Time Inc.*, 464.

36. Laura Z. Hobson, *Gentleman's Agreement* (New York: Simon and Schuster, 1947), 205–6.

37. Warren I. Susman, ed., *Culture and Commitment, 1929–1945* (New York: George Braziller, 1973), 318–19.

38. Walter LaFeber, "American Exceptionalism Abroad: A Brief History," *Foreign Service Journal* 77 (March 2000): 26, 27.

39. Steel, *Walter Lippmann*, xiii, 404; Walter Lippmann, "The American Destiny," *Life*, June 5, 1939, 47, 72–73; Baughman, *Henry R. Luce*, 132; Barton J. Bernstein, "Walter Lippmann and the Early Cold War," in *Cold War Critics: Alternatives to American Foreign Policy in the Truman Years*, ed. Thomas G. Paterson (Chicago: Quadrangle, 1971), 19.

40. Baughman, *Henry R. Luce*, 132.

41. Brinkley, "To See and to Know Everything," 52.

42. Luce, *American Century*, 37.

43. Quoted in Baughman, *Henry R. Luce*, 22.

44. Eric Hobsbawm, *Interesting Times: A Twentieth-Century Life* (New York: Pantheon, 2002), 404, 410.

45. Ibid., 404, 410.

46. W. T. Stead, *The Americanisation of the World* (London: "Review of Reviews," 1902); Richard Pells, *Not Like Us: How Europeans Have Loved, Hated, and Transformed American Culture since World War II* (New York: Basic Books, 1997), 7; David Forgacs, ed., *The Gramsci Reader: Selected Writings, 1916–1935* (New York: New York University Press, 2000), 277–80; Adams, *Epic of America*, 415; John Cassidy, "Happy Days," *New Yorker*, December 15, 2003, 41.

47. Louis Uchitelle, "When the Chinese Consumer Is King," *New York Times*, December 14, 2003.

48. Matt Forney, "Tug-of-War over Trade," *Time*, December 22, 2003, 44.

49. Uchitelle, "Chinese Consumer."

50. Quoted in *The Ideas of Henry Luce*, ed. John K. Jessup (New York: Atheneum, 1969), 7.

51. Herzstein, *Henry R. Luce*, 420; O'Neill, *Democracy at War*, 7; Pico Iyer, "A Flower Made of Steel: Madame Chiang Kai-shek, 1898–2003," *Time*, November 3, 2003, 47.

52. Alan Brinkley, "The Concept of an American Century," in *The American Century in Europe*, ed. R. Laurence Moore and Maurizio Vaudagna (Ithaca, N.Y.: Cornell University Press, 2003), 7–10, 19.

53. Indeed his vision was so compelling that "The American Century" should be classified with the most important essays in the nation's history—below, say,

Thomas Paine's "Common Sense," Henry David Thoreau's "Civil Disobedience," George Kennan's "The Sources of Soviet Conduct," or Martin Luther King Jr.'s "Letter from the Birmingham City Jail," but perhaps of the same stature as Alexander Hamilton's "Report on Manufactures," Ralph Waldo Emerson's "The American Scholar," or Jane Addams's "The Subjective Necessity for Social Settlements."

MAE M. NGAI

★ ★ ★ ★

★ The Unlovely Residue of Outworn Prejudices

★ *The Hart-Celler Act and the Politics of Immigration*

★ *Reform, 1945–1965*

It is to the Hart-Celler Immigration and Nationality Act of 1965 that we generally attribute the vast changes in the demographics of the United States of the last quarter century. Hart-Celler opened up new chains of migration from the third world: Latinos became the fastest growing ethnoracial minority group in the United States, by the year 2000 representing 12 percent of the total United States population; no less phenomenally, the number of Asian Americans increased almost tenfold between 1965 and 2000. Since 1980, 90 percent of new immigrants to the United States have come from areas of the world other than Europe.[1]

Congress did not anticipate these changes in migration patterns, so scholars commonly refer to Hart-Celler as an example of the law of unintended consequences. In this essay I locate an explanation for this unintentionality in the pluralistic brand of Americanism that liberals advocated during the Cold War era. Because the intent of social actors is not always transparent, I approach this problem by way of examining the intellectual underpinnings of the political and legislative discourse on immigration reform during the two decades following World War II. I am especially interested in the influence of postwar liberal commitments to pluralism and equal rights and the engagement of these ideas with nationalism as they were applied to immigration policy.

The problem of unintentionality might be productively approached by examining the set of paradoxes to which the idea of unintended consequences gestures without actually explaining them. In the case of Hart-Celler, the first paradox concerns the principle of equal quotas for all nations, which is commonly understood as the principal feature of the act. Equal quotas did not, in fact, lead to an equal number of immigrants from each country. Rather, Hart-Celler produced vastly asymmetrical patterns of migration.

The second paradox has to do with the qualitative and quantitative aspects of immigration policy. After World War II, many liberals believed that the national origins quotas were an illiberal and racist anachronism: as the Harvard historian Oscar Handlin described the quotas in 1953, they were "the unlovely residue of outworn prejudices."[2] Yet most critics of the quota system treated numerical restriction as a normative feature of immigration policy. In fact, both were initiated in the Johnson-Reed Immigration Act of 1924 as part of a single thrust aimed at limiting migration from southern and eastern Europe. So, we might ask, why did reformers attack one part of that proposition but naturalize the other?

And, in a related vein, we might ask, why have historians and other scholars of immigration continued, to this day, to focus their attention on Hart-Celler's repeal of the national origins quotas, to the near exclusion of its other features—most important, the overall ceiling on admissions and the unprecedented imposition of numerical quotas on countries of the Western Hemisphere?

I argue that these paradoxes may be understood by considering Hart-Celler as a product of liberal nationalism, a central feature of postwar Americanism. Here I use "liberal nationalism" to describe a historically specific ideology, which conjoined liberal pluralism with economic and geopolitical nationalism (as distinguished from the concept's recent use in multicultural citizenship debates). I highlight the marriage between liberalism and nationalism because scholars have recognized Hart-Celler as an expression of the former but not the latter—reflecting, I think, the enduring influence of American exceptionalism in our historical consciousness generally and the normative nature of nationalism in modern immigration policy more specifically. That is to say, the idea that citizens have a "national interest" that exists above and against the interests of noncitizens, is an unquestioned assumption in our thinking, not a matter that we subject to critical analysis.

Postwar liberal nationalism comprised a number of interrelated strands in immigration policy: first, a liberal pluralism that emphasized the equal rights of all citizens, regardless of race, ethnicity, or ancestry; second, an economic nationalism that sought to maintain and enhance the privileged position of the United States in the postwar global economic order; and, third, the nationalism of geopolitics, specifically the imperatives of Cold War foreign policy. In this essay I will focus mainly on liberal pluralism, after first briefly discussing the influence of Cold War politics and economic nationalism.

Cold War and Economic Nationalism

Cold War politics influenced the course of reform variously. Most notably, reformers argued that the discriminatory nature of the national origins quota system tarnished the overseas reputation of the United States as a champion of democracy. America's anti-Communist allies, from Greece to Japan, smarted under the sting of discrimination that attached to low quotas; like Jim Crow segregation, the quota system was fodder for Soviet propaganda about American racism. Reformers invoked Cold War imperatives to give legitimacy to their agenda. In a typical statement, for example, New York congressman Emanuel Celler asked, "Is the way to destroy an iron curtain . . . to erect an iron curtain of our own?" American geopolitical interests also informed the refugee provision of the law, which applied only to those fleeing Communist countries and the Middle East, not more broadly to those who suffered or feared persecution according to internationally recognized standards.[3]

The economic nationalism of Hart-Celler was evident in the overall low numerical ceiling (290,000, which as a percentage of population was lower than the quotas established in 1924) and in the law's preference for professional and highly skilled workers. These were particularly conservative measures in light of the expanding postwar economy and labor shortages in both skilled and unskilled occupations. But organized labor had become an important constituency of the postwar Democratic Party coalition and liberal elites and labor-union officials increasingly influenced each other's thinking. During the 1950s the trade unions, which now had many European ethnics in their ranks and in leadership positions, abandoned their longtime nativist stance and adopted the liberal position for abolition of the national origins quotas; but, at the same time, the unions remained opposed to alleged competition from immigrant labor and worked to incorporate this view into liberal thinking on immigration. For example, speaking in 1959 when he was in the U.S. Senate, John F. Kennedy endorsed an annual ceiling on immigration of 250,000 on grounds that "labor leaders have stated that this number could not conceivably cause any dislocation in the labor market, and there need be no fear of displacement of any workers."[4]

The significance of the economic preferences was plain enough to observers in 1965. The American Legion, long a bulwark of restrictionism, endorsed Hart-Celler because, it predicted, the law "well may add significantly to the wealth and power of the United States." Similarly, but from a different angle, the magazine *Commonweal* expressed disappointment in the legislation because it kept a low ceiling on admissions and because "the present prejudice on the basis of race will become a prejudice against the unskilled." In other words, it said, "Give me your poor Ph.D.'s, your huddled graduate engineers." Another journal concluded, "The golden door to America . . . is not likely ever to open again. . . . No more wretched refuse for these shores."[5]

Liberal Pluralism and the Valorization of the Citizen

Although the geopolitical and economic dimensions of American nationalism were evident to contemporaries, they have not been adequately appreciated in the historical scholarship on Hart-Celler. This is in large part because our understanding of the act has been dominated by its repeal of the national origins quotas. It is this aspect of the law that is most widely known and celebrated; it is why historians link immigration reform to the civil rights legislation of the same period and describe them together as "climactic achievements . . . of universalist principle" and the "high-water mark in the national consensus of egalitarianism."[6] There is much that is true in this account, but I argue that there is a more complicated story to tell. Considered in a framework of nationalism, liberal pluralism emerges as a more problematic element in immigration policy.

Central to the conventional narrative of immigration reform were ethnic European Americans who had, by World War II, become visible and vocal constituents of the New Deal political order. They wished for immigration reform in order to shed the badge of inferior status that the quota laws had imposed on them, as well as by practical desire to admit more immigrants from their countries of origin, especially their relatives. Thus did American Jews, Italian Americans, Greek Americans, and other groups demand their equal place in American society.[7]

That immigration reform and civil rights were cut from the same cloth of democratic reform in the same historical moment seems undeniable. Immigration reformers were deeply influenced by the civil rights movement, both by its broad appeals for social justice and human freedom and by its more specific conception of formal equal rights. Yet these strong similarities have perhaps obscured some important differences.

Take, for example, the question of citizenship. The civil rights movement was incontrovertibly about winning full and equal citizenship for African Americans, but citizenship occupied a more ambiguous and problematic position in immigration policy and reform discourse. Immigrants are aliens, not citizens—a fundamental distinction in legal status that bears on the scope of rights held by each class of persons, beginning with the right to be territorially present. Citizenship for immigrants was a possibility, but just that: a possibility. When immigration reformers spoke of equal rights, they referred *not* to the rights of migrants but to the rights of existing American citizens, those ethnic Euro-Americans who believed immigration policy was a proxy for their domestic social status. This was an important elision that would have consequences for how immigration reform was conceptualized. Indeed, the persistence of numerical restriction in the postwar period, with its emphasis on territoriality, border control, and the deportation of illegal aliens, suggests that in some respects immigration reform only hardened the distinction between citizen and alien.

It might be, as well, that liberals' valorization of citizenship in the postwar period constructed alienage as a lack, as citizenship's opposite. Earl Warren, chief justice of the Supreme Court and one of the era's greatest champions of liberal citizenship, spoke of citizenship in direct contrast with alienage in his dissenting opinion in *Perez v. Brownell* (1957), a denationalization case: "Citizenship *is* man's basic right for it is nothing less than the right to have rights. Remove this priceless possession and there remains a stateless person. . . . His very existence is at the sufferance of the state within whose borders he happens to be. In this country the expatriate will presumably enjoy, at most, only the limited rights and privileges of aliens, and like the alien he might even be subject to deportation and thereby deprived of the right to assert any rights."[8]

Writing at the end of Warren's tenure on the court, the constitutional scholar Charles L. Black Jr. believed this "neglect of the rights of aliens among us" was a problem that represented "part of the unfinished business of the Warren Court."[9] More recently, the legal scholar Peter Schuck also considered it anomalous that the Warren Court checked "governmental authorities on behalf of politically vulnerable groups [but] was abjectly deferential in the context of immigration law."[10]

The reason for this discrepancy is not transparent in the record of liberal discourse or the legislative history of immigration reform, for within the archive the alien's lack is asserted in large part by means of indirection or in silences. But if the alien lurked as the citizen's silent double, nationalism was the ground on which this duality was produced. We can see a shadowed relationship between citizen and alien in the writing of liberal reformers of the day. For example, in his classic history of American immigration, *The Uprooted*, Oscar Handlin alluded to a double character of the immigration laws. Referring to the quota laws of the 1920s, Handlin wrote:

As the purport of the deliberations in Congress became clear, the foreign-born could not escape the conclusion that it was *not only the future arrivals who were being judged but also those already settled*. The objections to further immigration from Italy and Poland reflected the objectors' unfavorable opinions of the Italians and Poles they saw about them. . . . Restriction gave official sanction to the assertions that the immigrants were separate from and inferior to the native-born, and at the same time gave their isolation a decisive and irrevocable quality.[11]

Thus, said Handlin, the quota laws "confirmed and deepened the alienation" that the immigrants experienced, which alienation, of course, was the central theme of *The Uprooted*.[12]

Handlin had more than a historical interest in the matter. When he published *The Uprooted* in 1951, he was an active public intellectual, writing extensively about pluralism and group life, civil rights, assimilation and the problem of Jewish identity, and, notably, immigration reform. He was a consultant to Truman's Presidential Commission on Immigration and Nationality, writing a critical analysis of the national origins quotas that would be published in the commission's report, *Whom We Shall Welcome*. Handlin was also an adviser to New York senator Herbert Lehman, the leading advocate for immigration reform in the Senate in the early and mid-1950s, consulting on policy and reviewing the senator's draft reform legislation.[13] He was also influential in more indirect and unofficial ways: his brother-in-law, Sam Flug, was an associate of Emanuel Celler.[14] Handlin's thinking on immigration policy is instructive because it both reflected and shaped the course of reform in the postwar period. He provided a cogent articulation of the liberal nationalism that framed the reform legislation ultimately passed in 1965, as well as the law's historical legacy.

But, first, it must be pointed out that, in the immediate postwar years, Handlin advocated a different policy: he called for a return to open immigration. In an article written in January 1947, "Democracy Needs the Open Door," Handlin criticized the racist national origins quotas but did not advocate replacing them with a system of equal quotas. He called more generally for "reopening" immigration, arguing that "the growth of population that would come from relaxation of immigration restrictions would make room for [expansive] energies and add new vigor to our economy." It was America's historical expansiveness, diversity, and openness to change that made the nation great, he contended. Handlin warned against nationalist thinking that would "forfeit opportunities for imaginative leadership in order to safeguard what we have." He argued it was "illusory [to expect] that the composition of American population will remain as it is" and added:

> Within our territorial limits and without, we shall more frequently brush up against outsiders and more frequently face the compulsion to make room. And to get by at the internal or the international level will call for the identical qualities of tact, tolerance, and vision. The needy people of the earth—and almost all the people of the earth are needy—now look to the United States for omens of these redeeming qualities. . . . Their anxiety turns about a single point: Is our belief in democracy coupled with the reservation that it is viable only in favored climes and in the hands of favored men, or does it have the inner energy for continued, untrammeled expansion?[15]

Handlin's perspective reflected a progressive, cosmopolitan sensibility that flourished during the war and the immediate postwar years. It was part of the same impulse that linked African American freedom with the liberation of African and Asian peoples from European colonialism. In the realm of immigration policy, it found expression at the highest levels of the Immigration and Naturalization Service. Immigration Commissioner Earl Harrison believed a looming international refugee problem posed the greatest challenge to American immigration law. In 1944 he suggested that "it might be well to consider the possibility of adopting a more flexible type of quota regulations which would enable us to meet situations of an urgent nature." Harrison's successor, Ugo Carusi (formerly commissioner of Ellis Island), was so inspired by the formation of the United Nations in 1945 that he called for extending the "new concept of international cooperation" to immigration policy.[16]

The Politics of Symbolic Reform

But by the late 1940s the Cold War had begun to reorganize world affairs into a bipolar frame, marginalizing internationalist and human rights discourses. The adjustments in the liberal argument for immigration reform were subtle at first. In 1952 Handlin continued to argue for "useful additions to our manpower," citing labor shortages and predictions of a declining birthrate. But there was a shift toward emphasizing the symbolic need for reform. The "most important" reason for reform, said Handlin, was that "the present system clashes with . . . democratic ideals." The quota system was "offensive to our allies and potential allies throughout the world and a slur on millions of our citizens." That last point received special emphasis: "The quotas cast the slur of inferiority [upon] . . . the grandfathers of millions of Poles and Italians and Jews, and of hundreds of thousands of others who, by their contributions to American life, have earned the right to be counted the equals of the descendants of the Pilgrims. . . . The Italian American has the right to be heard on these matters precisely *as* an Italian American. The quotas implicitly pass a judgment upon his own place in the United States."[17]

Handlin hoped that emphasizing the racist imputations of the quota system would mobilize Euro-American ethnic voters—who he believed were "apathetic"—to support immigration reform. "If the issue were presented in these terms," he argued, "many more would come to see a meaning in it that is now lacking for them."[18] But at another level the view that reform was symbolic was not merely strategic; symbolism became its principal content. Handlin and other reformers believed that repealing the national origin quotas would do little to change European migration patterns—for example, Britain hardly used its vast quota, and two-thirds of the total immigration during the 1950s was outside the quota system altogether. Handlin began to argue that the era of open immigration was over and would not return, even if all restrictions were lifted. In fact, Handlin was referring to migration from Europe. In more deliberative policy settings, he and other scholars acknowledged the difference in demographic trends between Europe and the developing world and advocated economic investment, not emigration, for overpopulated regions like Asia. However, these distinctions were lost in the popular and legislative discourse in the late 1950s and early 1960s, which focused on the symbolism of reform. Shortly after Hart-Celler was enacted, Handlin underscored the point again: "The change in our immigration law will have only minor quantitative significance. Revision is important as a matter of principle."[19]

The symbolic nature of reform was most evident in the case of American Jews, who played a leading role in the movement for immigration reform. Repealing the national origins quotas offered almost no direct material benefit for Jews, but it promised to eradicate the stigma that they carried. Immigration reform was part of a broader postwar campaign undertaken by organizations like the American Jewish Congress and the Anti-Defamation League to eliminate anti-Semitic prejudice in American society.

It was characteristic, as well, of American Jewish commitments to cultural pluralism that dated to the Progressive Era, when intellectuals like Louis Brandeis and Horace Kallen problematized Jewish ethnic identity and, more broadly, conceived of it as a prototype for American national identity. Throughout the 1950s and 1960s, the Anti-Defamation League of B'nai B'rith published scores of books, many commissioned from academics, that aimed to combat not just anti-Semitism but racism, nativism, and religious intolerance in general. One gets a sense of the project from the titles of some ADL publications: *Civil Rights and Minorities* (1956), by Paul Hartman; *Prejudiced—How Do People Get That Way?* (1959), by William Van Til; *Privacy and Prejudice: Religious Discrimination in Social Clubs* (1962); and *Negro American Intelligence* (1964), by Thomas Pettigrew. The prolific Oscar Handlin wrote for the ADL *Danger in Discord* (1949; about anti-Semitism), *American Jews: Their Story* (1958), and *Out of Many* (1964; on cultural pluralism).[20] These efforts were characteristic of the belief held by many postwar liberals and social scientists that prejudice was born of ignorance and could be resolved with education and persuasion. As the sociologist Francis Brown explained, "The whole problem of minorities must be approached from the point of view of modifying basic attitudes. The first step is knowledge of and appreciation for the contribution of each group."[21]

Toward this end, in 1958 the ADL proposed to Senator John F. Kennedy that he write a book on immigration history. It offered an outline written by Arthur Mann, one of Handlin's first doctoral students at Harvard and then an assistant professor at Smith College. Published over Kennedy's name as a modest pamphlet, *A Nation of Immigrants* departed considerably from the original outline by presenting more of a celebratory narrative of immigrant contributions to American life, featuring Carl Schurz, Andrew Carnegie, Samuel Gompers, and Albert Einstein, among others.[22] Although *A Nation of Immigrants* acknowledged that hardship and discrimination were part of the immigrant experience in America, it lacked the historical and sociological analysis of *The Uprooted*. Kennedy's writers promoted Handlin's famous thesis, that "the immigrants *were* American history," but only in a superficial way. They neglected Handlin's theory that the alienation and eventual assimilation of immigrants exemplified the more general process of Americans' transition to modernity. Handlin's view was not merely celebratory; in fact, he believed immigration history had already moved beyond the compensatory stage to yield larger lessons about American national development. Handlin bore an ultimate faith in assimilation and modernity but was also interested—perhaps more so—in the "tragic depths" of experience that accompanied America's "progress and growth," which were known to immigrants and native born alike: the breakup of communal life, the transformation of the family, the alienation induced by factory work and the city.[23] Historians have since debated whether European migrants in the late nineteenth century and the early twentieth were premodern people or whether they had, already, even as peasants, been shaped by capitalist market relations. But the point here is that Handlin's analysis was a critique. In a sense he was not unlike other historians of his time (Richard Hofstadter comes to mind) who subscribed to an exceptionalist view of American history yet found in that history much that was dark and unlovely.

However, Handlin's critique became erased in popular histories of immigration as well as in some of the scholarship on immigration. Perhaps the prosperity of the 1950s and 1960s all too easily sublimated the painful elements of social development of which Handlin spoke. The erasure led to an overemphasis on celebratory history and, perhaps more perniciously, to teleological histories that posited assimilation and inclusion as normative processes of American development. In this vein, *A Nation of Immigrants* exemplified the liberal pluralism of the times, which characterized racism and discrimination as anomalies in what Gunner Myrdal had famously called the "American creed."

Thus the new immigration history signaled the political arrival of ethnic Euro-Americans in the postwar political order, a kind of proto-multiculturalism. At the same time, there was as yet no parallel movement among non-European immigrant groups. Latinos and Asian Americans were almost completely absent from the immigration reform movement, reflecting the general state of their participation in politics, policy, and academia. They were also scarcely visible in popular histories of immigration; *A Nation of Immigrants* did not discuss Latino or Asian immigration at all, save for a brief paragraph on Chinese exclusion, which it said was "shameful." The exclusion of Latinos and Asians from the mainstream of politics and history meant that the reform movement had scant knowledge of Asians' and Latinos' experience and perspectives. Although liberals framed European immigration in terms of its impact on Euro-American ethnic group interests, they addressed Asian and Mexican immigration without considering the interests or viewpoints of Asian Americans and Mexican Americans. That is to say, they saw European immigration in terms of American citizens, whereas they perceived Mexican and Asian immigration in terms of foreigners.

Asian immigration was conceived almost entirely from the vantage point of U.S. Cold War foreign policy interests. Here the symbolism of reform was aimed not at Asian American citizens but at U.S. allies in East Asia. The "Asia-Pacific Triangle," the designation for a global race quota limiting Asian immigration to some 2,000 per year, was a "needless source of difficulty and a gratuitous insult to [Asian countries] who should be our allies," wrote Handlin.[24]

With regard to immigration from Mexico, Latin America, and the Caribbean, reformers also took a symbolic and abstract approach. In the early 1950s Handlin advocated, in the name of consistency, elimination of the quota exemptions historically enjoyed by countries of the Western Hemisphere.[25] However, throughout the 1950s and early 1960s, the reform movement supported continuing the nonquota policy for Western Hemisphere immigration, in deference to the State Department's commitment to Pan Americanism, a policy that was rooted in American state and business interests in Latin America and Canada. In fact, many believed that it was merely a policy of "Good Neighbor politeness" and that immigration from Mexico was already controlled by administrative means (since 1929 the State Department granted virtually no visas to Mexican laborers)—a belief that signaled Northern liberals' remove from the Southwest and their blindness to the effects of administrative control in generating illegal immigration.[26]

Equality and Inequality in Immigration Policy

Yet, having shifted immigration reform to the symbolic realm, liberals were not always clear about what exactly should *replace* the national origins formula. We have come to think that the only nondiscriminatory alternative was a system that distributed quotas equally to all countries. But that was not the necessarily the case. Most notably, in the early 1960s Michigan senator Philip Hart (who ultimately cosponsored the 1965 law) introduced legislation that used the nation as the basic unit for distributing visas; but rather than distribute quotas equally to all countries, Hart's formula took into account the needs of refugees and sending countries. Out of a total quota of 250,000, it allocated 20 percent for refugees and the balance to countries in proportion to the size of their population (32 percent) and in proportion to their emigrants to the United States (48 percent). Countries of the Western Hemisphere would have remained outside the quotas. Under Hart's plan, the only country that would have received a smaller quota than under the 1952 law was Great Britain. Hart's proposal is noteworthy because it did not consider the national interest of the United States in zero-sum opposition to the interests of other countries. It took into account a variety of factors: human rights, the needs of other countries, historical regional ties in the Americas, and American citizens' familial ties abroad. It was a more thoughtful policy that balanced numerous interests and needs.[27]

In fact, Hart credited the bill's design to the American Immigration and Citizenship Committee, an ad hoc coalition that had sponsored a two-year-long research project to devise a "humanitarian and nondiscriminatory" immigration policy. The committee comprised many liberal organizations that had been active in immigration reform in the early and mid-1950s, such as the American Jewish Congress, the National Council of Catholic Charities, and the United Auto Workers, as well as a growing constituency of voluntary organizations with experience in refugee resettlement, such as the American Council for Nationalities Services and the New York Association for New Americans. The bill also bore the imprint of Hart's chairmanship of the Senate Judiciary Committee's subcommittee on refugees and escapees.[28] To an extent these issues remained defined in terms of Cold War alliances. But insofar as refugee work impelled thinking on immigration reform, it opened up a way of approaching immigration policy that was not premised exclusively on nationalism.

In 1963 thirty-five senators and fourteen representatives cosponsored Hart's bill—not a small showing of support. *Life* magazine lauded its provisions for refugee admissions and urged Congress to pass it "for humanity's sake."[29] But President Kennedy's staff opposed it and pressured Hart to introduce the administration's more moderate bill. The Kennedy proposal allocated only 3.5 percent of total quota admissions to refugees, an extremely modest proportion. That change seemed to reflect the interests of the State Department, which was more concerned with the symbolism of reform as it enhanced foreign relations than it was with actual refugees. The administration bill initially exempted countries of the Western Hemisphere from numerical quotas, continuing past practice, and replaced the national origins quotas and Asia-Pacific Triangle with two broad preference categories: first, professionals whose skills were deemed in short supply in the United States and, second, relatives of existing citizens. According to the *Wall Street Journal*, this innovation came from the "youthful lawyers of the Kennedy Justice Department," whose preference for immigrants with professional skills "reflected President Kennedy's preoccupation with the ideal of quality in American life."[30]

Hart introduced the administration's bill while trying to keep his own in play. He acknowledged that both bills shared "the same fundamental objectives" but noted that they proposed "two alternate ways of removing the national origins quota system." Hart hoped that Congress would hold hearings on both, with the aim of crafting "the most creative and very best proposals." In fact, neither bill was reported out until after Kennedy's assassination and the reintroduction of his proposal by the Johnson administration. (The death in October 1963 of Francis Walter, who had controlled the House immigration committee throughout the 1950s, also gave Johnson more room to pass an immigration reform bill.) By that time, Hart's original bill had been swept aside, and the senator, along with Congressman Emanuel Celler, became a co-sponsor of the Johnson administration's bill.[31]

There was, in fact, a new symbolism in the Hart-Celler bill, which, in the context of the legislative battles taking place over civil rights, must have seemed irresistible to liberals: individuality, not nationality, counted most. Proponents of the administration bill emphasized that quotas were global, not national, and that admission would be determined according to the preference categories on a first-come, first-served basis. This meant that "in choosing between a Chinese doctor, an Italian doctor, or a Greek doctor," the date of application for the immigration visa would be the "final determining factor," according to Johnson's attorney general, Nicholas Katzenbach. The whole point of the reform, according to supporters, was to replace nationality and race with individual attributes (skills, family ties) as the criteria for entry. Country-based quotas were introduced indirectly, in the form of a provision that no single country could receive more than 20,000 visas. This limit was aimed at keeping the immigration stream diverse and at preventing "excessive benefit or harm to any country." Robert F. Kennedy called the system "basically simple[,] . . . sound[,] . . . and fair."[32]

The concept of "equality" was thus murky and inconsistent: the subject bearing equal rights was at once the u.s. citizen, the individual migrant, and the sending nation. Each subject's claim derived from a different epistemology of rights: civil rights in the liberal nation-state, human rights without reference to state membership, and the right of national self-determination, respectively. The discourse of formal equality elided these differences and, moreover, justified *both* liberalizing and restricting provisions of the law. It impelled repeal of the national origins quota system, but it also made the Western Hemisphere exemption from numerical restriction appear unfair. Thus liberals' support for Pan-Americanism collapsed when moderates in Congress, worried about population increases in Latin America, moved to slam shut the back door.[33]

Indeed, an immigration policy that treats all nations equally is substantively unequal: in a world of unequal conditions and power relations, such a policy means that a small country like Luxembourg will never use up its quota, whereas emigrants from larger and poorer countries like Mexico and China either have to wait many years for a visa or must enter the United States illegally. In addition, some countries have special relationships with the United States—colonial (Philippines), geographic (Mexico, Canada), war-generated (Vietnam)—that arguably justify privileged consideration in immigration policy. An equal-quotas-for-all structure also serves to limit, if not preclude, the possibility that the number of admissions from any given country might be determined diplomatically, through bilateral negotiations that consider migration in the context of the two countries' specific relationship, needs, and interests.[34]

The principle of equality in immigration thus involved a crucial slippage, in which a symbolic gesture of equality to citizens obscured an unequal policy toward noncitizens. The cost of this slippage has been an exaggerated notion of our immigration policy as generous and fair. In fact, Hart-Celler was numerically more restrictive than past policy; it gave impetus to the illegal immigration of the unskilled, especially from Mexico and Central America; it promoted a brain drain from the developing world; and it sustained the continuing resistance to humanitarianism as a policy imperative. Some progress was later made on these fronts: Congress established a refugee policy based on international norms in 1980; it legalized nearly 3 million undocumented immigrants in 1986; and it increased annual admissions by 35 percent in 1990, in response to the economic growth of the preceding decade.[35] But none of these policies were present in Hart-Celler. Moreover, none may be attributed to the principle of equal quotas. Rather, they came about as the result of greater international and domestic pressures for human rights, increased political activism among Latinos, and lobbying by business interests.

Oscar Handlin's was not the only voice in the immigration reform movement. Also involved were other academics, elected officials, jurists, clergy, trade unionists, and ethnic-group leaders. And even as pluralism's influence grew in the postwar years, it still lacked focus in the 1950s; it could not yet be translated into real policy. In the 1950s the time was not yet ripe for immigration reform.[36] But Handlin's contributions during that decade should not be underestimated. His writings, both scholarly and journalistic, provided an episteme for reform, a framework and a logic for critiquing old policy and for defining the contours of a new one. I do not mean to claim that Handlin established this framework alone or that he originated all the ideas. But his work was enormously influential. Handlin not only gave Euro-American ethnic groups voice and legitimacy, *as ethnics*. He gave them a central place in the master narrative of American history and argued that pluralism and group life were pillars of American democracy. The reform agenda was thus not just a matter of immediate political interests; it was a historical mission in the perceived telos of American democracy and in the construction of post–World War II Americanism. In this sense it was an analogue to the African American civil rights movement. To liberals in the postwar years, the similarities seemed irresistible and overshadowed the differences between them.

Handlin and other reformers successfully made immigration policy a test of pluralist politics, but the results were mixed. On the positive side, of course, they achieved repeal of the obnoxious national origins quotas. But their focused interest in securing symbolic equality for Euro-American ethnic groups also succeeded, albeit unwittingly, in crowding out from serious consideration two policies that would prove to be critical to the course of late twentieth-century immigration: open immigration in the Western Hemisphere and an internationalist responsibility toward refugees and asylum seekers. Of course, there were other reasons why these issues became marginalized in immigration policy. But it is worth wondering what might have happened, what kind of discussion there might have been, had more liberals pursued further and more consistently the democratic impulse that animated their own quest for reform.

Finally, it can be said that Oscar Handlin succeeded in setting down one of Hart-Celler's most enduring legacies: its place in the scholarship of postwar American history as a celebrated reform of liberal pluralism, its nationalist orientation and exclusionary dimensions erased from view. This was quite an extraordinary melding of history and historiography: in effect, Handlin wrote the history of an event in the midst of its making. Moreover, that line of interpretation was handed down to another generation of American historians trained by Handlin and his contemporaries; it was adopted and diffused across the field.

Another twenty years or so passed before Latinos and Asian Americans became a visible presence in politics and in the university. They were not, however, the newest immigrants admitted under Hart-Celler. Rather, they were, like Handlin's contemporaries at midcentury, of the second and third generation; they were also the children of the uprooted. And they too found in history their own usable pasts to work for new reforms, such as ensuring the rights of the undocumented, providing bilingualism in education, and establishing political representation. Thus the story of the postwar movement for immigration reform and the passage of Hart-Celler is not only a history of American politics. It is also about the politics of American history.

NOTES

This essay was written with the generous support of the Radcliffe Institute for Advanced Study at Harvard University. Earlier versions were presented at the Center for the Critical Analysis of Contemporary Culture at Rutgers University and the Charles Warren Center and Department of History Faculty Seminar at Harvard. I thank participants at both for valuable commentary and suggestions; I am also grateful to Oscar Handlin and David Handlin for sharing recollections with me.

1. U.S. Immigration and Naturalization Service, 2000 *Statistical Yearbook*, table 1, Immigration to the U.S., fiscal years 1820–2000; David Reimers, *Unwelcome Strangers: American Identity and the Turn against Immigration* (New York: Columbia University Press, 1998); Bill Ong Hing, *Making and Remaking Asian America through Immigration Policy* (Stanford, Calif.: Stanford University Press, 1990).

2. Oscar Handlin, "We Need More Immigrants," *Atlantic Monthly*, May 1953, 27–31 (quotation on 27). Immigration quotas based on national origin were established under the Johnson-Reed Act of 1924. The law apportioned quotas to countries in proportion to the number of Americans who could trace their "national origin" through immigration or through the immigration of their forebears. The law successfully met its intention to drastically limit immigration from eastern and southern Europe. On the invention of national origins and on the consequences of immigration restriction under Johnson-Reed, see Mae Ngai, *Impossible Subjects: Illegal Aliens and the Making of Modern America* (Princeton, N.J.: Princeton University Press, 2004).

3. Before 1965 the annual quota for Greece was 328, for Japan, 100. Celler cited in "The Consequences of Our Immigration Policy," December 5, 1955, file Immigration, box 478, Papers of Emanuel Celler, Library of Congress, Washington.

4. Press release, "Sen. Kennedy Introduces Three-Point Immigration Program," May 18, 1959, file 86th-1st, immigration: gen'l, box 630, Pre-Presidential Papers, John F. Kennedy Presidential Library, Boston (hereafter "JFK").

5. Deane Heller and David Heller, "Our New Immigration Law," *American Legion*

Magazine, Feb. 1966, 6–8; "Immigration Reform," *Commonweal*, June 1965, 341; "New Immigration Policy: Give Me Your Vigorous, Your Skilled," *New Republic*, February 27, 1965, 15–16.

6. Philip Gleason, "American Identity and Americanization," *Harvard Encyclopedia of American Ethnic Groups*, ed. Stephan Thernstrom (Cambridge, Mass.: Harvard University Press, 1980), 52; Roger Daniels, *Coming to America* (New York: Harper Collins, 1990), 338.

7. David M. Reimers, *Still the Golden Door: The Third World Comes to America*, 2nd ed. (New York: Columbia University Press, 1992); John Higham, *Send These to Me: Immigrants in Urban America* (Baltimore: Johns Hopkins University Press, 1975), 58–64.

8. *Perez v. Brownell*, 356 US 44, 64–65 (1958) (Warren, C.J., dissenting). It should be noted that alienage was not always the principal imagined opposite of citizenship. In late eighteenth- and early nineteenth-century America, citizenship comprised a range of status positions, with property-holding white men at the apex and slaves their most definitive opposite.

9. Charles L. Black Jr., "The Unfinished Business of the Warren Court," *Washington Law Review* 46 (1970): 3–46 (quotation on 8–9).

10. Peter Schuck, "The Transformation of American Immigration Law," *Columbia Law Review* 84 (1984): 1–90 (quotation on 16).

11. Oscar Handlin, *The Uprooted*, 2nd ed. (Boston: Little, Brown, 1973, 1951), 262 (emphasis added).

12. Ibid.

13. President's Commission on Immigration and Naturalization, *Whom We Shall Welcome* (Washington: GPO, 1953); sundry correspondence between Julius C. C. Edelstein and Oscar Handlin, 953, files C76-14 to C76-18, Legislative Files, Herbert H. Lehman Papers, Lehman Library, Columbia University, New York.

14. I thank David Handlin for this insight.

15. Oscar Handlin, "Democracy Needs the Open Door: Immigration and America's Future," *Commentary*, January 1947, 1–6 (quotations on 4, 6).

16. Harrison and Carusi cited by Robert Divine, *American Immigration Policy* (New Haven, Conn.: Yale University Press, 1957), 157. On World War II–era internationalist politics, see Penny Von Eschen, *Race against Empire* (Ithaca, N.Y.: Cornell University Press, 1997); Nikhil Pal Singh, "Culture/Wars: Recoding Empire in an Age of Democracy," *American Quarterly* 50, no. 3 (1998): 471–522.

17. Oscar Handlin, "The Immigration Fight Has Just Begun," *Commentary*, July 1952, 1–7 (quotations on 2, 6–7; emphasis in the original).

18. Ibid., 5–6.

19. Oscar Handlin and Mary Handlin, "The United States," in *The Positive Contribu-*

tion of Immigrants: A Symposium Prepared for Unesco by the International Sociological Association and the International Economic Association (Paris: Unesco, 1955), 47; Oscar Handlin, "Americanizing our Immigration Laws," *Holiday*, January 1966, 8–13. On the potential of mass immigration from "overpopulated" areas of the world, see, for example, Anthony T. Buscaren, *International Migrations since 1945* (New York: Praeger, 1963), 152–64; and Virgil Salera, *U.S. Immigration Policy and World Population Problems* (Washington: American Enterprise Association, 1960). Both Buscaren and Salera recognized that advanced industrialized nations like the United States would be unwilling to tolerate a level of immigration from Asia sufficient to have an appreciable effect on that continent's population problems. They advocated instead increased capital investment and economic development in the developing world.

20. Handlin also published *Adventure in Freedom* (New York: McGraw-Hill, 1954); *Chance or Destiny* (Boston: Little, Brown, 1954); *Race and Nationality in American Life* (Boston: Little, Brown, 1957); *Immigration as a Factor in American History* (Englewood, N.J.: Prentice-Hall, 1959); *The Newcomers: Negroes and Puerto Ricans in a Changing Metropolis* (Cambridge, Mass.: Harvard University Press, 1959); *The American People in the Twentieth Century* (Boston: Beacon, 1963); *Children of the Uprooted* (New York: Braziller, 1966); *A Pictorial History of Immigration* (New York: Crown, 1972); and many other titles.

21. See Stuart Svonkin, *Jews against Prejudice: American Jews and the Fight for Civil Liberties* (New York: Columbia University Press, 1997). Quotation from Francis J. Brown Jr. in *One America: The History, Contributions, and Present Problems of our Racial and National Minorities*, ed. Francis J. Brown and Joseph Slabey Roucek, rev. ed. (New York: Prentice-Hall, 1945), 622. On the evolution of ethnoracial group consciousness in the postwar period and implications for liberal democracy, see David Hollinger, *Postethnic America: Beyond Multiculturalism* (New York: Basic Books, 1994); and Nikhil Pal Singh, *Black Is a Country: Race and the Unfinished Struggle for Democracy* (Cambridge, Mass.: Harvard University Press, 2004).

22. John F. Kennedy, *A Nation of Immigrants* (New York: Anti-Defamation League, 1958; rev. ed., New York: Harper and Row, 1963). The revised edition, issued after the president's assassination and during renewed efforts to pass immigration reform legislation, was a larger and fancier volume, with lots of photographs and a new introduction by Robert F. Kennedy. It also added two paragraphs on Asian and Mexican immigrants and a number of photos of them.

23. Oscar Handlin, "Immigration in American Life: A Reappraisal," *Immigration in American History: Essays in Honor of Theodore Blegen*, ed. Henry Steele Commager (Minneapolis: University of Minnesota Press, 1961), 24. The first lines from *The*

Uprooted read: "Once I thought to write a history of the immigrants in America. Then I discovered that the immigrants were American history."

24. Handlin, "Americanizing our Immigration Laws," 12.

25. Oscar Handlin to Julius Edelstein, July 17, 1953, file Immigration C-76-18, Legislative Files, Lehman Papers.

26. "New Immigration Policy," 15–16; "New Immigrants," *New Republic*, September 25, 1965, 7; *U.S. News and World Report*, October 11, 1965, 55–57.

27. S. 3043, 87th Congress, 2nd session (1962); reintroduced as S. 747, 88th Congress, 1st session (1963).

28. *Congressional Record*, March 21, 1962, p. 4975.

29. Senate cosponsors of the Hart bill included Democrats and a half-dozen liberal Republicans, mostly from northeastern states, such as Kenneth Keating and Jacob Javits of New York, Clifford Case of New Jersey, and Claiborne Pell of Rhode Island. See *Congressional Record*, March 21, 1962, p. 4674, and February 7, 1963, p. 2021. *Life* magazine cited in *Congressional Record*, March 21, 1962, p. 8815.

30. Memorandum, William Welsh to Myer Feldman, April 19, 1963, file LE/IM, box 482, White House Central Subject File, JFK; Philip Hughes to Myer Feldman, March 6, 1963, ibid. (Hughes reported that Abba Schwartz, the State Department official whom the president asked to draft an administration bill, believed that the Hart bill did not "satisfactorily serve the Administration's purposes.") "Immigration Reform," *Wall Street Journal*, October 4, 1965. See *Congressional Record*, July 24, 1963, p. 13164.

31. *Congressional Record*, July 24, 1963, p. 13164; *Wall Street Journal*, October 4, 1965. The published record suggests that Hart was not entirely pleased with the Kennedy administration's maneuver, which used Hart against his own bill. I found no evidence that he was bitter about the pressure that was put on him, but I also found no evidence that Hart enjoyed the credit for Hart-Celler that was bestowed on him. Hart's authorized biography makes no reference whatsoever to the senator's work for immigration reform. His papers at the University of Michigan contain nothing on the legislative history of his immigration bills or Hart-Celler. See Michael O'Brien, *Philip Hart: Conscience of the Senate* (East Lansing: Michigan State University Press, 1995); e-mail message from Michelle Sweester, Bentley Historical Library, University of Michigan, Ann Arbor, to Mae Ngai, Nov. 26, 2003.

32. Testimony of Nicholas Katzenbach, *Immigration*, Hearings before the Subcommittee on Immigration, Senate Committee on the Judiciary, on S. 500, 89th Congress, 1st session, 2 vols. (Washington: GPO, 1965), 18; testimony of Robert F. Kennedy, ibid., 223. Hart-Celler followed the model established in legislation introduced by Herbert Lehman in the 1950s, which replaced the national origins

quotas with a first-come, first-served criterion and with no country receiving more than 10 percent of the total.

33. On deliberations over the Western Hemisphere quotas, see Ngai, *Impossible Subjects*, chap. 7.

34. It is worth noting that in the late nineteenth century Congress could not enact Chinese exclusion until it renegotiated the immigration provisions of the Burlingame Treaty with China and the U.S. Supreme Court gave Congress plenary, or absolute, power over the regulation of immigration. That move to statutory policy indexed the shift of immigration to the realm of nationalism and sovereignty. Notwithstanding the general unilateralist approach established in the late nineteenth century, the United States has on occasion used diplomatic agreements in matters of immigration, notably the U.S.-Japan Gentleman's Agreement of 1908 (by which Japan agreed to limit emigration of laborers); the U.S.-Mexico agreements authorizing the importation of agricultural contract workers (braceros) from World War II to 1964; and agreements with various Caribbean countries authorizing agricultural guest worker programs, some of which continue to the present.

35. Refugee Act of 1980 (94 Stat. 102); Immigration Reform and Control Act of 1986 (100 Stat. 3359); Immigration and Naturalization Act of 1990 (104 Stat. 4978).

36. Author interview with Oscar Handlin, November 4, 2003, Cambridge, Mass.

★ ★ ★ ★

★ In the Shadow of Vietnam

★ *Liberal Nationalism and the Problem of War*

From Theodore Roosevelt's charge up San Juan Hill in 1898, through the celebration of the multiethnic World War II platoon, to John F. Kennedy's Cold War patriotism, war figured centrally in the minds of Americans who wished to forge a liberal nation. Twentieth-century wars became occasions for celebrating America's greatness, intensifying popular devotion to its democratic ideals, and opening up the nation to groups that had been on the margins. Wars legitimated the idea of a liberal state, one authorized to remedy economic and social inequities in the name of justice and security. Wartime mobilizations also unleashed repressive instincts, as liberals sought to contain or eliminate those they labeled internal threats. Repression and democratization together bound liberal nationalism ever more tightly to the political dynamics of war.

But most liberals severed their historical connection to war in the 1960s and 1970s when they opposed American involvement in Vietnam. Simultaneously, many also repudiated nationalism, now seeing in it mainly a thrust toward the domination of weaker countries abroad and the subjugation of "lesser" peoples—minorities and women—at home. These liberals turned their political energies instead to a promotion of "multiculturalism" and of groups that Jesse Jackson included in his "Rainbow Coalition"—who gave their primary loyalty to identities grounded in race, ethnicity, gender, and sexuality rather than to the nation itself.

Many Americans outside the liberal camp associated this turn away from nationalism with their country's decline. Internationally, America had lost its swagger, unable to do much (or so it seemed) against enemies such as the Iranian militants who, in 1979, seized the United States embassy in Teheran and took scores of Americans hostage. Domestically, hyperinflation and growing unemployment accelerated the rusting out of the industrial heartland. When President Jimmy Carter told Americans, in 1978, that they would have to learn to live within limits, he seemed to be pronouncing the death of the American dream.[1]

Liberals' estrangement from war and from the American dream loosened their hold on national political power. Democrats won only a single presidential election between 1964 and 1992, and that one (Carter's victory in 1976) was due more to the Watergate scandal that forced President Richard Nixon's resignation in 1974 than to a liberal renaissance. By 1980 Republican Ronald Reagan, America's most important late-twentieth-century politician, had made pride in America critical to his appeal. His nationalism depended centrally on war—the Cold War—and on vanquishing an international enemy, the Soviet Union, that, in his telling, negated everything Americans held dear.

Reagan's success in winning two terms and securing the election of his legatee, George H. W. Bush, in 1988, convinced influential groups of liberals that the Democratic Party's return to power depended on re-embracing nationalism and wresting control of it away from the right. Liberal efforts to reappropriate nationalism entailed a variety of initiatives: talking about America in a prideful way; reconceptualizing multiculturalism as a story of diversity within an American unity; rethinking once hard liberal positions—a commitment to the welfare state, affirmative action, and deficit spending—in the interests of gaining support from an imagined American "heartland"; and fashioning a nationalism that was inclusive and tolerant and that did not depend for its appeal, as had earlier versions, on the denunciation and exclusion of "un-Americans."[2]

But what would these liberals do about the connection of their own history and historical icons—FDR and JFK, in particular—to war? Some believed that liberals who had led the nation into war had betrayed their best instincts and that nothing should be done to resurrect that tradition. In this view, the reformers who best embodied America's liberal ideals were activist-intellectuals who hated war such as Jane Addams, Randolph Bourne, Charles Beard, and a young Bayard Rustin. In the 1940s the historian Charles Beard became a maligned figure because he denounced America's entry into World War II. But in World War I he had been part of a robust and respected antiwar coalition of liberals and radicals. Such figures had argued that war profited big business, made the state too powerful and unaccountable, and undermined civil liberties and tolerance.[3]

Other liberals essentially ignored the historical connection between liberalism and war, presumably because they regarded it as no more than incidental to the evolution of their cause. Instead they focused on the positive in their efforts to rehabilitate the nation: building community, connectedness, and a vital center; reconciling multiculturalism with a commitment to core American values; and restoring a strong civic life that would tie Americans to each other, build pride in the nation, and expand support for liberal policies.[4]

That uplifting conception of Americanism seemed on the rise by the 1990s. Both the civil rights revolution of the 1960s, which delegitimated racial nationalism, and the collapse of the Soviet Union twenty years later, which removed America's principal adversary from the international arena, enabled many to claim that American nationalism had outgrown its racialist character and its association with war. It was now plausible to think that a kinder and gentler version of Americanism could flourish. But this thesis took a big hit on September 11, 2001. In the aftermath of that day of terror, militant nationalist sentiment in the United States surged, abetted by American-led wars in Afghanistan and Iraq. In light of these developments, the relationship of American nationalism to war deserves a fresh look.

A good place to begin is by examining a small group of celebrated nationalists who, in the 1990s, embraced, through representations of history, a liberal vision of war. We do not often think of these filmmakers, popular historians, and cultural impresarios as articulating a liberal point of view at all. But they did and still do. The leading figures—James McPherson, Stephen Ambrose, Ken Burns, Stephen Spielberg, Ted Turner, and Tom Brokaw—took it upon themselves, in the late 1980s and the 1990s, to immerse Americans in what were the two greatest, most decisive, and most liberal wars in U.S. history: the Civil War and World War II. In their eyes, liberals might reclaim nationalism by reigniting a fascination with liberal wars.

These "war and nationalism" liberals deserve more attention for their role in reinvigorating liberal nationalism than they have yet received. They undertook sophisticated efforts to imbue their war stories with liberal content. They possessed a better appreciation for the importance of war to the making of the American nation than did liberals who ignored the question. Most significantly, in the character of the citizen soldier, these liberals crafted an emblematic American who fought not out of hate or an urge to dominate but out of patriotic duty and a commitment to republican values. A tolerant and decent nationalism, they seemed to argue, could be achieved through wars fought for just goals and by altruistic warriors.

By recovering the figure of the citizen soldier and celebrating his exploits, these liberals drew attention to a critical, though largely ignored, development in the post-Vietnam American way of war: the turn away from the citizen soldier and the embrace, instead, of the professional warrior. When the Nixon administration discarded the draft and established an All-Volunteer Force in its place, it ended a tradition of citizen soldiering that had begun two hundred years before as a way to forestall the establishment of the kind of professional army we have today. "Standing armies"—the eighteenth-century term for professional ones—were thought to corrupt governments, encourage military adventurism, and undermine republics. By celebrating the citizen soldier, the "war and nationalism" liberals of the 1990s positioned themselves to launch a patriotic critique of the country's professionalized military—and of the kind of adventurist foreign policy that the establishment of such a military has helped make possible. In the process, they may have strengthened the credibility of a distinctly liberal approach to nationalism.

But such a critique did not, in fact, emerge. The "war and nationalism" liberals were reluctant or unable to grapple with the consequences of the Vietnam War for American society. That war had raised complicated, painful questions about what constitutes civic duty in a republic at a time of war and how citizen soldiers should behave during a war they deem to be dangerous to their country's future. No liberal nationalism can succeed in twenty-first-century America without confronting the civic and soldiering questions that Vietnam raised. Evading Vietnam did not render useless the kind of nationalism these liberals were trying to create. But it did make their nationalist narratives available to other groups on the political spectrum, particularly those intent on appropriating the narratives for conservative ends.

Interest in the Civil War and World War II ran high long before the 1990s, and books about them sold better than those on any other topics in American history. However, the publication in 1988 of James McPherson's *Battle Cry of Freedom: The Civil War Era* (which won a Pulitzer Prize) and in 1994 of Stephen Ambrose's *D-Day: June 6, 1944* markedly boosted the public's desire to learn about the history of those wars.[5] Ken Burns deepened the interest in the Civil War when, in 1990, he released what was to become one of the most popular documentaries ever shown on the Public Broadcasting System (it was titled simply *The Civil War*). Later that same decade, Stephen Spielberg, who was inspired by Ambrose's work, made the acclaimed, Oscar-winning film *Saving Private Ryan* (1998); he then teamed up with Ambrose and Tom Hanks to produce the HBO series *Band of Brothers* (2001). Ted Turner put the resources of his media empire behind the making of *Gettysburg*, which came out in 1993, and five years later Tom Brokaw embarked on an energetic and deeply personal print and television campaign to celebrate World War II soldiers and their contemporaries as the "Greatest Generation." By 2001 Brokaw's book trilogy of the same name had sold more than 5 million copies, and his television specials on World War II, often featuring Stephen Ambrose as a narrator or a talking head, had reached audiences in the millions as well.[6]

These figures did not have identical artistic or political agendas. The story of vanquishing an external enemy, Nazi Germany, could not be told the same way as that of the nineteenth-century conflagration that tore America apart. Feature filmmaker Spielberg approached his subject differently than did documentary filmmaker Burns. McPherson remained a more serious scholar than Ambrose. He resisted the lures of celebrity, the hiring of assistants to accelerate the production of his books, and the temptation to become a cheerleader for politicians in power. He also remained a stout liberal, as Ambrose drifted more and more into Republican circles. Nevertheless, these men were engaged in a common project: to place great wars at the center of American history; to find in those wars the leadership, character, and values that made America great; and to use the recovery of these wars' histories to bolster a nationalism that would serve liberal purposes.

The representations of war in the work of these authors and filmmakers shared several principles: first, war is hell, and its physical and psychological horrors have to be vividly conveyed; second, great wars have nevertheless been redeemed by the noble ideals for which they were fought—the elimination of slavery in the Civil War and the defeat of Hitler in World War II—and by the great leaders, such as Abraham Lincoln and Franklin D. Roosevelt, who were able to communicate to Americans what was at stake; third, even those Americans on the wrong side of the Civil War—Generals Robert E. Lee and James Longstreet, in *Gettysburg*, for example—fought with virtue and conscience; and, finally, and most important, great wars have been won by citizen soldiers.

The figure of the citizen soldier is crucial to understanding the liberalism of this war-centered nationalism. He is not a professional warrior and has no desire to become one. This sort of exemplary figure may be a gentle and reflective educator in civilian life: Captain James Miller, in *Saving Private Ryan*, is a Pennsylvania schoolteacher, and Colonel Joshua Lawrence Chamberlain, in *Gettysburg*, is a college professor from Maine. Neither is a military adventurer. They fight because their nation has called them to service, and their duty must be done. They want to keep America honest and democratic, and the restoration of peace is their goal. They harbor no dreams of imperial glory or of achieving the kind of Roman-scale conquests that motivated General George Patton.[7] Miller and Chamberlain have a clear understanding of what is at stake—in terms of both the war's overall purpose and the moral vulnerability of the men under their command. Yet they never lose an abhorrence of the death they must inflict and are periodically stricken by crises of conscience about the killing they must undertake. They keep themselves sane by looking forward to the day when their mission will end and they can return to their normal lives.[8]

Like most creations, this figure of the citizen soldier was fashioned out of preexisting cultural materials. Americans have long valued individuals who are thought to be uninterested in wealth, power, or authority but whose ethical core compels them to respond when their community is challenged. In popular culture, such characters have appeared most often in westerns, in the guise of a lone cowboy or gunman who is drawn into the defense of a town's ordinary citizens against outlaws or corrupt officials. The western loner is often a dark figure, or a morally complex one, his separateness intimately bound up with a personal history too painful or dangerous to share with other members of his community. By comparison, the citizen soldier of the war movies is a less complex and more socialized character. He is distinguished not by a past he feels compelled to hide but by the ordinariness of his civilian pursuits. He is simply a good citizen.[9]

Captain John Miller of *Saving Private Ryan*, played by Tom Hanks, is the most fully realized of these citizen soldiers depicted on screen. We encounter him coming ashore with his company of men during the first wave of assaults on the beaches of Normandy on June 6, 1944. From seeing the tremor in his hand as his boat approaches the beach and then watching as he is dazed and disoriented by an exploding mortar shell soon after he lands, we learn that he is not an indestructible superhero. Yet he collects himself and, through experience, decisiveness, and good judgment, organizes his men to overpower a German redoubt and leads them to safety.

This harrowing episode is merely a prelude to the real story of Spielberg's film: the search for Private James F. Ryan, a paratrooper dropped behind German lines on the eve of D-Day. Because three of his brothers have already died in combat, the top brass orders him to be removed from the theater of war. Captain Miller draws the assignment of finding Ryan and escorting him to safety. From the outset, Miller scorns his mission. He sees no good reason for risking the lives of his men to search for one unknown individual in an unfamiliar countryside swarming with thousands of enemy soldiers. Yet Miller does not hesitate to assemble a squad and to cross into enemy territory in pursuit of the spectral Ryan.

The search eerily transports the viewers of this World War II movie to another war, Vietnam. Spielberg's cameras linger on Miller's soldiers as they snake through rolling and unknown terrain. They have no idea when and under what circumstances they will find Ryan or encounter the enemy. They might as well be "humping the boonies"—a phrase from the Vietnam War used to describe the patrols of u.s. soldiers who ventured into enemy territory to draw fire, thereby to expose, engage, and defeat the Viet Cong. The climactic moment, when Miller's men threaten to desert him and the mission, also suggests that Spielberg's thoughts about Vietnam have shaped this World War II movie.

All wars generate instances when enlisted men rebel against their officers and sometimes kill them, but the incidence of such events in Vietnam exceeded that of every other war the United States has fought. The frequency of such actions in Vietnam came to symbolize the breakdown of the u.s. military, the despair that engulfed enlisted men who saw no purpose in what they were being told to do, and the repudiation of the values so closely tied to American nationalism—honor, duty, and a belief that it was worth fighting and dying for one's country. To suggest, as Spielberg does, that such sentiments may have entered the minds of the foot soldiers of the Greatest Generation is to enter a potentially subversive terrain of story-telling.[10]

In *Saving Private Ryan*, the near rebellion occurs when Miller orders his men to attack a nest of German machine gunners. They are reluctant to attack, but they do and they overwhelm the enemy. In the process, however, they lose one of their men, Private Irwin Wade, a medic, whose painful death constitutes one of the movie's most emotionally wrenching moments. Unnerved and enraged by Wade's death, Miller's men want to kill the German machine gunner they have captured. Miller intervenes to have the German soldier dig a grave for Wade and then to let him go. Infuriated by Miller's act, Private Richard Reiben, the squad's Irish American hothead, declares that he has finished serving on the Ryan mission. When Sergeant Michael Horvath, Miller's loyal noncom, pulls a gun on Reiben, the squad is on the verge of a Vietnam-style climax: American soldiers killing each other rather than obeying their captain and carrying on with their mission.

But Spielberg cannot allow that to happen—not in a movie about the

Greatest Generation. The leadership skills and ethical values of the citizen soldier save the day. Miller manages to subdue his trauma and collect his thoughts, and then he uses the occasion to reveal to his men a closely guarded secret, on which they have been laying bets: his occupation in civilian life. He announces that he is an English teacher in a small Pennsylvania town. To insulate himself against the charge that teaching English might be too effeminate a calling for an army captain, he tells them that he is a baseball coach too.

Miller's revelation catches his men off guard, breaks the murderous mood, and gives Spielberg the opportunity to deliver the film's most important message. Miller admits to his men that he has never believed in the Ryan mission. But if carrying it out earns him the right to go back to his wife, "well that," he says, "makes the mission worth it." In reference to the German machine gunner he refused to kill, he remarks: "Every man I kill, the farther away from home I feel." Moved by the spirit of their citizen-soldier leader, Miller's men all choose to stay with him. Not only will the squad remain unified, but it will find and save Private Ryan, even if the cost, in terms of their own lives, will be high.

It is an extraordinarily moving scene. Yet it also raises tough questions about the strategies Spielberg uses to rekindle patriotism. Two issues in particular invite scrutiny: first, the use of World War II nostalgia to overcome the bitter legacies of Vietnam and, second, the rehabilitation of the all-white, all-male platoon as a prime incubator of American greatness.

Growing up in the 1960s, Spielberg was deeply affected by the war in Vietnam. In a 1998 essay on American war movies written for *Newsweek*, he noted how Vietnam had ruptured his world, both personally and cinematically. Since childhood, he had been fascinated with American war films; indeed, his first movie, made at age fourteen, was an attempt to reenact the glorious World War II battles he and his friends had seen on screen. In that period of 1950s innocence, Spielberg did not doubt the virtue of the United States, the goodness of the wars it had fought, or the nobility and gallantry of those who gave their lives. But then war erupted in Southeast Asia, and, Spielberg recalled, "every Hollywood stereotype [was shattered] when the casualties from Vietnam stormed into our living rooms seven nights a week for nearly a decade." It was not simply that the unceasing stream of deaths disturbed Spielberg, but also "that a new kind of dying was moving our way, uncut and uncensored." Chaos, horrible killing, and cowardice were mixing, and perhaps overwhelming, bravery and glory on the battlefield. It was no longer easy to know what American soldiers were fighting for—or whether all of them were even fighting. Suddenly, separating the good guys from the bad became a much more complicated matter. In *Saving Private Ryan*, Spielberg's determination to reveal the confusion, brutality, and moral uncertainty of war reveals how profoundly Vietnam had shaped his approach to the subject.[11]

Why did Spielberg not make a film about the Vietnam War itself? With memorable Vietnam movies, such as *The Deer Hunter* (1978), *Apocalypse Now* (1979), and *Platoon* (1986), crowding the screens by the 1990s, Spielberg may simply have thought he could more easily make his mark with a cinematic exploration of World War II.[12] But we may also wonder whether Spielberg had another project in mind: to help Americans overcome the trauma of Vietnam by having them focus on a better war.

Several scholars have made this argument, stressing Spielberg's desire, in *Saving Private Ryan*, to end the post-Vietnam crisis of national identity by bringing Americans "home"—to a mythic nation, where individuals are good, republican and patriotic sentiments flourish, and the nation's political energies are harnessed to worthy causes.[13] The therapeutic power of the film, in this view, derives from Spielberg's ability to link his sensibilities about Vietnam—expressed in the gritty realism of the combat sequences— with his faith in American virtue. Spielberg leads his soldiers through the valley of death but comforts us with the knowledge that his young men, like the nation itself, will be redeemed. His soldiers are reluctant, imperfect heroes. But they are also, in his words, the "dogfaces who freed the world" and made America a great nation.[14]

Did the movie help viewers to exorcise the traumas that lingered from Vietnam and "find their way home" to an America they could love and embrace? It's hard to say. But even without knowing how this message was received, one can be troubled by Spielberg's attempt to use World War II to resolve a military and cultural crisis generated by Vietnam. In truth, a movie about World War II does little to help us comprehend what happened in Vietnam. It cannot lead us to understand the reasons for or the consequences of the American defeat in Indochina. It may actually have encouraged some viewers to evade hard questions about Vietnam and to immerse themselves in a nostalgia for the Good War and a better time, when American soldiers served honorably and successfully and made a worthy name for America in the world.

Saving Private Ryan makes no reference to the fact that the Greatest Generation served in a military organized on racist principles; not one African American appears in the three-hour-long movie. What is more, in the sixteen-plus hours of *Band of Brothers*, only one black face can be seen. In a narrow sense, this absence is defensible: of the 150,000 soldiers who landed on Normandy beaches on June 6, 1944, fewer than two thousand were African American, and they came ashore as support troops (driving trucks, unloading supplies, setting up barrage balloons) in later waves after the beachheads had been secured.[15] But hundreds of thousands of African American troops were in Great Britain at the time, building roads and airports, transporting supplies, and cooking food for the troops. Many wanted to fight—and to participate in D-Day—but were not allowed to. Not only had the army and the navy (and its marines) rigidly segregated their ranks along racial lines; they had also, by and large, barred blacks from combat roles. The u.s. high command determined that black soldiers could not be trusted to execute missions, especially when the nation's welfare was at stake.[16]

The bands of exclusively white brothers whom Ambrose, Spielberg, and Hanks celebrate were not naturally occurring formations. They resulted from a deliberate u.s. policy to separate black from white—at a great financial cost to taxpayers, who paid for the duplication of facilities and services, and at the risk of turning army bases into racial battlegrounds between white and black soldiers. At training bases, in particular, black soldiers increasingly expressed their anger at being asked to fight a war for democracy and against Nazism while living in a nation that denied them the basic rights and decencies of citizenship.[17]

It would not have been easy to address this matter in a movie focused on the first week in Normandy after D-Day.[18] A desegregated military would emerge late in the 1940s, partly because of protests by black soldiers and the growing revulsion of white Americans at the prevalence of Nazi-style racial practices in their own society. Over the next fifty years, the military became the most successfully integrated institution in America.[19] Still, there is something troubling about Spielberg's decision—following Ambrose's example—to choose racially homogeneous outfits and moments to celebrate the nation without pausing to note that this homogeneity was the product of a government policy. By reproducing historical patterns of internal exclusion without critiquing them, Spielberg and Ambrose may have helped to reinvigorate them.

Even if *Saving Private Ryan*, *Band of Brothers*, and Ambrose's books traffic in nationalist nostalgia for an era before Vietnam, when the United States fought a good war, military units stayed intact, and white men ruled America, such works still have something to offer those who would construct a liberal nationalism: the character of the citizen soldier. The historical recovery of this figure in the 1990s ironically occurred at a time when the U.S. military had all but abandoned him as an ideal around which to organize and legitimate itself. When instituted near the end of the Vietnam War, the shift toward a professional army had aroused little controversy. Republicans saw it as a way to escape the hammer of antiwar protest; they calculated, correctly, that domestic protests against foreign wars would decline when young American males no longer faced the prospect of conscription. Antiwar protesters viewed the end of the draft as a victory for their campaign to make it impossible for the United States to sustain its involvement in Southeast Asia. Military leaders worried that the new volunteer system would yield too few quality recruits, but they were reluctant to share their reservations with the public. Meanwhile, millions of young men, and their parents and siblings, were simply relieved to learn that Vietnam no longer threatened their future.[20]

What few understood at the time is how the shift to the All-Volunteer Force (AVF) would professionalize military ranks, make military service a specialized career rather than a widely shared civic duty, and narrow the social base from which soldiers were drawn. Popular connection to and control over the military declined, in part because most Americans no longer had a personal tie to it, and in part because the military, like most professions, developed a culture specific to its work and largely inaccessible to outsiders. That culture, inevitably, admires the professional soldier more than the amateur, the individual who demonstrates "real commitment" to his work rather than the "dabbler" who, as in the case of Captain John Miller, is eager to go home.[21]

To criticize the AVF is not to impugn the individual qualities of current and former military men and women. One can point to former generals, such as Colin Powell, Wesley Clark, and Anthony Zinni, who served well in both military and political roles. During the Second Iraq War, some officers expressed their reservations about the war's purpose and execution, the overextension of the army and the marines that it entailed, and the failure to prepare adequately for a long and bloody occupation.[22] The rank-and-file military contains many patriotic and well-trained men and women of various races and ethnicities who sincerely desire to serve their country and to make a proud vocation of their military life. The issue is not the quality of individual warriors and generals but the long-term social and political consequences of nurturing a professional military.

Certainly, earlier generations of Americans would have looked suspiciously on the kind of armed forces that twenty-first-century America has produced. Nothing rankled eighteenth-century revolutionaries more than the presence of Britain's "standing army" in their midst. This was an army thought to serve only the ambitions of the crown, inclining the king and Parliament toward imperial adventurism, corrupting their governing instincts, and strangling the liberties of the British people.

In designing their new nation, the founders of the American republic resolved not to create such a military force. The standing army of the United States would remain small. Its generals would serve in political capacities if called upon, but they would also know—following the example of Cincinnatus and George Washington—when to retreat into their private lives. One of the earliest and most enduring heroes of the Revolutionary War was the minuteman—the citizen soldier from Lexington and Concord who had mobilized to defend his new nation and then returned to his farm once his service was no longer needed.[23]

The decision to rely on citizen soldiers and state militias had its own dangers, of course. George Washington never liked them and was especially critical of the New England units for their reluctance to submit to his and the military's discipline.[24] Both during and after the Revolution, militiamen did not always wait for the government to call them into action and decided, instead, to take matters into their own hands—pursuing outlaws, thieves, and intruders and dispensing their own justice. Some of the individuals identified by nineteenth-century militias as "intruders" may have been genuine threats to public safety; others were marked as dangerous because of the color of their skin, their religion, their alleged lack of civilization, their itinerancy, or their poverty. Indians, Mexicans, and African Americans understood all too well that the line between honorable militias and vigilantes was often hard to fix. The night riders of the Ku Klux Klan adopted their own version of the militiaman image.[25] Meanwhile, the right to bear arms both strengthened the citizen-soldier tradition and denied governments a monopoly over the means of violence.

As the militia tradition declined in the early twentieth century, the meaning of citizen soldiery changed as well. It now referred less to militiamen—civilians who viewed military service as a recurring part of their civic duty and who kept their own weapons and cultivated an ethic of volunteering when asked to fight—and more to young, able-bodied male citizens whom the government called upon (or conscripted) to serve in its military.[26]

While acknowledging the dark side of the militia-citizen-soldier tradition, one can still say that it served the Republic well in one sense: it ensured that major wars would require assent from a broad cross section of the population. Even if political leaders did not seek a formal vote for war, they still had to generate a consensus that a particular war was worth the risk of losing husbands, brothers, and sons in battle. Of course, administrations bent on war have deployed all the tools of propaganda and persuasion they could muster, even if that meant misleading the public. But public skepticism was generally stronger and more probing when citizens had to weigh the value of war against the risk of losing a family member than it is today when the great majority of Americans face no such choice. With the exception of World War II, there had been a large opposition to every war in which the United States became involved, beginning with the Revolutionary War and concluding with Vietnam.[27] In February 2003 hundreds of thousands of Americans took to the streets to protest the impending war with Iraq. But once the war began, the numbers quickly dwindled.

The Bush administration's doctrine of preventive war—and the decision to invade Iraq—would probably have faced stiffer opposition had it been confronted by a military dependent for its man- and womanpower on citizen soldiers. Such soldiers and their families can provide a democratic check on the ambitions of rulers. It is hardly an accident that the most public and effective questioning of the war after hostilities began came from the ranks of National Guardsmen (and their families), men and women who carry on the citizen-soldier tradition in their own way: they are "weekend warriors" who must be available for military service in times of urgent need. General Creighton Abrams, army chief of staff when the AVF was introduced in 1973, restructured his service to ensure that units in future engagements would always include a mix of active and reserve units, the latter to be composed of National Guardsmen; it was his attempt to keep the army from becoming entirely detached from civilian America.[28] That decision explains why National Guard units played a prominent role in both the First and Second Iraq Wars.

Prior to the second war, the war-fighting component of National Guard service was not particularly prominent in the minds of its members. Most who joined the Guard in the 1980s and 1990s regarded it more as a second job than as a civic duty or military obligation: it provided a dependable supplemental income in return for a relatively low expenditure of time and energy. Guardsmen did not expect to be called to active duty, or, if they were, they anticipated their deployments would be brief and not too dangerous. Thus most Guardsmen were not prepared to question the Pentagon's decision to send large numbers of them to Iraq in 2003 and 2004.

But as their deployments in a theater of war dragged into months, and sometimes into years, many began to ask searching questions of themselves and of the military: As citizens first and soldiers second, how many months or years of service did they owe their country? Was this war winnable? Was it worth the sacrifice of their lives? Gradually, members of the Guard recovered the voices they had lost or never known: those of citizen soldiers. They became more willing to make their views heard precisely because they were citizens first and soldiers second.[29]

Given the public's enchantment with World War II and its citizen-soldier heroes, it is curious that a critique of the Bush administration's embrace of the professional military and its preemptive strike on Iraq did not develop sooner.[30] Why did the popular media's embrace of the citizen soldier have so little effect on public debate and political consciousness?

Three reasons suggest themselves. First, of course, is the destruction of the World Trade Center Towers and the loss of 3,000 lives—the most devastating single attack on U.S. civilians in American history.[31] In the aftermath of that national trauma, it was difficult to question how the country's military is organized and how its dependence on professional soldiers might undercut the vigor of its republican institutions. Indeed, popular thinking ran in just the opposite direction. The Bush administration used the wave of defensive patriotism to build support for a professional, efficient, and "shock and awe" military needed to protect America.

A second reason why the celebration of the citizen soldier had so little impact is that the books and movies about World War II produced in the 1980s and 1990s focused too narrowly on the individual at war. Stephen Ambrose was the main architect of this focus, having pioneered the writing of military history from the perspective of ordinary soldiers rather than that of generals.[32] Yet his social history is frustratingly constricted. Despite his love of the citizen soldier, Ambrose tells his readers almost nothing about his men as civilians—where they lived; the various families, neighborhoods, social circles, activities, and jobs in which they were enmeshed; or the political beliefs they brought with them when they entered the military. He only shows us his soldiers at war and in battle, and he is most interested in their reactions to stress and death. Filmmakers such as Spielberg, who followed Ambrose's lead, give viewers little more information about the civilian pasts of the soldiers, or they do so in a stylized and stereotypical sense that renders the fabric of past life almost meaningless.[33]

This preoccupation with citizen soldiers as embattled men at war lends itself more easily to discussions of manhood and warriorship than to ruminations that might address the relationship between military service and citizenship. Thus conservatives intent on reinstilling martial virtue into a society they perceive as having gone soft, and on restoring male power after a generation of feminist advance, have been able to turn Ambrose's and Spielberg's work to their own advantage.

A third reason why celebration of the citizen soldier did not translate into criticism of the AVF during a "war of choice" in Iraq has to do with Vietnam.[34] In one important respect, the Vietnam War belongs to the same historical moment as does World War II: the United States fought both wars with a citizen-soldier army built from mass conscription. During World War II, citizen soldiers contributed through their willingness to serve, fight, and sacrifice. Many made similar contributions in the Vietnam War, but other patriotic Americans offered a different civic contribution— by resisting the war. Some refused, on principle, to become soldiers in the first place; others, once drafted, refused to fight; still others fought but came home angry, disturbed, and determined to expose and denounce what the government had compelled them to do on the field of battle.[35]

To raise the issue of antiwar protest—especially in regard to a war that the United States lost—is to enter a complicated moral and philosophical terrain about what constitutes civic duty and what does not. What forms of resistance to war can truly be considered expressions of civic duty? Certainly filing for conscientious objector status and being willing to go to jail rather than serve in the military must be seen as civic acts. But what about fleeing to Canada rather than submitting to the draft? What about procuring a draft deferment on questionable grounds—by elaborately documenting phantom injuries or infirmities? What about desertion—or, most troubling of all, desertion in the midst of battle? Where do we draw the line between self-interest—saving one's own skin—and civic duty—doing what's right for the country?

This issue came into sharp relief during the Second Iraq War when, in October 2004, a group of nineteen reservists refused to risk their lives to deliver a shipment of fuel, arguing both that the fuel was contaminated (and therefore unusable) and that American commanders had failed to provide their truck convoy with the necessary protection. Was this a cowardly act of self-preservation or a courageous stand against a military bureaucracy and Department of Defense that had shown callous indifference to the lives of the men under its command?[36]

Or consider the Vietnam protesters in the streets of America in the 1960s. They had certainly risen above their self-interest, but many had also concluded that America was rotten and not deserving of their loyalty. Can you discharge a civic duty when you no longer want any part of the republic of which you are a citizen? This is a complicated question, but one thing seems clear: a healthy republic requires a mechanism for citizens to voice their displeasure about a war that is deemed to be unjust or not in the nation's interest. Sometimes the highest duty of a citizen soldier is to refuse to fight or, if he or she has already been to battle, to come home to speak out about that experience and to do everything one can to end the war. If the government cannot make a compelling case for war, then the war should become harder to prosecute.

John Kerry was once a citizen soldier (or, to be precise, citizen sailor). Never interested in becoming a professional warrior, he nevertheless volunteered with several buddies from Yale to serve in Vietnam. Kerry's service was valorous. He was a bit too grubby for medals, but not overly so in a war in which corruption pervaded the medal awarding system. He probably did take advantage of his class privilege to end his Swift Boat service after four months, instead of serving for the prescribed year. But in those four months he risked his life on a regular basis. On one occasion he saved the life of a fellow navy man while taking enemy fire. His Swift Boat mates clearly regarded him as an exceptional leader and a brave man.

After returning from Vietnam, Kerry joined the Vietnam Veterans against the War. It took courage for Kerry to go before the Senate Foreign Relations Committee, as he did in 1971, to tell the nation's leaders that the war was wrong, that it could not be won, and that it was corrupting the souls of the young men sent to fight it. His congressional speech and testimony are riveting and may constitute the most important civic deed of his long career.[37]

Yet, in Kerry's 2004 presidential campaign, he mostly refrained from discussing this second act of his time as a citizen soldier. When he accepted the Democratic nomination, he referred only to the first act: "I'm John Kerry, and I'm reporting for duty." He alluded to the great things that the 1960s generation had done, but he could not bring himself to defend his own antiwar activity.[38] During the campaign, he even distanced himself from the documentary film *Going Upriver: The Long War of John Kerry* (2004), made by his longtime friend George Butler, which celebrated his role in the antiwar movement.

Kerry thus engaged in an act similar to those of Ambrose and Spielberg:

he refused to confront the lingering divisions over the Vietnam War. To face them would have meant defending the claim he made in 1971, that U.S. involvement in that war was morally wrong. It would have meant articulating the obligation of citizens to protest, especially in times when governments have committed the nation to foolish and damaging wars. It might have helped Kerry define a strong case against U.S. involvement in the Second Iraq War, notwithstanding the political risk.

Kerry's reluctance to speak about his civic act of protest reveals how much the memory of Vietnam continues to influence the ideology of American nationalism. It also suggests that liberals who wish to reclaim the national faith can only do so by confronting the difficult lessons of that war.

Ironically, Ambrose, Spielberg, and the others have shown how this might be done—by making such powerful depictions of the citizen soldier. If the figure of the citizen soldier only becomes an excuse to glorify warriorship, it will be of little use to liberal nationalists. It will simply serve those who regard war as the essence of both manhood and nationhood. But if the celebration helps begin a discussion about the proper relationship between military service and civic duty, then it might become a way for liberals to recover their nationalist voice.

Such a discussion will not likely yield the nationalism-without-enemies that some liberals desire. But it holds out the possibility of creating a decent and popular nationalism with these principles at its core: that republics and their citizens should be slow to go to war and should make such decisions democratically; that citizens ought to deliberate about the possibility of war in the knowledge that family members not currently in the military may be called upon to fight; that dissent from war can be a patriotic act and must be defended as such; and that the best soldiers, in the broadest sense of the term, are not professionals who make the military a vocation but civilians who regard such service as a civic duty. Twenty-first century liberals would be well served by finding an analogue for the citizen soldier—in both his World War II and his Vietnam incarnations.

NOTES

I would like to thank Daniel Gerstle and Katrina Keane for their research assistance and Ira Berlin and Robert Chase for feedback on early versions of this essay. I also benefited greatly from opportunities to present this material to American studies scholars in Japan in 2003 (a presentation arranged by Jun Furuya) and American studies graduate students at Michigan State University in

2004. Finally, a special thanks to Michael Kazin and Joseph McCartin for their encouragement and expert editorial advice.

1. On the centrality of war to liberal nationalism before 1970 (and the turn away from war after 1970), see Gary Gerstle, *American Crucible: Race and Nation in the Twentieth Century* (Princeton, N.J.: Princeton University Press, 2001). On the Iran hostage crisis and Carter's emphasis on limits, see David Farber, *Taken Hostage: The Iran Hostage Crisis and America's First Encounter with Radical Islam* (Princeton, N.J.: Princeton University Press, 2004).

2. Gerstle, *American Crucible*, epilogue.

3. On liberal opposition to war, see Charles DeBenedetti, *Origins of the Modern American Peace Movement, 1915–1929* (Millwood, N.Y.: KTO Press, 1978); Thomas J. Knock, *To End All Wars: Woodrow Wilson and the Quest for a New Moral Order* (New York: Oxford University Press, 1992); Christopher Lasch, *The New Radicalism in America, 1889–1963: The Intellectual as Social Type* (New York: Knopf, 1965); Carl Resek, ed., *War and the Intellectuals: Essays by Randolph S. Bourne, 1915–1919* (New York: Harper and Row, 1964). On Rustin's pacifism during World War II, see John D'Emilio, *Lost Prophet: The Life and Times of Bayard Rustin* (New York: Free Press, 2003).

4. Arthur M. Schlesinger Jr., *The Disuniting of America: Reflections on a Multicultural Society* (New York: Norton, 1992); David A. Hollinger, *Postethnic America: Beyond Multiculturalism* (New York: Basic Books, 1995); Michael J. Sandel, *Democracy's Discontent: America in Search of a Public Philosophy* (Cambridge, Mass.: Belknap Press of Harvard University Press, 1996); Robert D. Putnam, *Bowling Alone: The Collapse and Revival of American Community* (New York: Simon and Schuster, 2000); Theda Skocpol and Morris P. Fiorina, eds., *Civic Engagement in American Democracy* (Washington: Brookings Institution Press, 1999).

5. James M. McPherson, *Battle Cry of Freedom: The Civil War Era* (New York: Oxford University Press, 1988); Stephen E. Ambrose, *D-Day, June 6, 1944: The Climactic Battle of World War II* (New York: Simon and Schuster, 1988).

6. *The Civil War*, directed by Ken Burns, PBS Home Video, 1990, DVD; *Saving Private Ryan*, directed by Steven Spielberg, Dreamworks SKG, 1998, DVD; *Band of Brothers*, directed by David Frankel, Tom Hanks, David Leland, Richard Loncraine, David Nutter, Philip Alden Robinson, Mikael Salomon, Tony To, HBO Home Video, 2001, DVD; *Gettysburg*, directed by Ronald F. Maxwell, Warner Home Video, 1993, DVD; Tom Brokaw, *The Greatest Generation* (New York: Random House, 1998); Tom Brokaw, *The Greatest Generation Speaks: Letters and Reflections* (New York: Random House, 1999); Tom Brokaw, *An Album of Memories: Personal Histories from the Greatest Generation* (New York: Random House, 2001).

7. On Patton, see Ladislas Farago, *Patton: Ordeal and Triumph* (New York: I. Obolensky, 1964); for a cinematic rendition, see *Patton*, directed by Franklin J. Schaffner, DVD, Twentieth Century Fox, 1970.

8. The key figure in *Band of Brothers*, Lieutenant (and later Captain) Richard D. Winters, fits this profile as well, though he has not been an educator in civilian life.

9. For insight into the lone cowboy or gunman as a figure in American culture, see Richard Slotkin, *Gunfighter Nation: The Myth of the Frontier in Twentieth-Century America* (New York: Atheneum, 1992); Arthur M. Eckstein and Peter Lehman, eds., *The Searchers: Essays and Reflections on John Ford's Classic Western* (Detroit: Wayne State University Press, 2004).

10. On "humping the boonies," "fraggings," and other aspects of the war in Vietnam, see Christian G. Appy, *Working-Class War: American Combat Soldiers and Vietnam* (Chapel Hill: University of North Carolina, 1993). On the collapse of military discipline, see also Robert D. Heinl Jr., "The Collapse of the Armed Forces," *Armed Forces Journal*, June 7, 1971.

11. Steven Spielberg, "Of Guts and Glory," *Newsweek*, June 29, 1998, 68.

12. A partial list of these prominent Vietnam movies includes *Coming Home*, directed by Hal Ashby, United Artists, 1978, DVD; *The Deer Hunter*, directed by Michael Cimino, EMI/Universal, 1978, DVD; *Apocalypse Now*, directed by Francis Ford Coppola, United Artists, 1979, DVD; *Rambo: First Blood Part II*, directed by George Pan Cosmotos, Lions Gates, 1985, DVD; *Platoon*, directed by Oliver Stone, Hemdale, 1986, DVD; *Full Metal Jacket*, directed by Stanley Kubrick, Natant, 1987, DVD; *Born on the Fourth of July*, directed by Oliver Stone, Fourth of July, 1989, DVD.

13. See, for example, A. Susan Owen, "Memory, War, and American Identity: *Saving Private Ryan* as Cinematic Jeremiad," *Critical Studies in Media Communication* 19 (September 2002): 249–82.

14. Spielberg, "Of Guts and Glory."

15. Ambrose, *D-Day*, 372.

16. Gerstle, *American Crucible*, chap. 5.

17. Ibid.; Daniel Kryder, *Divided Arsenal: Race and the American State during World War II* (New York: Cambridge University Press, 2000); David J. A. Hunter, " 'Jim Crow Abroad': American G.I.s and the Problem of Race in World War II Britain," unpublished seminar paper, 2003, University of Maryland, in author's possession.

18. It would have been easier to introduce the race question in a movie on the Battle of the Bulge, when Eisenhower, desperate for manpower, permitted black truck drivers to volunteer for combat; five thousand did so. Ambrose, *D-Day*, 372. The

makers of *Band of Brothers*, which has a long episode on the Battle of the Bulge, chose not to take up this opportunity—except to briefly show on screen a black truck driver.

19. On the history of integration in the military, see Morris J. MacGregor Jr., *Integration of the Armed Forces, 1940–1965* (Washington: Center of Military History, U.S. Army, 1981); Bernard Nalty, *Strength for the Fight: A History of Black Americans in the Military* (New York: Free Press, 1986); Charles C. Moskos and John Sibley Butler, *All That We Can Be: Black Leadership and Racial Integration the Army Way* (New York: Basic Books, 1996); Colin Powell, with Joseph E. Persico, *My American Journey* (New York: Random House, 1995).

20. David R. Segal, *Military Organization and Personnel Accession: What Changed with the AVF—and What Didn't* (College Park: Center for Philosophy and Public Policy, University of Maryland, 1981); Martin Binkin, *America's Volunteer Military: Progress and Prospects* (Washington: Brookings Institution, 1984); U.S. Senate, Committee on Armed Services, *Status of the All-Volunteer Armed Force*, Hearing before the Subcommittee on Manpower and Personnel, 95th Cong., 2nd sess., June 20, 1978 (Washington: Government Printing Office, 1978); Edward W. Brooke and Sam Nunn, *An All-Volunteer Force for the United States?* (Washington: American Enterprise Institute for Public Policy Research, 1977).

21. Peter D. Feaver and Richard H. Kohn, eds., *Soldiers and Civilians: The Civil-Military Gap and American National Security* (Cambridge, Mass.: MIT Press, 2001); Thomas W. Lippmann, "Socially and Politically, Nation Feels the Absence of a Draft," *Washington Post*, September 8, 1998; David R. Segal, *Recruiting for Uncle Sam: Citizenship and Military Manpower Policy* (Lawrence: University Press of Kansas, 1989); Jerald G. Bachman, John D. Blair, and David R. Segal, *The All-Volunteer Force: A Study of Ideology in the Military* (Ann Arbor: University of Michigan Press, 1977); Robert K. Fullinwider, ed., *Conscripts and Volunteers: Military Requirements, Social Justice, and the All-Volunteer Force* (Totowa, N.J.: Rowman and Allanheld, 1983); Eliot A. Cohen, *Citizens and Soldiers: The Dilemmas of Military Service* (Ithaca, N.Y.: Cornell University Press, 1985); Binkin, *America's Volunteer Military*. Andrew Bacevich has stressed how the All-Volunteer Force has given American elites (economic and educational) an excuse to opt out of military service. In 2000 only 6.5 percent of military enlistees between the ages of eighteen and twenty-four had had any college education. Bacevich, *The New American Militarism: How Americans Are Seduced by War* (New York: Oxford University Press, 2005), 28.

22. On the criticism by military officers (mostly retired) of the Bush administration, see "Group Urges Voters Not to Choose Bush," *New York Times*, June 14, 2004; Peter Slevin, "Retired Envoys, Commanders Assail Bush Team," *Washington Post*, June 17, 2004; "Retired Officials Say Bush Must Go," *Los Angeles Times*, June 13,

2004; Peter Slevin, "Group Seeks Change in Security Policy; Dignitaries Fault Bush Administration," *Washington Post*, June 13, 2004.

23. John Whiteclay Chambers II, *To Raise an Army: The Draft Comes to Modern America* (New York: Free Press, 1987), chap. 1. On the minuteman tradition, see Robert A. Gross, *The Minutemen and Their World* (New York: Hill and Wang, 1976).

24. Joseph J. Ellis, *His Excellency: George Washington* (New York: Knopf, 2004), 27–28, 76–77. Ellis endorses Washington's dim view of the militias. For a positive view of these militias, see David Hackett Fischer, *Washington's Crossing* (New York: Oxford University Press, 2004), 19–21.

25. For insight into the history of vigilantism, see Linda Gordon, *The Great Arizona Orphan Abduction* (Cambridge, Mass.: Harvard University Press, 1999). On threats that armed groups of white men posed to blacks, see Steven Hahn, *A Nation under Our Feet: Black Political Struggles in the Rural South from Slavery to the Great Migration* (Cambridge, Mass.: Belknap Press of Harvard University Press, 2003).

26. On the decline of the militia tradition, see Chambers, *To Raise an Army*, chaps. 2–3. See also Eliot A. Cohen, "Twilight of the Citizen Soldier," *Parameters* 31 (Summer 2001): 23–28.

27. It is estimated that a third of the colonials living in the thirteen colonies opposed the Revolutionary War. In the case of World War II, opposition to war only collapsed once the Japanese attacked Pearl Harbor. In the late 1930s antipathy toward getting involved in armed conflict and a reluctance to be drawn into Europe's second world war were popular sentiments in American society. For a perceptive portrait of the strength of antiwar sentiment in 1930s America, see Arthur M. Schlesinger Jr., *A Life in the Twentieth Century: Innocent Beginnings, 1917–1950* (Boston: Houghton Mifflin, 2000).

28. Bacevich, *New American Militarism*, 39–41.

29. See, for example, the May 1, 2004, radio address given by Paul Rieckhoff, a National Guard officer from New York City, who served ten months in Iraq with the 124th Infantry, Third Battalion. This address was given as the Democratic Party's response to Bush's radio address announcing that America had accomplished its mission in Iraq. First Lieutenant Paul Rieckhoff, "Rebuttal to G. W. Bush, Mission Accomplished," May 1, 2004 <http://www.foxnews.com/story/0,2933,118735,00.html>. See also Anthony Ramirez, "National Guard Officer Offers Criticism of Bush's Iraq Plan," *New York Times*, May 2, 2004; "Under Armored," a *NewsHour with Jim Lehrer* transcript, December 9, 2004, in which Rieckhoff discusses National Guardsmen concerns with moderator Ray Suarez

and Lt. Gen. Michael De Long (<http://www.pbs.org/newshour/bb/military/july-deco4/armor_12-9.html>); and "Troops' Queries Leave Rumsfeld on the Defensive," *New York Times*, December 9, 2004. For more on the Guard, see Jeffery Gettleman, "Anger Rises for Troops' Families as Deployments in Iraq Drag On," *New York Times*, July 4, 2003; Monica Davey, "Deadly Week Ends in Tears for the Fallen," *New York Times*, April 15, 2004; Eric Santora, "Families and Individuals Join in Anger and Frustration," *New York Times*, August 30, 2004; Thomas E. Ricks, "Strains Felt by Guard Unit on Eve of War Duty," *Washington Post*, September 19, 2004 (this includes a story on a Labor Day AWOL incident and low morale); Monica Davey, "For 1,000 Troops, There Is No Going Home," *New York Times*, September 9, 2004; Monica Davey, "Eight Soldiers Plan to Sue over Army Tours of Duty," *New York Times*, December 6, 2004; Matthew B. Stannard, "Citizen Soldiers on a Global Mission: National Guard General Says State's Force Stretched to Do All That's Asked of It," *San Francisco Chronicle*, December 12, 2004; John F. Burns, "With 25 Citizen Warriors in an Improvised War," *New York Times*, December 12, 2004.

30. Here and there we can detect traces of this line of thinking, but only traces: for example, in the proposal floated by Congressman Charles Rangel and other members of the Black Caucus in 2003 and 2004 to bring back the draft so that all American families would have to face the prospect of sending loved ones into harm's way; and in the work of a North Carolina security studies think tank that had been exploring the dangers generated by the growing gap in America between military and civilian society. Charles B. Rangel, "Bring Back the Draft" (op-ed piece), *New York Times*, December 31, 2002; Darryl Fears, "2 Key Members of Black Caucus Support Military Draft," *Washington Post*, January 3, 2003; Triangle Institute for Security Studies: Project on the Gap between the Military and Civilian Society, <http://www/poli.duke.edu/civmil/>. For other relatively early examples of this critique, see Michael Moore's argument with Bill O'Reilly, Fox News, "The O'Reilly Factor," July 27, 2004, <http://www.foxnews.com/story/0,2933,127236,00.html>.

31. I do not include the attack on the Pentagon here because the Pentagon is not properly considered a civilian target, even though many civilians work there.

32. Ambrose's glorification of the grunt rather than the brass (probably his oeuvre's most enduring contribution) sprang from the same populist sensibility that prompted liberal and left-leaning historians of the 1970s and 1980s to embrace "social history"—the history of ordinary men and women rather than that of presidents, diplomats, captains of industry, and brilliant artists and intellectuals. Perhaps nothing so clearly reveals Ambrose's affinity for left-liberal sensibilities

(other than his thirty-year friendship with World War II bomber pilot and Vietnam dove George McGovern) as does his zeal for writing a history of the World War II military from the "bottom up."

Ambrose was always interested in military history. He wrote his Ph.D. dissertation on Henry Wager Halleck, Lincoln's chief of staff, and then, in the early 1960s, became editor of the Eisenhower papers, a project that made his reputation as a historian. But his career as a military historian did not follow a conventional path. He had done his graduate work at the University of Wisconsin, where, by his own account, he had been influenced by the progressive-left spirit that animated intellectual life in Madison in the 1950s. As a student, he would later recall, he joined the Socialist Party, though he did not elaborate on how long he was a member or describe the kind of activism (if any) in which he became engaged.

This early exposure to radicalism intensified as the 1960s progressed: Ambrose grew his hair long, heckled President Nixon at Kansas State University in 1970 (an act that cost him an endowed professorship there), and supported McGovern in 1972. Among his heroes, in addition to McGovern, was Ernest Gruening (D-Alaska), one of the two U.S. senators to vote against the Gulf of Tonkin Resolution in 1964. Ambrose later wrote that in the 1960s he "was antiwar to such a degree" that he might "well have slipped into the pit that many doves fell into—blaming the United States for everything that went wrong here and abroad." In his book *Rise to Globalism*, he criticized Harry Truman for deciding to drop the bomb on Hiroshima more to scare the Soviet Union than to compel a Japanese surrender.

Ambrose's interest in social history fits with his liberal-left orientation in the 1960s. His movement to the right began, by his own account, in the 1970s during his work on the life and career of Richard Nixon, a man whom Ambrose had despised but, through the course of writing three volumes on him, came grudgingly to admire. See Stephen E. Ambrose, *To America: Personal Reflections of an Historian* (New York: Simon and Schuster, 2002), from which it is possible to reconstruct his political trajectory from the 1950s through the 1980s; the quote in the preceding paragraph comes from p. 135 of that book. See also "Interview with Stephen E. Ambrose, Ph.D.," Academy of Achievement: A Museum of Living History, May 22, 1998, <www.achievement.org/autodoc/page/amboint-1> (accessed June 30, 2005). The other works by Ambrose referenced above are *Halleck: Lincoln's Chief of Staff* (Baton Rouge: Louisiana State University Press, 1962); Ambrose, *Rise to Globalism: American Foreign Policy since 1938* (New York: Penguin Books, 1971); and *Nixon*, 3 vols. (New York: Simon and Schuster, 1987–91).

33. Thus Spielberg alludes to the ethnic origins of the soldiers in Miller's platoon by naming one Richard Reiben (Irish), a second Adrian Caparzo (Italian), a third Michael Horvath (eastern European Christian), and a fourth Stanley Mellish (Jewish). And in demonstrating how all these soldiers made common cause, Spielberg gestures toward the World War II theme of the platoon as a multi-ethnic crucible of Americanization and solidarity. (For more on this theme, see Gerstle, *American Crucible*, chap. 5.) But the cultures (and neighborhoods) out of which these soldiers emerged seem indistinguishable from each other. Spielberg does not pause to examine them, to give them color or texture, or to make them a factor in the life and death of platoon members. The only scene from the United States that Spielberg puts on screen (other than a scene involving George Marshall in U.S. military headquarters) concerns the visit of an army officer and chaplain to the Ryan home to report to Mother Ryan on the deaths of three of her sons. The Ryan farm (huge golden wheat fields) and the Ryan house (a meticulous, perfectly kept Victorian farmhouse) are pure cliché.

The only character, besides Ryan, whose cultural background seems to make a difference to events in the movie is Mellish. Mellish dies at the hands of a German because a fellow U.S. soldier, Timothy Upham (a Gentile), is frozen by cowardice. Spielberg may have meant this episode to be a metaphor for the cowardice of the Gentile world in failing to confront Nazism and the Holocaust. In general, however, Spielberg, like Ambrose, is most interested in the qualities that World War II soldiers displayed while under the stress of battle—toughness, courage, plainspokenness, stoicism, and sometimes skepticism, cowardice, and brutality.

34. Some scholars stress a fourth reason why interest in the citizen military has declined, and that has to do with its alleged obsolescence in an age of high technology and limited wars. Armies of citizen soldiers, Eliot Cohen has argued, are best suited to mass wars in which technological requirements are low (and thus the need to train poorly educated recruits is minimal). But Cohen is too quick, perhaps, to advance arguments grounded in technological determinism and too reluctant to examine the political motivations that impelled the Nixon administration, in the 1970s, to free itself from a citizen soldiery and embrace a professional military. See Cohen, "Twilight of the Citizen Soldier," 25–26; for a contrary view, see Bacevich, *New American Militarism*, 217–20.

35. On the history of the antiwar movement, see Nancy Zaroulis and Gerald Sullivan, *Who Spoke Up? American Protest against the War in Vietnam, 1963–1975* (Garden City, N.Y.: Doubleday, 1984); Charles DeBenedetti, with Charles Chatfield, *An American Ordeal: The Antiwar Movement of the Vietnam Era* (Syracuse, N.Y.: Syracuse University Press, 1990); Michael S. Foley, *Confronting the War Machine:*

Draft Resistance during the Vietnam War (Chapel Hill: University of North Carolina Press, 2003); and Maurice Isserman and Michael Kazin, *America Divided: The Civil War of the 1960s* (New York: Oxford University Press, 2003).

36. Neela Banerjee and Ariel Hart, "Inquiry Opens after Reservists Balk in Baghdad," *New York Times*, October 16, 2004; "When Soldiers Say No," *New York Times*, October 19, 2004, editorial page. The punishment meted out by the military to these refuseniks was surprisingly mild.

37. On Kerry's wartime and antiwar experiences, see Michael Kranish, Brian C. Mooney, and Nina J. Easton, *John F. Kerry: The Complete Biography by the Boston Globe Reporters Who Know Him Best* (New York: Public Affairs, 2004); Douglas Brinkley, *Tour of Duty: John Kerry and the Vietnam War* (New York: William Morrow, 2004); and *Going Upriver: The Long War of John Kerry*, directed by George Butler, Swiftboat Films and White Mountain Films (2004). For the charges leveled against Kerry by John O'Neill and other Vietnam Veterans, see John E. O'Neill and Jerome R. Corsi, *Unfit for Command: Swift Boat Veterans Speak Out against John Kerry* (Washington,: Regnery, 2004). Excerpts of Kerry's 1971 Senate Foreign Relations Committee testimony can be found in William A. Williams, ed., *America and Vietnam: A Documentary History* (Garden City, N.Y.: Anchor Press/Doubleday, 1985); visual excerpts are available in *Going Upriver*.

38. John Kerry, Nomination Acceptance Speech to the Democratic National Convention, July 29, 2004, <http://www.washingtonpost.com/wp-dyn/articles/A25678-2004Jul29.html>.

★　★　★　★

★ Religious Diversity

★ *The American Experiment That Works*

Mention the word "diversity," as people do all the time these days in the United States, and one thinks immediately of questions concerning race. When the subject is broadened beyond race, moreover, it often extends to other categories of human existence—including ethnicity, gender, or sexual orientation—that are to some degree like race, in the sense that the categories themselves signify characteristics that lead some people to discriminate against people who possess those characteristics. To say that America has not responded well to the challenge presented by diversity is to say that it has failed in its mission to treat everyone with equal respect and dignity.

There is a good reason why discussions of diversity in America are generally cast in the language of failure. When we consider how much racial discrimination has persisted in American life, even those who are optimists about how far we have come since the days of Jim Crow—I consider myself one such optimist—can hardly speak in triumphant terms, for so much remains to be done before America is free of the taint of racism. Few are the number of Americans so convinced that the American record on race is unblemished that they would go around the world touting the United States as a model for all countries to follow.

One subject that is frequently left out of discussions of diversity in America, however, is the question of religion. On the face of it, religious diversity ought to be even more difficult to achieve than racial diversity. In post-Westphalian European history, there is little evidence of commitments to religious diversity. If the king was Catholic (or, for that matter, Protestant), so were the people; and societies that were divided by religion were constantly at war. Nor is religious diversity a goal throughout much of the contemporary world. Pakistan, a Muslim state, seceded from India shortly after India won its independence from Great Britain and thereby created a society that is more than 95 percent Muslim. And the only other state created since World War II along specifically religious lines is Israel. Before its creation, Jews were always a religious minority wherever they lived, but now, in at least one country, they are a majority, and as such they are wrestling with questions of religious tolerance unprecedented in Jewish history.

Although religious diversity has not been a defining characteristic of numerous societies around the world, it has been a feature of American life since our earliest days. "Providence," wrote John Jay in *The Federalist Papers*, "has been pleased to give this one connected country to one united people—a people descended from the same ancestors, speaking the same language, professing the same religion, attached to the same principles of government, very similar in their manners and customs, and who, by their joint counsels, arms, and efforts, fighting side by side throughout a long and bloody war, have nobly established general liberty and independence."[1] Jay, however, was wrong. Not only were small numbers of Catholics and Jews present in eighteenth-century America; the Protestants were hardly of one mind: they were divided into different sects that disagreed on everything from the role of scriptural authority to the place of the liturgy in worship. Americans have never, at least in any meaningful sense, professed the same religion. The refusal of the founders to establish a church in this country meant that we would always have competition for souls and thus a bewildering variety of different faiths and traditions determined to attract believers to their particular conceptions of the truth.

As America grew, so did its religious diversity. Catholics became the largest Christian denomination in America during the nineteenth century, and the Jewish presence in this country expanded from a small number of generally Sephardic and German Jews to massive numbers of Russian and Polish ones. By the 1950s Will Herberg was calling attention to the "triple melting pot" of Catholic, Protestant, and Jew, and sociologists such as Robert Bellah were talking about a "civil religion" that included broad, nondenominational references to America as a redeemer nation.[2] These trends were only exacerbated by the Immigration Reform Act of 1965, which brought unprecedented numbers of non-Christians and non-Jews to our shores. Religious diversity, as William Hutchison has pointed out, is a fact of life in contemporary America.[3] The clearest sign of our diversity is that we no longer know what to call ourselves. We are no longer Judeo-Christian, given significant numbers of Muslims. But even the term "Abrahamic," which includes Muslims, excludes Sikhs and Jains. Concerned about the extent of religious diversity, scholars like Samuel P. Huntington warn against opening the borders to ever-greater numbers of immigrants, but, for most Americans, religious diversity is a challenge to be met, not a disaster to be rolled back.[4]

Despite this remarkable diversity, some observers believe we remain as uncomfortable about religious diversity as we are about racial diversity.[5] America, from their point of view, treats anyone who does not belong to the dominant Christian religion with the same forms of invidious discrimination that it treats racial minorities. For them, the attacks on Muslims after September 11—or, even more damning, the attacks on Sikhs out of the mistaken belief that because they wear turbans, they must be Muslims—is proof positive of how sorry our record on religious diversity is. As is the case with race, these people believe, we still have a long way to go.

Yet there is reason to challenge this depressing view of religious diversity in America. While our record is by no means perfect—attacks on religious minorities after September 11 were truly disgraceful—the American record on religion is one that ought to make us proud. Here we do have the right to hold up our society as a model. We were the first society in the world to avoid religious wars through a guarantee of religious freedom. And we have managed to bring together people of many different faiths into one society better than any other country with which I am familiar.

Contrast, for the moment, our record with those of European societies generally believed to be the most tolerant countries in the world: Holland, France, and Denmark. Holland is widely known—praised by some, condemned by others—for its liberalism: it looks the other way when young people smoke marijuana on the street, regulates rather than prohibits prostitution, and has even gone so far as to allow dying patients the right to have their lives ended. France is often viewed as the most enlightened country in the world, having long ago committed itself to secularization and the ideals of human reason. And Denmark is world famous for the tolerance it demonstrated during World War II when, alone among all the nations of western Europe, it saved its Jewish population from certain death by organizing a brigade of boats that allowed all Danish Jews to escape to Sweden until the war ended.

Yet none of these societies has been able to deal effectively with religious diversity, especially in the aftermath of Muslim immigration. France has responded by banning all significant religious symbols in schools, forbidding large crosses and Jewish skull caps in order to make sure that Muslim women are prevented from wearing the *hajib*. In 2002 Denmark elected a right-wing government based on an anti-immigrant program. This government believes that Denmark, where Lutheranism is the state-sanctioned religion, should be a Christian society and that Muslims have no place as Danish citizens. Indeed, because the government owns all church land—that is what happens when a society does not have separation of church and state—Muslims cannot have religious burial in Denmark despite the fact that 250,000 of them live there. (They can accept burial in a Christian cemetery and thus never face Mecca, or their bodies can be shipped to their countries of origin.) And Holland has been much in the news because one of its most liberal politicians—a libertarian advocate of eliminating drug laws—was also a determined opponent of Muslim immigration to the Netherlands. He was recently assassinated.

By comparison, the United States does not look so bad. In the aftermath of September 11, the U.S. Department of State asked my wife and me—my wife, now an American citizen, was born in Denmark, and we both speak Danish—to go to Copenhagen to explain how our country practices separation of church and state. I began my remarks at various venues by saying that when it came to the welfare state, Americans have a great deal to learn from the Danes; they insure everyone, provide extraordinary social benefits, and have no significant poverty to speak of. But when it comes to religious toleration, I went on, Danes have much to learn from Americans, since we have no politician anywhere in sight who has made anti-immigration central to his message. (The only such person is Patrick Buchanan, and he has become a marginal force in American politics; President Bush does not share the anti-immigrant sentiment found in some quarters of his party, and Democrats generally benefit from the immigrant vote.) The Danes did not want to hear my message. Like many people around the world, they believe that the United States is a gun-toting, capital punishment–happy, racist society, and they simply cannot accept that we may do something right. And they are also so convinced of their own superiority that they have little tolerance for people whose values differ from their own.

Two aspects of the ways Americans treat religious diversity require elaboration if we are to understand why the United States has chosen a different, and, in significant ways, more liberal, path than its western European friends. The first is to explain how we arrived at where we are, for the historical record in this country has not, in contrast to our present experience, been very positive. The second is to consider the implications of our approach to religious diversity for the issue of how we accommodate believers from lands that are neither Christian nor Jewish—because this is, in many ways, the single biggest challenge we will face as we deal with the global realities around us.

Of all the societies in the world, the United States has been for the longest time—and, without doubt, to the strongest degree—committed to the principle of religious freedom. It was not only that our revolution, in rejecting the sovereignty of the British monarch, by necessity rejected the establishment of the Anglican Church. It was also that we guaranteed the principle of religious liberty. Our society would not tolerate religious tests for office, oaths of fidelity, and the excommunication of apostates. Here, unlike anywhere else in the world, people would have the license to worship God as they best saw fit.

Yet could a people who were given the gift of political freedom also become so completely separated from religion that faith played no significant role in their lives? George Washington expressed his concern in his Farewell Address: "Of all the dispositions and habits which lead to political prosperity, religion and morality are indispensable supports. . . . What ever may be conceded to the influence of refined education on minds of peculiar structure, reason and experience both forbid us to expect that national morality can prevail in exclusion of religious principle."[6]

It is not difficult to understand why people who believed in political freedom understood religion as central to the life of the Republic. It was because people were free in so many aspects of their lives that they required the wisdom, if not the omnipotence, of a supreme being. As he did in so many areas of American life, Alexis de Tocqueville understood this relationship perfectly. "For my own part," he wrote, "I doubt whether man can ever support at the same time complete religious independence and entire political freedom. And I am inclined to think that if faith be wanting in him, he must be subject; and if he be free, he must believe."[7] One of Tocqueville's great fears was that democracy and equality would lead to the naked clash of self-interest. Religion, in his view, contained a softening ingredient that would tame the clash and bring all sides involved in political warfare to recognize a higher interest.

Yet if one believes that religion is central to the proper and restrained exercise of freedom, which religion should it be? A religion general enough to include people of many different beliefs will lack the content that is capable of inspiring fierce devotion among its followers. On the other hand, a religion that speaks to particular followers will of necessity exclude from the common morality those who follow other faiths and is thus inappropriate for a society committed to respecting many different religions within its boundaries.

This dilemma divided the founders right from the start. Some, such as Thomas Jefferson, were children of the Enlightenment. For them, religion tended toward sectarianism and dogmatism, which meant that the best hope for America lay in the advancement of reason and knowledge. For others, however, the Enlightenment solution was no solution at all, for it meant the eventual abandonment of faith. Their task, as they understood it, was to uncover a set of moral principles grounded in a specific religion, but general enough to apply to all. In pursuit of this goal, they had one great advantage: their own religion, Protestanism, emphasized the importance of each individual finding voluntarily his or her own way to God. In that sense, Protestant morality seemed fully compatible with a more general American commitment to political freedom.

And so despite the religious diversity that existed here from the start of the Republic, the common morality of America's first century and a half was Protestant morality. The ideas that guided our country until the period right after World War I—one can consider the Scopes trial of 1925 as the watershed event—were Protestant in nature. For more than half of its existence, in other words, the United States, whose constitution officially made impermissible the existence of an established religion, nonetheless informally established Protestantism for the purpose of guiding its affairs. Consider just a few examples.

As I have already suggested, the very principles by which church and state were separated in the United States were founded on Protestantism. John Locke, who did so much to shape our ideas of political liberty, also shaped our understanding of religious liberty. For Locke, a Catholic emphasis on hierarchy and obedience was subversive of religious tolerance, and Jews, he wrote, had no commitment to the separation of religion and politics because God had given them their own state.[8]

The concepts of democracy, political participation, and equality, moreover, all owed their particular character to the revivalist tradition of evangelical Protestantism. The tent meeting was the precursor of the modern media campaign and the modern election campaign. In America, religion would be synonymous with enthusiasm, not with theological debate.

In addition, America's educational institutions—from colleges and universities down to public schools—were shaped in the image of Protestantism.[9] Massachusetts became the home of the public school because its Protestants, who called themselves "know-nothings," so distrusted Catholic schools. Without Catholic immigration, the American commitment to public education would have been in doubt. After they attended state-run Protestant schools during the day, children were expected to populate YMCAs in the afternoons and on weekends.

Even the single greatest challenge to America—the Civil War—was defined for Americans by the greatest political speech ever given in this country, Lincoln's Second Inaugural, a speech filled with Protestant understandings of sin and redemption. So was the winning of the West—Manifest Destiny, as it came to be called—like the expansion of American power around the world, was cast in specifically Protestant terms. Along the same lines, America's first great experiment with social reform—the Social Gospel—was inspired by Protestant theologians before it had its significant impact on Progressive politicians and thinkers.

Despite the importance of religious freedom in America, the Supreme Court managed to avoid handing down any decisions in this arena until 1947, when cases involving the Jehovah's Witnesses began to draw the distinctions capable of balancing the importance of common moral principles with respect for the freedom of individual religious believers.[10] One of the reasons the Court entered this arena so late was because the unofficial Protestant establishment lasted so long. Non-Protestant religions either separated from the dominant society to create their own institutions— Catholic schools are the obvious example—or, as was true of much of American Judaism, they confined their religious beliefs and practices to the private realm and thus acceded to Protestant domination in the public realm. In the United States, in short, we separated church and state, but we never separated church and culture. Our culture of individualism was so thoroughly imbued with Protestant ideals that, as late as the 1960s, Americans wondered aloud whether a Catholic could really become president of the United States.

How and when, then, did the period of Protestant domination of our culture come to an end? The answer I propose is that Protestant culture contained within itself a contradiction that eventually contributed to its demise. Although premised on one religion's outlook on the world, Protestantism's affinity for individualism, its relatively nonhierarchical organizational style (in contrast to Catholicism), and—especially in its evangelical form—its commitment to reaching out and spreading the Word helped transform American culture in directions that made it all but impossible for one religion to insist on a privileged status in relationship to others.

Consider, to take just one example, the question of religious establishment. There are established Protestant churches throughout Europe, and there were some in the colonies and (for a time) the states of America. But because Protestants in this country insisted on the idea of *sola scriptura*— that only the Bible, not a theological authority such as the pope, held the truth of God's teachings—most Americans reacted negatively to the idea that the state should have a monopoly over faith. Put another way, our founders created an unprecedented approach to religion that was modeled on the American economy. Adam Smith argued in 1776—the same year as the start of the American Revolution—that a free market is the best guarantee of efficiency because competition ensures that monopolies will not be allowed to suppress innovation. That is exactly what has taken place in the religious sphere. In European countries that have an official state church— including even a very liberal society like Denmark—the state's monopoly on faith causes the majority religion to become complacent and to fear competition from any new faiths. But, in America, all religions benefit from religious freedom. The majority religion benefits because, unable to take its dominance for granted, it has to reinvent itself continually in order to fend off challenges from newcomers. And newcomer religions benefit because they have room to practice their faith and to seek adherents. The First Amendment guarantees that we can believe in what we want. It turns out that it also guarantees that what we want will be many different things.

In other words, long before immigrants from non-Protestant lands began to arrive in this country in large numbers, Protestantism itself had already prepared the ground for religious diversity. And once those immigrants did come, it became all the more difficult to hold the line against religious differentiation. The process worked in two ways. On the one hand, non-Protestant faiths adopted aspects of Protestant worship; all religions in America, it has been suggested, eventually become congregational religions, so strong is the spirit of voluntarism first identified by Tocqueville. And, on the other hand, Protestants themselves, after initially greeting Catholics and Jews with a distinct hostility, began to realize that in America secularism could become the enemy of all religion, thus bringing together all creeds, regardless of their theological differences. By the 1960s a combination of civil religion, assimilationist Judaism, and Catholic political success had created a society in which religion was still seen as the key to morality, but also one in which no single and specific religion could be singled out for special mention in fulfilling that objective.

One can ask whether a model that was developed to apply primarily to Christians—and, to a lesser extent, Jews—can also work when it has to deal with Muslims, Hindus, Buddhists, and all the other followers of "new" religions—which are actually rather old—now to be found in the United States. Because, unlike Canada, we do not ask for people's religious identity on the census—our tradition of separation of church and state militates against that—we can never know exactly how many people belong to different religious traditions. Still, there is no doubt that there are now more Muslims in America than Episcopalians and that there may be more Buddhists here than Muslims. The challenge of religious diversity has clearly entered a new phase.

Sizable numbers of immigrants from non-Christian lands have not been in the United States for more than a generation or two, yet already we can answer the question of whether the free-market model works for them. It does. Let me offer some evidence for my optimistic conclusion.

One often overlooked fact about immigration is that many people who come to the United States from non-Christian, or Christian-minority, societies become Christians on their arrival in the United States. Koreans are the most striking example; only 25 percent of native Koreans are Christian, but the overwhelming majority of Korean immigrants to the United States belong to Christian faiths.[11] Moreover, not only are they Christians; they are conservative Christians. They generally belong to evangelical churches closely linked to conservative forms of Presbyterianism, and—like other evangelicals—they tend to frown on sexual freedom, to insist on firm discipline in the raising of children, to believe that homosexuality is a sin, and to insist on a strict reading of the Bible.

Conservative Christians often say that they are born again, that they have experienced through their faith a new appreciation of Jesus. Immigrants, we need to recall, are also born again; they leave one society to start an entirely new life in another, facing a new language, a new way of life, and new careers. When a Buddhist or a Confucian comes to America and changes her religion, that change is part of an entirely new way of life. This person is saying that she wants to start again and that the best place to start again is the United States. America is filled with people for whom religion is not what sociologists call an example of "ascribed status"—something into which you are born—but rather an "achieved status"—something you decide for yourself. That is one way in which religious freedom contributes to tolerance, for it allows people to pick the religion of their choice.

Muslims in America are very different from Koreans because they very rarely convert to another faith; in fact, far more American Christians convert to Islam than Muslims do to Christianity. (As many as half of the Muslim population in America are converts, and well more than half of them are African American.) Yet, despite this difference, there is much in the story of recent Muslim immigration to America from which we can learn.[12]

The mere fact that there is Muslim migration to North America and Europe, in the first place, is remarkable. Throughout much of Islamic history, Muslims were expected to live in Muslim-majority societies. This was not always possible because sometimes only part of a country was conquered by Islam or because Muslim traders out of economic necessity had to live in non-Muslim countries. But it is only in recent times that millions of Muslims have decided, of their own free will, to move to countries where Islam is not the dominant faith. To understand how revolutionary this is, one first has to recognize that Islam is a way of life and a system of law and not just a religion. When Muslims live in non-Muslim countries, they have to accept that religious law and civil law are not the same thing—and that is an important accomplishment in its own right.

Islam in the West cannot be practiced the same way that it is in Muslim-majority societies. In September 2002 I led a program on behalf of the U.S. Department of State that brought thirteen Muslim scholars from the Islamic world to the United States, where, it was hoped, they would learn about the separation of church and state and we would learn about their societies. As part of the program, we attended Friday religious services at a mosque in Orange County, California. The service began with a ritual: a young American man from Los Angeles had chosen to convert to Islam, and we all watched as he vowed to obey the laws of the Prophet. The next morning we had breakfast with a group of religious leaders in Pasadena, and one of the Muslim scholars, a woman from Tanzania, told them they she had never before witnessed a conversion ceremony. "Is that because you come from a Muslim-majority society in which people do not convert?" one of the religious leaders asked. "No," she replied, "it is because at home I am not allowed into the mosque."

Women constitute at least half the believers in Islam, and their experiences are often quite different in the United States than they are in their countries of origin, as this person from Tanzania's comment indicates. Not only are women allowed in mosques here—although, to be sure, they often sit only in the balcony or on the side—but their voices are heard in many different capacities. Islam in America is experiencing what Catholicism and Orthodox Judaism in America experienced before it. When patriarchal religions experience the gender equality so prevalent in American culture, they inevitably bend to accommodate it. This does not mean that Islam is a hotbed of feminism, just as it does not mean that the American Catholic Church is free to admit women as priests. But it does mean that a significant number of believers are freer to participate in the leadership and activities of their religion here than they would be in other places.

Women are not the only members of the Islamic faith whose religion has been transformed by the move to the United States. In the Islamic world, imams and other religious leaders are primarily scholars charged with the interpretation of the Qur'an and the hadith, the teachings of the Prophet. Here, like their counterparts in other American religions, they are called on to become marriage counselors, to engage in interreligious dialogue, to lead tour groups, or even to give talks about their faith vis-à-vis American culture. Indeed, during my time with the Muslim scholars, we were addressed by one imam who is a leader in the Los Angeles community, and he told our guests from the Muslim world that he was freer to practice his faith than he was back home. To understand why he said that, we need only recall that in the long war between Iran and Iraq, or in the civil war in Afghanistan, Muslims killed Muslims. Here, Sunnis and Shiites live together, and no one cares whether you originally came from Iran or Iraq, even if it is because no one knows the difference.

So far I have discussed two kinds of situations in which believers come from non-Judeo-Christian societies and discover America: in one, they convert to one of America's historical religions; and, in the other, they adopt their faith to American ways of life. There is a third possible situation as well: people who are neither Christian nor Jewish come to the United States and discover massive numbers of Americans so receptive to their faith that they convert to it.

This kind of conversion has happened primarily with respect to Buddhists.[13] The 1965 immigration reforms and, subsequently, the end of the war in Vietnam led to the arrival of as many as 2 or 3 million Buddhists, primarily from Asia. Here they have been met by famous movie stars, psychotherapists, writers, and other religious seekers, many of them Jewish, who search for wisdom through ancient Buddhist rituals. There is not always a meeting of the minds between these two groups. Asian immigrants think of Buddhism as a religion. They often pray before statues and wear traditional dress. Their monks try to practice celibacy. They tend to belong to traditions that emphasize chanting. American converts, by contrast, are fleeing from the religions of their birth and seeking spirituality. They generally prefer meditation to chanting. Buddhism, for them, involves a search for inner peace, not a cosmological understanding of how the world came to exist. It is no wonder that immigrant Buddhists and native-born Americans who embrace Buddhism tend to practice the religion in such different ways.

Still, the fact that many Americans have been converting to religions other than Christianity and Judaism suggests how far we have come from the days when the United States was a primarily Protestant society. Instead of turning away from the foreign and exotic in disgust, significant numbers of Americans welcome foreign faiths precisely because they are different. There are now so many religions in America, and so many Americans who switch back and forth between them, that toleration has become something like an insurance policy. If you do not know what religion you might adopt tomorrow, let alone the faith of the potential spouse your child has brought home, you had better be kind to all of them. Once a society is committed to religious freedom, it will find itself unable to confine that freedom to people from one faith while denying it to people from other faiths. That is the true lesson of the religious diversity we have experienced since large numbers of people began coming to the United States from all over the world.

Let us return to the question of diversity with which I began. We live at a time when large numbers of people throughout the world talk about how they fear America. Our European allies are traditionally resentful of us, no matter how much they depend on us for support. Our wealth makes us the envy of the world and causes many in the poorer parts of the globe to resent the values for which we stand. As we have learned from September 11, some people hate us so much that they will stop at nothing to kill as many of us as they can. Given the sizable global opposition to the American invasion of Iraq, with people around the world taking to the streets to manifest their opposition to American foreign policy, this is evidently not a good time to insist that America's bad reputation is undeserved.

Yet, in at least one area, I believe that it is. I confess to a certain exasperation when I hear people from societies that have never had to wrestle with the problem of religious pluralism lecture us about our blindness and arrogance. Unlike their societies, we welcome the challenge of finding ways in which people with radically different faiths can live together in the same society. It is a terribly difficult matter to do successfully, and we have not always done it well. But we are doing it well now. With the exception of a few spewers of hate—such as conservative Christians à la Jerry Falwell who pronounce Islam a false religion and attack its prophet as a pedophile—the overwhelming majority of Americans want their fellow citizens to know that they are not going to judge them as infidels or heretics because their beliefs are different from everyone else's.

Now if only we could learn how to apply our success in achieving religious diversity to our attempts to promote racial diversity. But that is a subject for another discussion, and when that discussion takes place, I hope that its participants will keep in mind the fact that diversity in an area as contentious as religion has been ought to make diversity in other areas possible as well.

NOTES

1. *Federalist* no. 2, <http://memory.loc.gov/const/fed/fed_02.html>.

2. Will Herberg, *Protestant Catholic Jew: An Essay in American Religious Sociology* (1955; repr., Chicago: University of Chicago Press, 1983); Robert N. Bellah, *Varieties of Civil Religion* (San Francisco: Harper and Row, 1980).

3. William R. Hutchison, *Religious Pluralism in America: The Contentious History of a Founding Ideal* (New Haven: Yale University Press, 2003).

4. Samuel P. Huntington, *Who Are We? The Cultural Core of American National Identity* (New York: Simon and Schuster, 2004).

5. Diana Eck, *A New Religious America: How a "Christian Country" Has Become the World's Most Religiously Diverse Nation* (San Francisco: HarperCollins, 2001).

6. "Washington's Farewell Address to the People of the United States (1796)," <http://www.yale.edu/lawweb/avalon/washing.htm>.

7. Alexis de Tocqueville, *Democracy in America*, 2 vols., trans. Henry Reeve (New York: Bantam Classic, 2000), 2:532.

8. *John Locke, A Letter Concerning Toleration, in Focus*, ed. John Horton and Susan Mendus (New York: Routledge, 1991).

9. Charles Glenn, *The Myth of the Common School* (Amherst: University of Massachusetts Press, 1988).

10. See, for instance, *Everson v. Board of Education*, 330 U.S. 1 (1947), in which the Court found that the First Amendment means at the least that neither a state nor the federal government can set up a church. Neither can pass laws that aid one religion, that aid all religions, or that give preference to one religion over an-

other. Neither can force or influence a person to go to or to remain away from church against his will; neither can compel him to profess a belief or disbelief in any religion.

11. For background, see Ho-Youn Kwon, Kwang Chung Kim, and R. Stephen Warner, eds., *Korean Americans and Their Religions: Pilgrims and Missionaries from a Different Shore* (University Park: Pennsylvania State University Press, 2001).

12. I have relied here on Yvonne Yazbeck Haddad and John L. Esposito, eds., *Muslims on the American Path?* (New York: Oxford University Press, 2000); and Linda S. Walbridge, *Without Forgetting the Imam: Lebanese Shi'ism in an American Community* (Detroit: Wayne State University Press, 1997).

13. See Paul David Numrich, *Old Wisdom in the New World: Americanization in Two Immigrant Theravada Buddhist Temples* (Knoxville: University of Tennessee Press, 1996); Penny Van Esterik, *Taking Refuge: Lao Buddhists in North America* (Tempe: Arizona State University Press, 1992); and Wendy Cadge, "Taking Refuge: The Practice of Theravada Buddhism in America" (Ph.D. diss., Princeton University, 2002).

II

Americanism in the World

ALAN McPHERSON

★　★　★　★

★ **Americanism against American Empire**

Critics of U.S. territorial expansion, wars, and cultural influence abroad have rarely spoken of their views as a form of "Americanism." Perhaps they should have done so. After all, they offered their criticisms as guideposts for the moral revitalization of U.S. national identity. In February 2003, right before the guns of Gulf War II blared, Michael Kazin argued, for instance, that "the best dissent has never been anti-American." He accurately expressed the dismay of many on the left of American politics to the effect that patriotism was largely absent from the peace movement in the so-called war on terrorism. He recalled that "progressives once had such a [patriotic] vision. . . . They articulated American ideals—of social equality, individual liberty and grass-roots democracy."[1]

The recurring argument for a positive oppositional patriotism among critics of U.S. foreign affairs—abroad as well as at home—has been one of the richest traditions in the history of Americanism. Following the advent of a century of U.S. world power around 1900, two domestic groups who sympathized with foreign critics became particularly important to this discourse: the first one was composed of prominent, mostly white Americans who commented on the U.S. land war in the Philippines; forming the second were African Americans who opposed U.S. occupations in nations of color, especially Haiti after 1915. These two groups were salient for several reasons: they were made up of respected public figures whose words reached the masses as well as policymakers; they expressed some of the earliest and most spontaneous homegrown opposition to U.S. expansion; they witnessed the full tactical and geographical range of U.S. imperial reach, from crude land grabbing to more subtle cultural hegemony and from the neighboring Caribbean to the far-off western Pacific; and, finally, taken together, they underscored the continuing fault line of race in U.S. public discourse about foreign relations.

These Americans, white and black, reaffirmed what they considered to be the core values of their nation, which they saw betrayed by the brutal tactics, broken promises, and devastating policies of U.S. troops, officials, merchants, and missionaries. In observing the withering morality of Americanism, white critics expressed a deep sense of shock and shame at its corrosive effect on the "soul" of America. Convinced that their nation was rapidly changing for the worse, they defined Americanism as a return to traditional national values of restraint and fair play. Black critics were equally saddened, if less surprised. Their persistent—and, in the case of Haiti, pathbreaking—focus on the inherent racism of U.S. empire did not assume positive core values. For that very reason, their "Americanism" may have been greater still because it expected more from America than a mere return to a fabled past. It demanded a commitment to equality matched by action. Taken together, these influential critics of U.S. actions and attitudes abroad articulated a vision of an America transformed by world power into a nation perhaps more disillusioned but also more mature and, they hoped, still idealistic.

However, despite their visionary, steadfast criticism, both whites and blacks trod on dangerous ground by insisting there had to be a virtuous "America" abroad. The danger lay not so much in striving for the unattainable as it did in perpetuating a discourse of dissent that revolved around the harm done *to* America through its foreign interventions instead of around the far greater harm done *by* America. The history of Americanism against American empire suggests that, however touching and politically wise may be the call for dissenters on the left to create, as Kazin wrote, "a privileged place in one's heart" for the nation, it presents the risk of turning debates over foreign policy into an inward-looking distraction that may perpetuate the arrogance of which America is so often accused.

Americanism, Anti-Americanism, and Non-Americans

The history of a dissenting "Americanism" often suggests a reappropriation of the word "anti-Americanism." In this sense, "anti-Americanism" stands not for a lack of patriotism but rather for a positive historical tendency to reform U.S. national identity through scrutiny of U.S. actions abroad. Its history examines patterns of discourse in those who gave a resounding "no" to U.S. wars of expansion or imperial occupations on the basis that such ventures corrupted national values.

From the very birth of the nation in the late eighteenth century, Federalists and Republicans fought a symbolic tug-of-war over the label "Americanism," and both based their definitions partly on their views of events abroad. Adversaries Thomas Jefferson and John Adams each used the word, which for the former meant an assertion of independence from Britain and for the latter signaled an affirmation of friendship with Europe.[2] Then, through the War of 1812, the Mexican War, the World Wars, the Vietnam

War, and the Gulf Wars of 1991 and 2003, many rejected the proposition "my country, right or wrong," and redefined national goals out of moral values rather than the other way around. (Military hero Stephen Decatur uttered the original phrase "our country, right or wrong," after the War of 1812, but his lesser-known words preceding it were "Our country! In her intercourse with foreign nations, may she always be in the right.")[3]

As Jürgen Gebhardt has argued, "Americanism" in this sense was not strictly blind patriotism but a broader moral conviction, "a form of American civil theology, which appeared with the claim of truth. . . . God, the world, humanity, society, and history all existed within the cosmos of American observances."[4] "Anti-Americans" who thus saw themselves imbued with the mission of making their nation obey a higher authority than its own sovereignty stood firmly against prevailing authorities and overwhelming odds. They usually lost the policy struggle in which they were engaged, but they consistently had a short-term impact on public opinion and a long-term impact on "Americanism," whether or not they used the word.

The jury is still out, however, on whether the construction of Americanism should be left in the hands of Americans alone. After all, the signatories of the Declaration of Independence claimed in 1776 "a decent respect to the opinions of mankind," thereby asserting that what the rest of the world thought about u.s. identity mattered. Humankind's definitions of Americanism, moreover, may be more important than its definitions of other nations' identity—for two reasons. First, Americans long felt that foreign policy should be an idealistic expression of national identity, and so defining the morality of that policy meant defining the morality of all Americans. Observing this tendency midway through the nineteenth century, Alexis de Tocqueville noted that his American interlocutors tended to display "irritable patriotism" in the face of foreign criticism. Even the lowliest citizen, he explained, "taking part in everything that is done in his country, feels a duty to defend anything criticized there, for it is not only his country that is being attacked, but himself." The "vanity" that Tocqueville wrote about—which foreigners these days call arrogance—soon extended to u.s. world power; individuals divorced from the exercise or benefit of that power nevertheless felt wounded when it was criticized.[5] The second reason why u.s. foreign relations needed criticism from outside was the combination of the unique length of u.s. tentacles and the alleged universality of u.s. values. Americans *could* and *would* change the world along the lines of privatization, Christianity, racial hierarchy, and

Western liberal values. So since Americans claimed that foreigners should follow their civilizing model, one could suppose that foreigners might want to have a say in that model.

And they *have* wanted a say. Foreign critics of the United States have long been more than willing to help it come to terms with its national identity by suggesting their own definitions of Americanism. Foreign dissenters have pointed out contradictions, hypocrisies, and unintended consequences of u.s. empire. In other words, they have held the United States to its own standards, which are meant to be grounded in equality before the law, self-determination, liberal democracy, universal human rights, and free markets. Thus the anti-Americanism of foreigners, like that of domestic critics of u.s. expansion, was also a reminder of the high ideals of Americanism.[6]

The War of 1898 and the u.s. occupations that followed proved a watershed for the reassessment of those ideals among both Americans and non-Americans. Through the nineteenth century, except for, in part, the War of 1812 and the Mexican War, u.s. citizens had been free from foreign hostilities so major that they could force a reexamination of national identity. Criticisms of Americanism instead touched on what could be considered domestic affairs: the evils of slavery, the corruption of the spoils system, the treatment of American Indians, the savagery of capitalism, the decadence of lowbrow culture. Foreigners who participated in this criticism, such as Tocqueville, said little about foreign affairs. Moreover, they were predominantly Europeans, and therefore not exactly victims of empire but rather competitors in it. It took the dramatic, violent, long-term commitments to world power entered into in such places as the Philippines and Haiti after 1898 to set off the search for the "soul" of America both at home and abroad.

Americanism "Tangled" in Asia

The u.s. "liberation" of the Philippines from Spanish empire sparked an existential crisis of sorts for many Americans that peaked in 1899 and 1900. Arguably, for the first time in u.s. history, events around the globe produced an anguished reappraisal of American national identity. The sudden ascent to—or, as critics said, descent into—world power forced many to come to terms with the brutal realities of imperialism: its "barbaric" violence, its repression of freedoms abroad and at home, and the limits of u.s. reach despite overwhelming superiority of arms. The Philippines debate over U.S. national identity shattered the previous view of Americans as "innocents abroad."

It took the bloodshed of the Philippine-American War to shake the seemingly secure foundations of Americanism: four thousand U.S. troops died, not to mention the more than two hundred thousand Filipinos who met the same fate. In the late 1890s, "Americanism" had been a sturdy concept, one that domestic debates about citizenship, Catholicism, and immigration had reaffirmed as white, native born, Protestant—and good. As a measure of that consensus, most of the thousands who later wrote, rallied, and sang against the Philippine issue—from socialists who advocated revolution to industrialist Andrew Carnegie—had originally been quiet when the United States went to war against Spain in Cuba in the spring of 1898.[7] *That* war seemed in line with U.S. ideals: it hurried the collapse of an Old World empire, propped up self-determination for Cuban patriots, and ended the cruelty of Spanish *reconcentración*, the sweeping up of Cubans into concentration camps. The turn away from these ideals in Cuba came only with the passage of the Platt Amendment of 1901, which denied the island its independence in foreign affairs. By that time, however, the stirring over the Philippines had begun in earnest.

In the Philippines in 1899, American actions contradicted not only abstract values of Americanism but also the U.S. goals that were stated at the outset of the struggle. For a few months, everything went as planned: Admiral Dewey smashed the Spanish forces in the spring of 1898, and by midyear American warships brought the exiled Filipino patriot Emilio Aguinaldo back to his home islands to help finish off the Spanish, whom Aguinaldo had been fighting since 1896. What followed, however, was by almost every account a travesty of justice. On January 4, 1899, Major General Elwell S. Otis unilaterally declared himself governor of the Philippines, thus breaking the pledge of upholding sovereignty that Dewey made to Aguinaldo. The following day, Aguinaldo accused the United States of actions "foreign to the dictates of culture and the usages observed by civilized nations." Seizing on a soon-to-be-common idea, Aguinaldo noted American hypocrisy: "My government can not remain indifferent in view of such a violent and aggressive seizure of a portion of its territory by a nation which arrogated to itself the title champion of oppressed nations."[8] Ignoring this contradiction, by February 1899 U.S. forces signed the Treaty of Paris with Spain, redesignated Aguinaldo and his rebels as the newest, greatest threat to American interests on the archipelago, and attacked their positions. In the next year or so, armed with superior firepower and imbued by a racist fervor for annihilation akin to that directed against American Indians, U.S. forces imitated the departing Spaniards by resorting to *reconcentración* in order to crush Aguinaldo.[9]

Few disputed that the occupation disregarded the principle of self-determination; President William McKinley and others simply declared Filipinos incapable of it. One supporter of the president, in a book titled *Americanism in the Philippines*, published in 1900, even defended "Americanism" as a *denial* of self-government. "Just powers of government are not necessarily derived from the consent of the governed," he wrote, "but rather from the source whence originated the necessity for government. The best thing that can be done for people, in many instances (and this is one of them), is to govern them against their consent."[10]

Filipino rebels were quick to point out this bold inversion of the logic of Americanism. The message that the Filipinos most consistently drove home to their U.S. audience was that the occupation had made a mockery of a principle for which Americans themselves had fought. Aguinaldo insisted that Dewey had promised self-government for the Filipinos "in full good faith" despite not writing it down. Now the feeling of betrayal was in the air.[11] "Can you wonder our people mistrust you?" wrote one of Aguinaldo's representatives to American readers. "They do not even regard you as being serious—a nation which professes to derive its just power of government from the consent of the governed." "I claim," said another, displaying a mastery of American themes, "in the name of the Filipine [*sic*] nation, the fulfillment of the solemn declaration made by the illustrious William McKinley, president of the republic of the United States, aggrandizement and extension of national territory, but only in respect to the principles of humanity, the duty of liberating tyrannized people and the desire to proclaim the unalienable rights, with their sovereignty, of the countries released from the yoke of Spain."[12] Aguinaldo and his men vowed to fight anyone, including Americans, to defend their "American" right.

The pragmatist philosopher and psychologist William James articulated the meaning of this betrayal for the American psyche perhaps more meaningfully than any other American observer. As Carrie Tirado Bramen has argued, James belonged to a generation caught between diversity and unity, the twin desires of Americanism. He embraced the burgeoning plurality of modernity, yet he longed for his nation to maintain some of the moral oneness of Victorianism.[13] The turn of the century was a time of flux for the nationalism of many domestic observers of the American scene, some of whom wished to reconstitute a multicultural nation before embarking on empire, while others saw U.S. racial hierarchy itself threatened by empire.[14] Perhaps this ambivalence moved James to qualify the U.S. war in the Philippines as a "tangle" in a famous letter to the *Boston Evening Transcript* published on March 1, 1899, right after the signing, in Paris, of the "peace" treaty with Spain. In his letter, James warned of danger to the American creed. U.S. troops were acting as "pirates, pure and simple," and robbing Aguinaldo's forces, "an ideal popular movement," of the right to govern that they clearly had won. "We are destroying down to the root every germ of a healthy national life in these unfortunate people," he wrote. "It is horrible, simply horrible."[15]

James was also devastated about what world power was doing to "national life" in the America that he loved. "Imperialism and the idol of a national destiny, based on martial excitement and mere 'bigness,' keep revealing their corrupting inwardness more and more unmistakably." This was all happening too quickly, he thought, for Americans: "The process of education has been too short for the older American nature not to feel the shock. . . . The worst of our imperialists is that they do not themselves know where sincerity ends and insincerity begins. Their state of consciousness is so new." James's only hope lay in combining Filipino force of arms with U.S. force of ideals: "If the Filipinos hold out long enough, there is a good chance . . . of the older American beliefs and sentiment coming to their rights again. . . . Let every American who still wishes his country to possess its ancient soul—soul a thousand times more dear than ever, now that it seems in danger of perdition—do what little he can."[16]

Because there was little that critics *could* do, the emotion that primarily emerged from the pages of anti-imperialist writings was not anger or outrage but rather sorrow. Sorrow settled in on James and others from the realization that empire had become a way of life for the United States. The emotion was most unsettling for a people used to conquering and feeling good about it.

Sorrow meant tragedy, and tragedy, in turn, evoked dark comedy. The sadness brought on by the sense of betrayed ideals often took the shape of brilliant satire and sarcasm, two forms of humor that ridicule hypocrisy and, as such, were ideally suited to protest the Filipino folly. The titles of certain anti-imperialist writings spoke volumes; "Stories of 'Benevolent Assimilation,'" "Onward, Christian Soldier!" "A Provisional Settlement," and "The New Freedom" all dripped with sarcasm. Many of these works mourned specific losses. Ernest Howard Crosby, for instance, bade a doleful farewell to the American claim to leadership in anticolonial struggles:

Americans, you once were free—

. . . .

And then, after your Revolution, you led the world.

. . . .

Think you to lead again by dint of armies and navies and coast defenses?
Not so is the world mastered.
Spread your frontiers, take Cuba and Hawaii, beguile Canada if you can,
     push on over the great Southern Hemisphere;
Will these lands be yours?
There is only one possession in them worth the capturing, and that is
     the hearts of men.

William Lloyd Garrison Jr., the son of the great abolitionist, mourned the passing of Christian values of charity and bemoaned their replacement by proselytizing violence:

The Anglo-Saxon Christians, with Gatling gun and sword,
In serried ranks are pushing on the gospel of the Lord.
On Africa's soil they press the foe in war's terrific scenes,
And merrily the hunt goes on throughout the Philippines.

. . . .

Then onward, Christian soldier! Through fields of crimson gore,
Behold the trade advantages beyond the open door!
The profits on our ledgers outweigh the heathen loss;
Set thou the glorious stars and stripes above the ancient cross![17]

With their collective call for a return to traditional values of self-denial and self-reliance, these and similar poems attempted a positive reevaluation of the core of America. In this sense, they confirmed the judgment of the *New York Evening Post* that "Anti-Imperialism is only another name for old-fashioned Americanism."[18]

The most influential satire of the anti-imperialist movement was Mark Twain's "To the Person Sitting in Darkness." Twain was a late convert to anti-imperialism, having approved of the war in Cuba. Once he read the Treaty of Paris, however, he changed his mind: it gave the United States near-imperial power over Cuba, Puerto Rico, Guam, and the Philippines, and even guaranteed the property of hated Spanish friars. Twain spoke out in 1900, published "Darkness" early the next year, and worked for the Anti-Imperialist League for the following decade. According to the historian Jim Zwick, the publication of "Darkness" "sparked an intense controversy that revitalized the movement" and made Twain "the most prominent opponent of the Philippine-American War." The text was reprinted several times and proved to be the league's most popular publication.[19]

"To the Person Sitting in Darkness" pulled no punches. Like Garrison's poem, it made satirical use of the Christian mission of uplift. Twain sarcastically announced "glad tidings" of the news of missionaries' inflicting Draconian punishments on Chinese Boxers or other Asians who resisted proselytizing. Twain hinted that Asians were no longer "in darkness" but rather newly enlightened as to the corrupting effects of American civilization. Dropping the sarcasm, he wrote, "What we want of our missionaries out there is, not that they shall merely represent . . . our religion, but that they shall also represent the American spirit." He called the Philippines an "error," indicating that, like James, he thought Americanism could be salvaged. He said that McKinley had abandoned the "*American* game" that worked so well in Cuba for the European game in the Philippines. He concluded that "there must be two Americas: one that set the captive free, and one that takes a once-captive's new freedom away from him, and picks a quarrel with him with nothing to found it on; then kills him to get his land."[20]

The concept of an America bifurcated by brutal policies in Asia resonated with later generations. Throughout the twentieth century, multiple wars in Asia—the Pacific War against Japan in World War II and the dropping of atomic bombs, the Korean War, and especially Vietnam—caused similar traumas of disbelief and disillusionment among Americans. Asia tended to combine specific elements—"jungle" terrain and guerrilla warfare, a determined enemy who often took no prisoners, an "inscrutable" language and culture—that made these wars bloody, racist, and total. Prominent individuals and groups feared that such brutal on-the-ground contests precipitated the moral implosion of America—the internment of Japanese Americans, accusations of disloyalty, and the censorship of news from the front.[21] Veterans, especially those of the Vietnam War, eventually took the lead in defining "Americanism" as the protection of civil liberties, especially the right to dissent.[22]

In one of the more controversial instances of this vein of dissent, in the 1960s Senator William Fulbright (D-Ark.), chair of the Foreign Relations Committee, broke with President Lyndon Johnson's Vietnam buildup partly on the basis that such a brutal war created—here it was again—"two Americas":

> One is generous and humane, the other narrowly egotistical; one is self-critical, the other self-righteous; one is sensible, the other romantic; one good-humored, the other solemn; one is inquiring, the other pontificating; one is moderate, the other filled with passionate intensity; one is judicious and the other arrogant in the use of great power. Both are characterized by a kind of moralism, but one is the morality of decent instincts tempered by the knowledge of human imperfection and the other is the morality of absolute self-assurance fired by the crusading spirit.

Twain's desperate plea was revived: this could not be happening; there *must* be two Americas, the more virtuous being the older. Recalling Twain's exact words, in fact, Fulbright recast doubts about the "Blessings-of-Civilization Trust." His solution? A "Higher Patriotism" that integrated dissent into foreign policy making.[23]

Like Fulbright in the 1960s, American critics of the Philippine War around 1900 largely focused on endangered national identity at home. "The wounds which our love of country received in those days," said James after most of the fighting was over, "are of a kind that do not quickly heal." He seemed chastened to learn that Americans abroad were ordinary sinners who needed, from time to time, a cleansing of the soul. "Angelic impulses and predatory lusts divide our heart exactly as they divide the hearts of other countries. It is good to rid ourselves of cant and humbug, and to know the truth about ourselves." And it was not just "cant and humbug"—presumably, non-American traits—that James thought should be gotten rid of. He also questioned whether far more solemn principles were still relevant in light of recent events. "The country has once and for all regurgitated the Declaration of Independence and the Farewell Address, and it won't swallow again immediately what it is so happy to have vomited up." Americans, he seemed to suggest, had practiced the tyranny they had rejected in the first of these documents, and they had renounced the neutralism of the second. A new era was afoot, at the core of which was a loss of innocence.[24]

One unfortunate consequence of the dissenters' Americanism, therefore, was to relegate Filipinos to the background. James, Twain, and others, of course, were deeply outraged about the injustices done to Aguinaldo, and their humanitarianism was heartfelt. The fact that their arguments were primarily concerned with healing America's soul, however, was a testament to the contortions they had to perform to keep their domestic audience. After all, their main strategy was to limit the damage of imperialism by winning the election of 1900. As Cornel West has noted, James's anti-imperialism revealed much "about his own class and white fellow citizens."[25] In the end, anti-imperialism had ambivalent consequences. On the one hand, it provided a powerful American critique of the Philippine War. Aguinaldo himself acknowledged as much when he later commented: "I do believe that we Filipinos contributed a great deal to the return of America to normality, sobriety and morality. . . . We made the Americans realize that our love of freedom was akin to their own—that it was over and above our lives, our fortunes and our sacred honor."[26] On the other hand, the America-centered discourse of the anti-imperialists relegated Filipino aspirations to a secondary status, converting them into weapons in a fight over the meaning of the American national creed rather than taking those aspirations on their own terms. As events in Haiti would later show, black reformers could fall prey to this tendency just as easily as whites.

Race, African Americans, and Americanism

African Americans have tended to see u.s. empire as a natural extension of race prejudice rather than as an aberration in the "love of freedom." And the "two Americas" to which they often refer are divided by race, not by ideological traditions. These are only a couple of the differences that make African American perspectives useful to historians who wish to reconstruct competing visions of Americanism. While whites, especially prominent literary figures or politicians, attempted to revive Americanism through appeals to the distant past, African Americans reached forward, rarely finding inspiration in days gone by. The nearly twenty-year u.s. occupation of Haiti, begun in 1915, was not the first incident to bring forth African American concerns about the racism of u.s. imperialism, and it would not be the last. But it was an incident so ignored by mainstream America that African American "anti-Americans" felt compelled to alert the rest of the nation to a racially charged drift in national ideals.

To be sure, African American critics of the Haiti occupation reiterated several themes of Americanism that arose during the Philippine struggle. Among these were the denial of self-determination, the greed of u.s. corporations, and the militarism of u.s. administrators. But the African American critics set themselves off by redefining Americanism in an idealistic way, as incorporating racial egalitarianism, or at the very least racial solidarity among those of African origin. Leading African Americans made of Haiti a cause célèbre and a new venue for expressing their vision of Americanness. Once again, however, critics of U.S. occupation were less concerned with resolving a conflict in a foreign land than they were with healing deep wounds in America.

Compared with the war in the Philippines, the U.S. occupation of Haiti did not involve an obvious crisis of "Americanism," and that was the case for several reasons. First, from 1915, when the occupation began, to about 1920, Haiti remained a tiny sideshow to the dramatic events in Europe. Second, Americans broadly saw the Haitian intervention as altruistic racial "uplift." The historian Mary Renda, in her masterful *Taking Haiti*, has detailed the salience of U.S. paternalism in the Haiti occupation, an authoritarian mind-set that flattered the U.S. sense of civilizing mission.[27] And, third, much of the Haitian elite were initially grateful to U.S. intervention for ending political massacres and restoring fiscal and governmental regularity. An editor in Port-au-Prince, Charles Moravia, wrote on August 25, 1915, four weeks after U.S. forces landed in his town, that "the Americans are enemies of despotism, and to prevent its return, they invaded the country." He even claimed that, "of all the peoples of the white race, the Yankee people is that which has done the most for the rehabilitation of the black race."[28] With support from intellectuals such as Moravia, elite politicians, and the Catholic Church, U.S. officials quickly dictated the nature of the next Haitian government and, in October 1915, rammed through the parliament a convention that made Haiti a virtual protectorate of the U.S. government.

Soon enough, however, the realization of contradictions and betrayals inherent in U.S. empire set in. Back in 1913, President Woodrow Wilson had clearly stated in a speech in Mobile, Alabama, that the United States would no longer seize Latin American territories.[29] Now, not only had U.S. officials engaged in a seizure, but they were hanging on. Haitians loudly proclaimed that their national dignity was being trampled on and reminded all who would listen of their heritage of resistance to foreign powers. Relations on the ground also soured: U.S. officials acted as overseers in government, imposed new loans on Haiti, evicted squatters from their land, and revived a system of forced labor that looked, to Haitians, a little too much like slavery. One white U.S. administrator called the practice of corvée "un-American."[30] To underscore how U.S. policymakers were contradicting Americanism, several Haitian newspapers periodically reprinted the Declaration of Independence.[31] Peasant, or *caco*, rebels preferred using guns and machetes to signal their resistance to u.s. rule in the countryside.[32] The most important *caco* chief was Charlemagne Péralte. Before his death at the hands of u.s. counterinsurgents in 1919, he rejected not only imperialism but also the hypocrisy that seemed particularly identified with American imperialism: "[In 1915] we were ready to accept the Convention and to execute our obligations under it, but the false promises made by the Yankees when they landed on our soil have become clearer after nearly four years of endless insults, unspeakable crimes, assassinations, outright robbery, and barbaric acts the secret of which, among all the peoples of the world, *only* the American possesses."[33]

The African American response to such accusations was sympathetic. "SHAME ON AMERICA!" wrote W. E. B. Du Bois as early as October 1915. Mirroring the Filipino episode in 1898, the high hopes raised by the initial intervention in Haiti only compounded the disillusionment that soon followed. Like many other African Americans, Du Bois criticized the Haitian occupation as a morally repugnant exercise in globalizing white supremacy. "The lynching and murder in Port-au-Prince is no worse than, if as bad as, the lynching in Georgia," he wrote. "Hayti can, and will work out her destiny and is more civilized today than Texas."[34] Throughout the occupation, African American missionaries, journalists, academics, educators, writers, communists, church groups, political groups, and club women kept up a steady stream of support, both material and moral, for the cause of Haitian independence.

African Americans were not simply against intervention. They also identified with Haiti's potential for economic progress and democratization by and for a nation of color. "Haiti is the one best chance that the Negro has in the world to prove that he is capable of the highest self-government," claimed the writer James Weldon Johnson, who traveled to Haiti for the National Association for the Advancement of Colored People (NAACP) and who, along with Du Bois, had Haitian forebears or family.[35] African Americans identified with Haitians as blacks and set aside domestic political disputes as American reformers of empire. If Haiti developed, it might set an example for America, and so the occupation itself offered a chance for America to reinvigorate its own national identity. It was one of the more important instances in which African Americans saw themselves as what Brenda Gayle Plummer calls "brokers in matters that concern other peoples of color."[36] In a telegram to President Herbert Hoover requesting the appointment of African Americans to any commissions sent to Haiti, the NAACP expressed the overlapping racial and national identities of black Americans: "Twelve million American citizens of Negro descent are deeply and vitally interested in the matter which touches their legitimate racial pride and the fate of over two million fellow black folk."[37]

However, for all the conviction, imagination, and unity that African Americans displayed during their Haitian protests, there existed an underlying failure to accept *Haiti*'s self-image. In two key areas where the u.s. treatment of Haiti seemed to have lost its moral compass—politics and education—black Americans misunderstood Haitian realities and too easily imagined Haitian conditions would be improved if transformed according to African American ideals. African Americans lived their own liberation vicariously through Haitians, and so Americanism in matters of foreign relations was, once again, American centered.

In the political arena, where black Americans expected Haitians to show solidarity against empire, they instead confronted the persistence of intrarace factionalism among Haitians. Johnson felt it most stingingly. As a French-speaking former consular officer in Latin America, Johnson thought he was prepared to understand Haitians. He was also willing to put aside any divisions he had with other African Americans. In this vein he wrote to Marcus Garvey, the leader of the United Negro Improvement Association with whom the NAACP had long had disputes, and argued that, this time, "it was exceedingly necessary that the colored people of America unite with their brothers in Haiti."[38]

Johnson's trip to the black republic in 1920 was a success in many ways. It reinvigorated the nationalism of several Haitians, who then modeled a major opposition group, the Union Patriotique, on Johnson's NAACP. It produced a series of devastating articles in the *Nation*[39] and the *Crisis*.[40] It even got the attention of Republican presidential candidate Warren Harding, who funded the Johnson trip and used its findings to fuel his successful campaign against the Democrats in 1920. Johnson's work, finally, helped give the u.s. government a scare that prompted an investigation and eventually a curbing of the worst abuses.[41]

Johnson, however, felt a chill when he interviewed Haitians. Two leading political figures, Sudre Dartiguenave and Louis Borno, were "guarded," he thought. Most of his suggestions for self-improvement along the African American path met with little interest. He was also unable to set up a formal chapter of the NAACP in Haiti. His suggestion that Creole be formulated into a written language with the aim of educating peasants, he recalled, "was politely received, but aroused no enthusiasm."[42] Most disillusioning to Johnson was this apparent unwillingness among Haitians to bridge the divide between the few French-speaking, educated, paler-skinned urbanites and the overwhelming majority of Creole-speaking, illiterate, darker-skinned peasants and workers. To be sure, he argued sincerely in the *Crisis* that "the Americans have carried American prejudice to Haiti. Before their advent, there was no such thing in social circles as race prejudice."[43] But he knew that, while there had been no official segregation prior to the arrival of the Americans, there certainly was social prejudice, and its depth and pervasiveness largely kept Haitians from imagining themselves part of an open political system that defended equal rights for all. Again and again, white and black U.S. visitors came back with tales of the mutual disdain between blacks and "mulattoes" in Haiti.[44] As members of a society where distinctions among blacks based on color were minor compared to sharp white-black segregation, Americans expressed surprise at what they found in Haiti. The writer Langston Hughes, for instance, observed years later, "It was in Haiti that I first realized how class lines may cut across color lines within a race, and how dark people of the same nationality may scorn those below them."[45] Nor were African American leaders themselves exempt from such scorn. One Haitian publication, for example, disparaged Marcus Garvey as a "workman who does not possess . . . that beautiful Latin culture, that civilization of which we are so proud and which distinguishes us from all the other Negroes in the world."[46]

Hopes for American-style changes faced a challenge in education similar to the one they faced in politics. Booker T. Washington and his Tuskegee Institute had developed agricultural and industrial training programs that U.S. administrators attempted to reproduce in Haiti. But Haitian elites roundly rejected them on the grounds that they were imperialistic *and* inspired by black America. In prescribing "common school, agricultural, and industrial education" for Haiti in 1915, Washington was ironically right when he predicted that "the racial lines drawn in this and other countries will not be tolerated in Haiti."[47]

In 1930 an all-black group commissioned by Hoover and headed by a successor of Washington, Robert Russa Moton, produced the most important report on the needs of Haiti in the field of education.[48] Throughout the process, however, the Moton Commission suffered discrimination from all sides. Hoover sent these black educators to Haiti in a commission separate from a more prominent, all-white commission. Then the U.S. Navy failed to provide passage back to America. Haitian elites also showed their disdain for Moton by suggesting to Washington the segregation of the commission to begin with and by ignoring its recommendations once they were made.[49] The Moton Commission members, therefore, were embarrassed to recommend an American system of education that they perceived to be beneficial for blacks while they remained second-class citizens in the very process of making that recommendation. Americanism was again contradicting itself abroad.[50]

The reaction of Haitians to educational reform was perhaps most disappointing. Once again, the social divide between Haitians manifested itself. The elite benefited from a belles lettres education that was elevating to them but useless to the large majority of Haitians. Of the 95 percent who were not of the elite, perhaps fewer than five out of every thousand school-age children received an education. Visitors to Haiti, black and white, remained astounded at the spoils and inefficiency that ruined what education there was among the poor. Haitians on the whole, however, rejected the materialism and utilitarianism of an "Anglo-Saxonized" Tuskegee education.[51]

As demonstrated in the cases of the Philippine War, the Haitian occupation, and countless other episodes, American critics' vision of a United States that could improve its identity through a reform of its behavior abroad has a robust heritage. It is robust partly because black and white visions, though often separate, were also complementary. While whites searched the nation's past for values to preserve or resurrect, blacks looked to create new values in the future. Whites forged their Americanism through nostalgia; blacks, through hope.

There exists an irony in U.S. criticism of empire. Americans open to foreign criticism often became so concerned with proving their patriotism, with reshaping American identity, that they distorted serious suffering abroad, understanding it primarily in light of ongoing struggles to define a more progressive Americanism in the United States rather than on its own terms. The disconnect was a testament to the enduring distance—cultural, political, and material—between "anti-Americans" abroad and their putative allies in America.[52] Few noticed that those two groups could also be complementary.

For most of the twentieth century, the dynamics of disconnection held. Rarely did American critics of their nation's foreign relations break free of an America-centered discourse and encounter foreign critics of Americanism on their own terms. Yet, in the Vietnam War era, Reverend Martin Luther King Jr.'s antiwar stand at least pointed to the possibility that they might begin to do so. The complementarities explored in this essay—white and black, American and non-American—came together in one great speech in April 1967 in which King denounced the war in Southeast Asia. He spoke of a widely shared disillusion among whites with the materialism, paranoia, and cruelty of the U.S. war machine. He also articulated the particular African American critique of the war—that blacks were fighting for a democracy abroad that was denied to them at home, that proportionately more blacks than whites were drafted and dying, that devoting so many resources to war weakened antipoverty programs at home.

King also spoke of a diseased Americanism. "The war in Vietnam," said King, "is but a symptom of a far deeper malady within the American spirit." To convey the seriousness of this sickness, he recognized the importance of seeing American hypocrisy through the foreign gaze, in this instance through the eyes of the Vietnamese. "They [Vietnamese] must see Americans as strange liberators," he said. "What must they think of us in America[?]" "How can they believe in our integrity[?]" "How can they trust us[?]" "How do they judge us[?]" "What must they be thinking[?]" He quoted a Vietnamese Buddhist who shared his disillusionment: "Each day the war goes on the hatred increases in the hearts of the Vietnamese and in the hearts of those of humanitarian instinct. . . . The image of America will never again be the image of revolution, freedom and democracy, but the image of violence and militarism." King called for a "revolution in values" to stamp out "those who possess power without compassion, might without morality, and strength without sight."[53]

It was a prescient, wise speech—and an unusual one in that it incorporated the perspectives of foreigners into a patriotic criticism of U.S. world power. King's vision remains the standard against which Americans' criticism of U.S. foreign policies ought to be judged. Today, if the American left ignores King's call to view the United States through the eyes of the victims of American power, its efforts to build a patriotic peace movement may seem increasingly out of date to many around the world. Perhaps it would be wiser to look for a union of Americanism's ideals with the best ideals of other civilizations around the world, in a truly forward-looking redefinition of an American as an open and compassionate citizen of the world.

NOTES

1. Michael Kazin, "The Best Dissent Has Never Been Anti-American," *Washington Post*, February 9, 2003.

2. Jürgen Gebhardt, *Americanism: Revolutionary Order and Societal Self-Interpretation*

in the American Republic, trans. Ruth Hein (Baton Rouge: Louisiana State University Press, 1993), 230; see also Andrew W. Robertson, " 'Look on This Picture . . . and on This!' Nationalism, Localism, and Partisan Images of Otherness in the United States, 1787–1820," in "AHR Forum: Creating National Identities in a Revolutionary Era," *American Historical Review* 106 (October 2001): 1263–80.

3. Decatur in *The Oxford Dictionary of Quotations*, 5th ed., ed. Elizabeth Knowles (Oxford: Oxford University Press, 1999), 254.

4. Gebhardt, *Americanism*, x.

5. Alexis de Tocqueville, *Democracy in America*, ed. J. P. Mayer, trans. George Lawrence (New York: Perennial/Harper and Row, 1988), 237.

6. A note here on historiography and methodology. In seeking the roots of Americanism in multinational debates over foreign policy, this essay responds to two integrative scholarly trends of late: the interlacing of the history of U.S. foreign relations with that of domestic affairs and the internationalization of American studies. As to the first trend, a collection of essays edited by Thomas Bender has epitomized the desire to recast the narrative of "America" free from the boundaries of the national and equally free from the sharp distinction between events abroad and at home: Bender, ed., *Rethinking American History in a Global Age* (Berkeley: University of California Press, 2002). A similar groundbreaking collection, about the integration of U.S. empire and U.S. culture, is Amy Kaplan and Donald E. Pease, eds., *Cultures of United States Imperialism* (Durham, N.C.: Duke University Press, 1993). A recent spate of books on the international causes and consequences of the African American freedom struggle has enriched scholarship on the Cold War just as it has exploded the once tidy periodization of the Civil Rights Movement as having occurred from 1954 to 1965. Examples include Thomas Borstelmann, *The Cold War and the Color Line* (Cambridge, Mass.: Harvard University Press, 2001); Penny Von Eschen, *Race against Empire: Black Americans and Anticolonialism, 1937–1957* (Ithaca, N.Y.: Cornell University Press, 1997); and Mary Dudziak, *Cold War Civil Rights: Race and the Image of American Democracy* (Princeton, N.J.: Princeton University Press, 2000). The second trend—the internationalization of American studies—is also decades old but has been revitalized in recent years by interdisciplinary integration and foreign voices. In mid-2003 Michael Hogan, a leading scholar of U.S. foreign relations, emphasized to his peers that American studies, as a discipline, had surpassed history in its ability to integrate. In 2000 several country-based associations of American studies had joined together as the International American Studies Association. In the United States, the American Studies Association and its *American Quarterly* began to internationalize. In the field of history, the Organization of Ameri-

can Historians and the *Journal of American History* had begun to do the same. Historians of U.S. foreign relations, argued Hogan, were particularly well positioned to influence the internationalization of American studies, which was, he announced optimistically, "turning our way." Hogan, "The 'Next Big Thing': The Future of Diplomatic History in a Global Age," a lecture delivered at the 2003 SHAFR conference in Washington, published in *Diplomatic History* 28 (Winter 2004): 1–21. See also Heinz Ickstadt, "American Studies in an Age of Globalization," *American Quarterly* 54 (2002): 543–62.

7. Philip S. Foner, introduction to *The Anti-imperialist Reader: A Documentary History of Anti-imperialism in the United States*, vol. 2, ed. Philip S. Foner (New York: Holmes and Meier, 1986), xiv.

8. Aguinaldo quoted in Teodoro A. Agoncillo, "Anti-Imperialism in the Philippines: The Filipino Plea for Independence," in *American Imperialism and Anti-imperialism*, ed. Thomas G. Paterson (New York: Thomas Crowell, 1973), 135.

9. E. Berkeley Tompkins, *Anti-imperialism in the United States: The Great Debate, 1890–1920* (Philadelphia: University of Pennsylvania Press, 1970), 233–35; Don Emilio Aguinaldo y Famy, president of the Philippine Republic, *True Version of the Philippine Revolution* (Tarlak, P.I., September 23, 1899); David Haward Bain, *Sitting in Darkness: Americans in the Philippines* (Boston: Houghton Mifflin, 1984), 177–78.

10. William A. Peffer, *Americanism and the Philippines* (Topeka, Kans.: Crane, 1900), 100.

11. Emilio Aguinaldo, with Vicente Albano Pacis, *A Second Look at America* (New York: Robert Speller and Sons, 1957), 50.

12. The first statement was from an unnamed official cited in the *American Review*, September 1899; the second was from Agoncillo, Aguinaldo's personal representative, cited in *Public Opinion*, January 5, 1899. Both statements are reproduced in *The Anti-imperialist Reader: A Documentary History of Anti-imperialism in the United States*, vol. 1, ed. Philip S. Foner and Richard C. Winchester (New York: Holmes and Meier, 1984), 359, 356.

13. Carrie Tirado Bramen, *The Uses of Variety: Modern Americanism and the Quest for National Distinctiveness* (Cambridge, Mass.: Harvard University Press, 2000), 58–59.

14. Walter Benn Michaels, "Anti-imperial Americanism," in *Cultures of United States Imperialism*, ed. Amy Kaplan and Donald E. Pease (Durham, N.C.: Duke University Press, 1993), 365–91.

15. William James, "The Philippine Tangle," *Boston Evening Transcript*, March 1, 1899, <http://www.boondocksnet.com/ai/ailtexts/tangle.html> (July 16, 2003).

16. Ibid.

17. Ernest Howard Crosby, "The New Freedom," from *Plain Talk in Psalm and Parable* (1899), and William Lloyd Garrison Jr., "Onward, Christian Soldier!" from *Liberty Poems* (n.d.), both reproduced in Foner, *The Anti-imperialist Reader*, 2:59, 81.

18. Cited in *Mark Twain's Weapons of Satire: Anti-imperialist Writings on the Philippine-American War*, ed. Jim Zwick (Syracuse, N.Y.: Syracuse University Press, 1992), xl.

19. Zwick, *Weapons of Satire*, xix, xvii. See also Foner, *Anti-imperialist Reader*, 2:xxxiii–xxxv.

20. Emphasis in the original. Mark Twain, "To the Person Sitting in Darkness," from *North American Review* (February 1901), in Foner, *The Anti-imperialist Reader*, 2:195–207.

21. See Lawrence S. Wittner, *Rebels against War: The American Peace Movement, 1941–1960* (New York: Columbia University Press, 1969); John W. Dower, *War without Mercy: Race and Power in the Pacific War* (New York: Pantheon, 1986), 119–20; Nancy Zaroulis and Gerald Sullivan, *Who Spoke Up? American Protests against the War in Vietnam* (Washington: University Press of America, 1981); David W. Levy, *The Debate over Vietnam* (Baltimore: Johns Hopkins University Press, 1991); Kenneth J. Heineman, *Campus Wars: The Peace Movement at American Universities in the Vietnam Era* (New York: New York University Press, 1993); Michael C. C. Adams, *The Best War Ever: America and World War II* (Baltimore: Johns Hopkins University Press, 1994); Robert Buzzanco, *Masters of War: Military Dissent and Politics in the Vietnam Era* (Cambridge: Cambridge University Press, 1996); and Melvin Small, *Antiwarriors: The Vietnam War and the Battle for America's Hearts and Minds* (Wilmington, Del.: SR Books, 2002).

22. Rodney G. Minott, *Organized Veterans and the Spirit of Americanism* (Washington: Public Affairs Press, 1962).

23. J. William Fulbright, *The Arrogance of Power* (New York: Random House, 1966), quotations on 245–46 and 20. See also Fulbright's later, less controversial books, *The Crippled Giant: American Foreign Policy and Its Domestic Consequences* (New York: Random House, 1972) and *The Price of Empire* (New York: Random House, 1989).

24. William James, "Address on the Philippine Question," from *Proceedings of the Fifth Annual Meeting of the New England Anti-Imperialist League*, December 1903, in *William James: Writings, 1902–1910*, comp. Bruce Kuklick (New York: Library of America, 1987), 1130–35.

25. Cornel West, *The American Evasion of Philosophy: A Genealogy of Pragmatism* (Madison: University of Wisconsin, 1989), 63.

26. Emilio Aguinaldo, with Vicente Albano Pacis, *A Second Look at America* (New York: Robert Speller and Sons, 1957), 131–32.

27. Mary A. Renda, *Taking Haiti: Military Occupation and the Culture of U.S. Imperialism* (Chapel Hill: University of North Carolina Press, 2001).

28. Charles Moravia, from *La Plume*, August 25, 1915, in Suzy Castor, *L'occupation américaine d'Haïti* (Port-au-Prince: Maison Henri Deschamps, 1988), 75; and Moravia, writing a few days after the occupation, in David Healy, *Gunboat Diplomacy in the Wilson Era: The U.S. Navy in Haiti, 1915–1916* (Madison: University of Wisconsin Press, 1976), 121. See also B. Danache, *Le président Dartiguenave et les Américains*, 2nd ed. (Port-au-Prince: Les Editions Fardin, 1984; orig. pub. 1950), 22, 33.

29. The Wilson speech of October 27, 1913, is in Dana G. Munro, *Intervention and Dollar Diplomacy in the Caribbean, 1900–1921* (1964; repr., Westport, Conn.: Greenwood Press, 1980), 270–71.

30. Colonel W. T. Waller cited in Roger Gaillard, *Hinche mise en croix: 1917–1918*, vol. 5 of *Les blancs débarquent* (n.p., 1982), 27 ("non-Américain").

31. Hans Schmidt, *The United States Occupation of Haiti, 1915–1934* (1971; repr., New Brunswick, N.J.: Rutgers University Press, 1995), 195–96.

32. For details, see Healy, *Gunboat Diplomacy*, 45; Dantès Bellegarde, *La résistance haïtienne: L'occupation américaine d'Haïti* (Montreal: Éditions Beauchemin, 1937); Kethly Millet, *Les paysans haïtiens et l'occupation américaine d'Haïti (1915–1930)* (La Salle, Quebec: Collectif Paroles, 1978); Georges Michel, *Charlemagne Péralte and the First American Occupation of Haiti*, trans. Douglas Henry Daniels (Dubuque, Iowa: Kendall/Hunt, 1996); and the invaluable series of books by Roger Gaillard, which have appeared as vols. 3–7 of *Les blancs débarquent*: *Premier écrasement du cacoïsme: 1915* (n.p., 1981); *La république autoritaire: 1916–1917* (n.p., 1981); *Hinche mise en croix: 1917–1918* (n.p., 1982); *Charlemagne Péralte le caco: 1918–1919* (n.p., 1982); *La Guérilla [sic] de Batraville, 1919–1934* (n.p., 1983).

33. Emphasis added. Open letter from Péralte to the French minister in Haiti, in Gaillard, *Charlemagne Péralte le caco*, 201–2.

34. W. E. B. Du Bois, "Hayti," *Crisis*, October 1915, 291.

35. James Weldon Johnson, "The Truth about Haiti: An NAACP Investigation," *Crisis*, September 1920, 223; Leon D. Pamphile, *Haitians and African Americans: A Heritage of Tragedy and Hope* (Gainesville: University Press of Florida, 2001), 104, 109.

36. Brenda Gayle Plummer, "The Afro-American Response to the Occupation of Haiti, 1915–1934," *Phylon* 43 (June 1982): 125–43 (quotation on 126); Schmidt, *United States Occupation of Haiti*, 120–21; Henry Lewis Suggs, "The Response of

the African American Press to the United States Occupation of Haiti, 1915–1934,"
Journal of Negro History 73 (Autumn–Winter 1988): 33–45; Pamphile, *Haitians and African Americans*, 102–22.

37. Quoted in Pamphile, *Haitians and African Americans*, 123.

38. Quoted in Plummer, "Afro-American Response," 133.

39. James Weldon Johnson, "Self-Determining Haiti: I. The American Occupation," *Nation*, August 28, 1920. 236–38; "Self-Determining Haiti: II. What the United States Has Accomplished," *Nation*, September 4, 1920, 265–67; "Self-Determining Haiti: III. Government of, by, and for the National City Bank," *Nation*, September 11, 1920, 295–97; and "Self-Determining Haiti: IV. The Haitian People," *Nation*, September 25, 1920, 345–47.

40. Johnson, "Truth about Haiti"

41. In "James Weldon Johnson and Haiti," *Phylon* 32 (Winter 1971): 396–402, Rayford W. Logan called Johnson's *Nation* series "a classic exposé of an inglorious episode in United States imperialism," which "laid a foundation" for U.S. changes in foreign policy (396).

42. James Weldon Johnson, *Along This Way: The Autobiography of James Weldon Johnson* (1933; repr., New York: Da Capo Press, 2000), 347, 353.

43. Johnson, "Truth about Haiti," 223.

44. John Houston Craige, *Cannibal Cousins* (New York: Minton, Balch, 1934), 163–64.

45. Langston Hughes, *Autobiography: I Wonder as I Wander*, in *The Collected Works of Langston Hughes*, vol. 13, ed. Joseph McClaren (Colombia: University of Missouri Press, 2003), 61.

46. *Les annales capoises*, October 30, 1924, cited in Pamphile, *Haitians and African Americans*, 132. Garvey tried to declare October, 26 1924, a day to celebrate the restoration of Haitian independence, but only two hundred people attended the celebration.

47. Booker T. Washington, "Haiti and the United States" (letter to the editor), *Outlook*, November 17, 1915, 681.

48. Plummer, "Afro-American Response," 134, 136, 141. Educators who accompanied Moton included W. T. Williams and the presidents of Howard University and Georgia State Industrial College.

49. Robert M. Spector, *W. Cameron Forbes and the Hoover Commissions to Haiti (1930)* (Lanham, Md.: University Press of America, 1985), viii, 160.

50. Plummer, "Afro-American Response," 141–42; Leon Denius Pamphile, *L'éducation en Haïti sous l'occupation américaine 1915–1934* (Port-au-Prince: Imprimerie des Antilles, 1988), 111, 115.

51. Haitians also had more substantial reasons for rejecting U.S. administration of their education. See Spector, *W. Cameron Forbes*, 168–72; Pamphile, *L'éducation*

en Haïti, 37, 45, 46; Plummer, "Afro-American Response," 136: Rayford Logan, "Education in Haiti," *Journal of Negro History* 15 (October 1930): 410–19; Ludwell Lee Montague, *Haiti and the United States, 1714–1938* (Durham, N.C.: Duke University Press, 1940), 257; Emily Greene Balch, ed., *Occupied Haiti* (1927; repr., New York: Garland, 1972), 104.

52. That distance may be part of a greater process. Debates over the patriotism of the right or the left in foreign policy may be operating in a quaint antechamber off from the real debate in the parlor—about the disappearance of "America" itself due to globalization. Accusations that good old-fashioned "Americanism" has eroded in the field of foreign relations, after all, have, at least since 1898, sprung from the erosion of national borders that imperialism causes. See Martha C. Nussbaum, "Patriotism and Cosmopolitanism," in *For Love of Country?* ed. Joshua Cohen (Boston: Beacon Press, 2002), 3–17.

53. Martin Luther King, Jr., "Declaration of Independence from the War in Vietnam," Riverside Church, Manhattan, April 1967, <http://www.commondreams.org/views04/0115-13.htm> (February 4, 2004).

★ ★ ★ ★

★ Japanese Intellectuals Define America,
★ from the 1920s through World War II

Since Commodore Matthew Perry's Black Ships sailed into Edo (now Tokyo) harbor in 1853, the United States has been the indispensable measuring rod for reaffirming Japan's international status and its place in world history.

Perry's ships appeared suddenly on the Pacific horizon to impress Japan's ruling elite and common people with the overwhelming military and scientific supremacy of Western civilization. In the course of building a modern state, the Japanese encountered another face of America distinct from its military power and its economic and technological might. For officials and civilians rushing headlong into modernization, America's "soft power"—represented by missionaries, technicians and teachers brought to Japan as "hired foreigners"—assumed enormous importance. Embodying "Western learning," these Americans made significant contributions in nearly every field—from science to the history of thought, from theology to pedagogy.

As a polity, the United States also influenced how the "founding fathers" of the Meiji period (1868–1912) understood the goals of the modern Japanese state they were building. Even though the members of the Meiji elite borrowed their new governing structure from the Prussian, French, and British systems, they were well aware that the ideals articulated in the Declaration of Independence, the U.S. Constitution, and Alexis de Tocqueville's *Democracy in America* were partly responsible for the swift rise of the United States to world power.

After World War I, such new features of American culture as jazz music and ballroom dancing began to reshape Japanese urban customs and sensibilities. This popular culture—at once free and exuberant and efficiently commercialized—showed a different aspect of Americanism. When coupled with the mass production system pioneered by Henry Ford, it spurred Japan's rapid development of industry and consumption after World War II.

One can thus define Japan's path to "modernity" over the past century and a half as a process by which Japan's politics, economy, society, and culture have been "Americanized"—often voluntarily, at times forcefully. But Japanese intellectuals with connections to government did not always find the United States a model worth emulating. There were significant periods when America's political ideology and culture were viewed as models to avoid, at whatever the cost.

In general, Japanese hostility was triggered by nationalist thinkers who believed in the superiority of the Japanese race and the distinctive polity it had developed. The era of the Pacific War and, to a lesser extent, the decade of Japanese-U.S. trade frictions from the late 1970s through the 1980s saw the apex of anti-American nationalism.

Of course, the specific issues dividing the two nations have changed over time. But one can discern certain continuities in the negative opinions that Japanese intellectuals have held about the United States. Mindless materialism, a dearth of history and tradition, and the triviality of popular culture are seen as essential characteristics of the Other. This essay focuses on a period during which anti-Americanism took a particularly virulent form in Japan—from the late 1920s through the end of World War II. Favorable images of the United States were turned on their head, as the Japanese press and academia dedicated themselves to singing jingoistic, self-serving praises of the Japanese state. This understanding (or mis-understanding) of Americanism has made something of a comeback at the turn of the twenty-first century, amid the U.S. war in Iraq and the continuing expansion of American popular culture.

What is clear is that throughout the relationship between the two nations, Americanism has provided a crucial reference point, in both a positive and a negative sense, for Japanese thinkers and officials in their attempts to conceive of their nation's unique, significant place in the world. The idea of Japanese exceptionalism was framed, in part, by the need to grapple with what seemed distinctive about America.

As a result of their victory in the 1904–5 war with czarist Russia, the leaders of the Japanese government became confident they could hold their own among the world's imperialist powers. In East Asia, this attitude helped drive an increasingly adversarial relationship with the United States. In addition, the discriminatory treatment meted out to Japanese immigrants in the United States—school segregation and laws against alien land-owning were its most egregious forms—generated mass outrage back home. The sense of wonder about and admiration for American civilization that dated back to the early Meiji period began to fade. Gradually, a "cultural conflict" that spanned the Pacific came to dominate intellectual debates about Japanese-U.S. relations.

Amid this rising nationalistic spirit, Japanese intellectuals began to express their uneasiness about some aspects of Americanism, its republican founding principles in particular. Their critique developed in the context of a discovery of Japan's unique "national polity" (*kokutai*) and its "state founding spirit."

A typical, quite influential example of this point of view was a book published in 1926, *Return to the Spirit of the Founding of the Japanese State* by Nagata Hidejiro. Nagata was a leading member of the House of Peers and of a private right-wing organization that, two years before, had helped establish a "Festival for the Creation of the Japanese State" (*Kenkokusai*). His goal in writing this slim monograph was to promote the festival by clarifying the meaning of the creation of the Japanese state.[1]

Nagata closely linked the founding of the state with the Shinto myth of the "Descent of the Divine Grandson." The myth centered on Jimmu, Japan's first emperor, whose grandmother, the story goes, was the sun goddess Amaterasu. Jimmu initiated a royal line in about 660 B.C. that remains unbroken. According to Nagata, the state represented a trio of transcendent ideals: the "ideal of the peace-loving noble mind," the "ideal of conducting public affairs based on public opinion," and the "ideal of the concert between the ruler and the ruled, and equality among the country's four classes." Such principles, Nagata argued, "are true for all times . . . constant verities that should not be violated anywhere, at home or abroad." He urged his fellow leaders to bear in mind "that ways must be found to adapt them to the modern age." He hoped the festival would mobilize the population to revere the state and follow its wise, generous rulers.[2]

Nagata's emphasis on the antiquity and uniqueness of Japan's divine creation stemmed from a deep sense of anxiety about his nation's position in the world. To a large extent, his views were shared by Japanese government leaders from the eve of World War I through the 1920s—the Taisho and early Showa periods.[3] Nagata wrote that Japan's situation in the mid-1920s was "more perilous than that in the period of the Sino-Japanese War or of the Russo-Japanese War." He deplored its isolation in world politics since the abrogation of the Anglo-Japanese alliance in 1923. He bridled at the "national humiliation" caused by the U.S. Congress in 1924 when it passed an immigration law that barred every Japanese citizen from settling in the United States. Under American leadership, a regime of white supremacy was rapidly being established throughout the world: "The freedom and equality and opportunities that the Americans preach endlessly are concepts that apply only to the whites and are not extended to the yellow race. Australia too does not allow in immigrants of the yellow race on the basis of its 'white Australia' policy."

Asia was no less hostile to Japanese interests in the 1920s. The British, reported Nagata, "are building a new base in Singapore." China was a hotbed of anti-Japanese sentiment. Soviet Russia was not just challenging Japanese claims to territory in the Far East but was also promoting revolution against the state itself as part of the strategy of the Third International. Nagata predicted, "No matter which country Japan might go to war with in the coming years, no country in the world would wish us a victory." This was "a terrible feeling to have."[4]

Nagata, one should note, was not crudely self-defensive. He warned against a "narrow and exclusive patriotism" and preached that the true spirit of the Japanese state did not allow intolerance, either inside or outside the country. Yet he emphasized the uniqueness of Japan, not its universal qualities of spirit. Every successful state, he maintained, based itself on a national creed rooted in that country's particular history and traditions. Japan's creed, of course, was centered on the imperial family.

Such relativism allowed Nagata to retain a certain degree of objectivity about foreign countries. He believed, for example, that England's national creed was rooted in its parliamentary system. Here, he argued, was the origin of the vaunted English spirit of self-rule.

Nagata's view of America was quite favorable, which is something of a surprise given his assessment of the U.S. role in the world. The American creed, he wrote, rested on a faith in practical individualism and adherence to the Constitution. Nagata singled out Herbert Hoover, then the celebrated secretary of commerce, as a pillar of both self-reliance and social service. He praised U.S. society for allowing citizens to advance as far as their intellect, character, and talents would take them. He also lauded laws to regulate corporate trusts. Americans' reverence for the Constitution, in his mind, provided institutional stability to what remained a young and energetic nation.[5]

Nagata's book reflected the transitional nature of the time in which it was published. There was nothing of the imperial ethnocentrism or crude stereotypes of "American and British brutes and savages" that would become routine by the late 1930s. Also absent, however, were the sort of views held by Meiji-era intellectuals who had admired America's open civilization and hoped that Japan might soon become an intermediary between East and West. While Nagata's perspective on Americanism was relatively favorable and accurate, he did not think Japan should learn from, much less emulate, the progressive modernity of the United States. The title of his concluding chapter was telling: "Imitation Is Suicide."

During the 1930s Japanese policymakers at first tried to repair their country's deteriorating relations with the United States. In the Foreign Ministry, diplomats were assisted by such pro-American intellectuals and businessmen as Nitobe Inazo and Kiyosawa Kiyoshi. Several of these men had once studied in the United States and retained a fascination for the foreign culture and political system they had encountered in their youth.[6] But Japan's invasion of Manchuria in 1931 had set the two nations on an adversarial course, and these pro-American figures could do little but plead vainly for compromise.

At the same time, Japanese officials showed a good deal of interest in the New Deal. In common with the rest of the industrial capitalist world, Japan was in the throes of a depression, and Franklin Roosevelt's program seemed to be a possible path to economic revival. Japanese leaders, who were increasingly authoritarian, had no interest in the democratic principles that underpinned the New Deal. They focused instead on the expansion of presidential powers and on Roosevelt's use of an intellectual "brain trust" to supply him with policy ideas.[7]

Given the fierce rivalry between the two countries, this effort by the Japanese elite must be classified as learning from an enemy. How, Tokyo officials wondered, would their nation match up against an economy superior both in natural resources and in the output of its factories?

By the mid-1930s the kind of ambivalence Nagata Hidejiro represented had gone out of fashion. Japanese leaders and the intellectuals who bolstered their rule conceived of America as a nation that entirely lacked the deep spirituality and long traditions of Japan. In their eyes, the United States stood naked as a monster spewing out raw materialism and rampant modernity. Few Japanese authors still thought it worthwhile to examine the intellectual and cultural roots of American democracy, which had fascinated their predecessors. The urgent questions of American intentions toward Japan and the possibility of war between the two nations dominated their work.

On occasion, a solitary intellectual lodged a modest protest against this state of affairs. In March 1941 a writer using the pseudonym "Hida Buntaro" concluded sadly that most recent studies of the United States were "fragmentary and subjective in nature" and seldom "written in the spirit of scientific inquiry." But his call to examine American institutions using statistical techniques fell on deaf ears.[8]

Instead, almost without exception, Japanese writings on America during the "Fifteen Years War" (from 1931 to 1945) were topical in nature and were often aimed at ingratiating their authors with the shepherds of the militarized state. The reigning discourse about Americanism sought to force a complex historical experience into a simplistic picture and, on that basis, to establish Japan's cultural and intellectual superiority. The image of Japan's polity was refined and elevated partly to create a false contrast with all things American.

Thus the numerous studies on the u.s. enemy at the start of the Pacific War failed to meet the basic—and urgent—need of Japanese policymakers to measure accurately America's military might, not to speak of its cultural strengths. Most intellectuals asked whether Japan could defeat the United States and quickly answered that because it had to, it would.[9] Amid this blind jingoism, past scholarship about America was ignored, and any doubts about war with the United States were suppressed.

Ironically, one of the few Japanese figures who accurately evaluated America's power was Yamamoto Isoroku, commander in chief of the national fleet. Yamamoto, who had graduated from the u.s. Naval Academy and studied at Harvard, appreciated the sheer size of the American military and warned the public that a war was unwise. It was a great tragedy that a man with such deep doubts about the possibility of a Japanese victory was chosen to lead the attack on Pearl Harbor.[10]

On the other side of the Pacific, most u.s. leaders and intellectuals avoided such one-dimensional, polarized opinions of the future enemy. While officials in the Roosevelt administration were clearly worried about Japan's rising jingoism, they were also curious about its origins and questioned how deeply it was rooted in the traditional culture of the island nation. How to treat Japanese soldiers and civilians both during and after a war also became a subject for debate.

Soon after the shooting began, the Office of War Information initiated an extensive program of Japanese studies. Bright American students were trained in Japanese language and culture, and groups of officials began to plan the democratization of postwar Japan. Ruth Benedict's *The Chrysanthemum and the Sword* (1946), a classic anthropological study, was a leading product of this enterprise.[11] Whereas Japanese who wrote about the United States peddled wishful thinking and dichotomous images, Americans who studied Japan engaged in scholarly research about the history and society of a hostile nation.

In Japan, evaluations of the enemy revealed a deep-seated desire to preserve what was deemed to be an exceptional society. On July 23 and 24, 1942, several leading intellectuals held a symposium on the theme of "Kindai no Choukoku" (overcoming modernity), the proceedings of which were quickly published in the September and October issues of the literary magazine *Bungakukai*. According to Takeuchi Yoshimi's postwar recollection, "Kindai no Choukoku" was at that time a vogue phrase that functioned almost as a spell, together with the hope for a "Greater East Asia Co-Prosperity Sphere" shaped by Japan's power and "Asian" values.[12] Japanese leaders, buoyed by temporary military success, were anxious that they be able to replace Western imperialists as the creators of a new regional order. A variety of intellectuals eagerly lent legitimacy to this endeavor by drawing as stark a contrast with Americanism as possible.

A typical argument was made by the film critic Tsumura Hideo in an article that he bluntly titled "What Should Be Torn Up?"[13] Tsumura first drew a curious distinction between "the old European civilization suffused with the spirit of modernity" and the United States, which had "developed by assimilating the currents of the modern spirit while rebelling against them." Europe, in this formulation, had some hope of redemption. Tsumura argued that, in order for Japan to "recover [its] own intellectual and organic life," it would have "to escape from the spirit of the new age." To Tsumura, this spirit was "Americanism" itself, and it represented something more dangerous than simple modernity. He tried to explain:

> The American-style of individualism and hedonism is intertwined with the spirit of the new age. It is true that the spirit of the new age has benefited from the spirit of science, a legacy of modernity. But it is tricky to attach the word "spirit" to the word "scientific." While the spectacular development of natural sciences and applied sciences is associated with this new age, we ought to remember that sciences have functioned as a breeding ground for the materialistic-mechanistic civilization. By chanting the words "scientific spirit," we become caught up in a type of Western rationalism that takes us away from the origin of the human spirit.[14]

A few participants in *Bungakukai*'s symposium sought to qualify this one-sided picture. Suzuki Shigetaka, a historian of medieval Europe, spoke of the puritanical strain in American culture that led millions to reject the theory of evolution and to support the prohibition of alcoholic beverages.[15]

But this was a departure not taken. The dominant theme in the 1942 symposium was of intellectual combat with an implacable, "mechanistic" foe. As Tsumura declared, "I don't concede that there is any value in America that needs to be passed on to posterity. America is . . . a monster that infects man with its facility, inevitability, and accessibility."[16] The "overcoming modernity" debate succeeded in stripping from Americanism any element of idealism or intellect. This helped make the war with the United States easier to justify to the Japanese public and among Japanese intellectuals themselves.

Even serious scholars of ideas fell into the trap of reducing America to its drive for empire and material aggrandizement. Take, for instance, the 1943 article on "American national character" published in a pamphlet by Watsuji Tetsuro, a leading ethicist, philosopher, and cultural historian.[17] Watsuji's academic expertise lay in German philosophy, and he had been at work, since the mid-1930s, on an original system of ethics inspired by Wilhelm Windelband, Martin Heidegger, and others. A first-rate scholar, Watsuji represented the mainstream of Japanese intellectual life.[18]

But his conclusions about the United States were, by 1943, both derivative and delusional. Watsuji alleged that the "American ambition for world conquest" had triggered the war in the Pacific. The Americans, he wrote, "ventured into the Pacific with the attitude of gambling scoundrels and were trying to conquer Asia. Impudent and self-righteous, [they] clung to the might of machines for their sole support." Since the Japanese could deploy machines more adeptly, the United States had to fall back on what Watsuji mockingly called the "pure American spirit"—the sheer abundance of its resources. But "quantity" alone could not defeat a people whose moral spirit was strong. Watsuji concluded that the impatient "scoundrels" would be surprisingly easy to destroy.[19]

This prominent intellectual came to his views through an idiosyncratic examination of America's philosophical roots, stretching back to the colonial era. For Watsuji, the spiritual foundations of modern America could be traced to a pair of seventeenth-century English thinkers, Francis Bacon and Thomas Hobbes. Bacon, the father of the "scientific method," believed, according to Watsuji, in the production of useful commodities rather than "the moral improvement of man or the leavening of culture." His inductive technique was a landmark contribution to science, but it also promoted a mechanistic civilization.²⁰ For his part, Hobbes was guilty of promulgating natural laws based on the existence of a perpetual "war of everyone against everyone." According to Watsuji, his ideas gave English pioneers a clear conscience as they butchered Indians and took their lands.²¹

The intellectual historian felt no need to provide evidence that the early colonists imported Bacon's and Hobbes's views into the New World; nor did Watsuji show that those views were at the root of America's national character. He leaped instead to the assumption that because Indians were in a state of nature and African slaves outside the social covenant, the cruelties meted out to them could be viewed by early Americans as compatible with justice if they were imbued with Hobbesian rationalizations.²²

Watsuji linked Bacon with the struggle against climate and space from which, in his view, was born the crass and intellectually narrow society of machines in which Americans were fated to live. Benjamin Franklin perfectly exemplified what America was missing. Watsuji granted that Franklin's "spirit of discovery" had promoted a form of practical education. But such learning, he wrote, "did not produce the kind of culture that we can respect. What it did was to lower the cost of housing, food, and clothing and further stimulate the tendency to hedonism. For Americans, there is no civilization without machines. They cannot live without them. However, there is no culture for those who are slaves to machinery."²³

It was just a short step from this statement to a sweeping denunciation of American diplomacy. Watsuji interpreted every American initiative from Perry's Black Ships to the Washington Treaty of 1922 and U.S. criticism of Japan since the Manchurian invasion as due either to a Hobbesian national character or to a culture excessively dependent on machines and "devoid of ethical meaning." In the 1960s Black Panther Party leader Huey Newton declared, in an analogous way, that "the spirit of the people is greater than the Man's technology."²⁴ That is the common reaction of a nationalist intellectual from a developing country or an exploited race who is both awed and angered by America's might and its leaders' arrogant expression of their ideals.

Watsuji directly contrasted Americanism with the virtues of the character of his own nation. In the pamphlet in which his analysis of American character appeared, he included another essay, "The Way of Japanese Subjects." Here, he elaborated on ideas Nagata Hidejiro had first sketched out in the 1920s. The sacred, if primitive, nature of Shintoism was held up as the religious basis of the emperor system. Following this faith, the Japanese, according to Watsuji, elevated collectivity over individuality, spirituality over materialism, and loyalty over personal fulfillment. The spirits of Japanese *gemeinschaftlich* culture and American *gesellschaftlich* civilization were not just opposites in nature; they were hostile. They could never be reconciled.[25]

This was an intellectual pit into which anti-American patriots often fall. Watsuji, for all his erudition, had only reaffirmed the internal unity of Japanese society. He made no serious attempt to understand Americanism itself; nor did he examine its historical development or its attraction for many people in the United States and elsewhere. The wages of blind intellectual combat were counted out in ignorance.[26]

From the early Meiji period to the World War II era, the history of Japan's receptivity to Americanism came full circle, starting with uncomplicated interest and imitation and ending with ahistorical condemnation. In these changing views of America, one can see how the imperatives of power politics can silence the claims of rationality. Gradually, the needs of wartime leaders squelched the sense of wonder and lively interest about the United States and an empathetic view of its history. Scholarly writings aimed at gaining a deeper understanding of American ideas were replaced by polemics.

The circumstances of history made an alternative all but impossible. Long before the Fifteen Years War, Japanese thinkers who took pro-American views were an isolated breed. The hardening of the emperor system after the Meiji period made it difficult for intellectuals to openly profess sympathy for either Christianity or republicanism. During the 1930s and early 1940s, thinkers who did so became pariahs. At no time did pro-Western intellectuals have real partners either in America or in most of Europe with whom they could forge a spirit of solidarity. They had contact only with a small circle of diplomats and a few academics who studied Japan. So they were imprisoned by the traditional dualism that pitted their national "spirit" against American materialism, Japanese tradition against the corrosive engine of modernity.

Such intellectuals were also isolated from other Asians. They rejected the notion that the Japanese empire could produce a harmonious "whole world under one roof" or a "Greater East Asia Co-Prosperity Sphere." But neither were they able to propose a more humane, less hegemonic mode of solidarity with weaker nations on the continent. So they could not transmit to their neighbors aspects of Americanism with which they had a good deal of sympathy and understanding.

To have been able to do so, they would have had to transcend the simplistic notion that the behemoth of the West was either purely benign or purely menacing, full of either sincere idealists or deeply hypocritical ones. In reality, Americanism is not an abstract faith. It must be understood in the context of the human networks that function in the United States, with the rules and traditions that govern those relationships. Americans have never been just the proud upholders of republican principles. Some are vulgar; others are racist, selfish, or cunning. By focusing on such negative characteristics, one can derive the view of America that most Japanese intellectuals articulated during the Fifteen Years War. But neither this dark portrait nor the light-filled one promoted during the seven-year U.S. occupation that followed World War II is realistic or a source of insight. To array these stereotypes side by side only impedes understanding.

In the world after September 11, 2001, Japan once again confronts two opposing views of America and its national ideals. Now, however, Japan is so firmly a U.S. ally that it has sent a small contingent of troops to back up the invasion of Iraq. Inevitably, the government in Tokyo focuses on the positive aspects of Americanism and ignores all the others. Intellectuals and scholars on both sides of the Pacific must be willing to discard such tendentious modes of thought in order to listen to more profound, if weaker, voices.

NOTES

1. Nagata Hidejiro, *Kenkoku no Seishin ni Kaere* (Return to the founding spirit) (Tokyo: Jitsugyo no Nihon Sha, 1927), 4.
2. Ibid., 11–13.
3. The Taisho era corresponded to the reign of Taisho Emperor, 1912–26, and the Showa era to the reign of Showa Emperor, 1926–89.
4. Nagata, *Kenkoku no Seishin ni Kaere*, 2–4.
5. Ibid., 32–37.
6. Nitobe studied at Johns Hopkins University from 1884 to 1887. In Baltimore he became a Quaker and married an American. After teaching at various institutions in Sapporo and Tokyo and working as the head of Industrial Bureau in Taiwan, he became the undersecretary-general of the League of Nations in 1920, serving in that capacity until 1926. As an internationalist, a Christian, and a liberal, he was opposed to militarism and jingoistic nationalism, and, until his

death in Vancouver in 1933, he advocated amicable relations between the United States and Japan. Jun Furuya, "Graduate Student and Quaker," in *Nitobe Inazo: Japan's Bridge Across the Pacific*, ed. John F. Howes (Boulder, Colo.: Westview, 1995), 55–76. Kiyosawa was much younger than Nitobe and a self-trained journalist. He studied at Whitworth College in Spokane, Washington. After returning to Japan in 1920, he constantly advocated, as a liberal, cooperation with the United States. Kitaoka Shinichi, *Kiyosawa Kiyoshim*, 2nd ed. (Tokyo: Chuo Koronsha, 2004).

7. See, for example, the following articles: Tsurumi Yusuke, "Ruuzuberuto no Seisaku to Sono Eikyo: Amerika no Fukyo to Tekunokurashii no Igi" (Roosevelt's policy and its influence: The American depression and the significance of technocracy), *Jitsugyo no Nihon*, March 1, 1933, 25–27; Shishimoto Hachiro, "Tekunokurashii kara Mita Amerika Kinyuukyoko" (The American financial crisis from a viewpoint of technocracy), *Jitsugyo no Nihon*, April 15, 1933, 40–45; Takahashi Kamekichi, "Saikin ni okeru Sekai Shihonsugi no Shin tenko" (The recent new shift of world capitalism), *Kaizo*, March 1934, 2–25; Ishibashi Tanzan et al., "Beikoku zaikai mondai hokokukai (toron kiroku)" (Proceedings of a seminar on American business circles), *Shukan Toyo Keizai Shinpo*, November 25, 1933, 25–47; Ooyama Ikuo, "Beikoku Shin Daitoryo Dokusaiken no Kakuritsu e" (Establishing a new presidential dictatorship in America), *Chuo Koron*, August 1933, 109–27; Masaki Chifuyu, "Keiki Seisaku to Amerika" (Policies for business adjustment and America), *Chuo Koron*, October 1933, 19–26; Abe Isamu, "Ruuzuberuto no Hijoji Taisaku" (Emergency policies of Roosevelt), *Chuo Koron*, February 1933, 79–93. See also Sakai Saburo, *Showa Kenkyukai: Aru Chishikijin Shudan no Kiseki* (Showa Kenkyukai: A history of an intellectual group) (Tokyo: Chuko Bunko, 1992), 13–14.

8. Hida Buntaro, "Nichibei Mondai to Hyoronka" (The Japan-U.S. problem and its critics), *Kaizo*, March 1941, 218–21. *Kaizo*, a high-quality journal, assembled a group of American specialists into a discussion group and featured their debate in its March 1941 edition, but the discussion was superficial and failed to analyze fundamental trends of American society and culture.

9. See, for example, Matsushita Masatoshi et al. in "Zadankai: Amerika Kousen ryoku no Kitei" (A round table: The fundamentals of American military power), *Kaizo*, January 1942, 66–84, in which even leading American specialists warped their scholarly judgment by engaging in jingoistic wishful thinking.

10. Asahi Shinbun sha, ed., *Nihon to Amerika* (Japan and America) (Tokyo: Asahi Shinbun sha, 1971), 86.

11. Ibid., 113; Ruth Benedict, *The Chrysanthemum and the Sword: Patterns of Japanese Culture* (Boston: Houghton Mifflin, 1946), chap. 1.

12. "Tokushu: Kindai no Choukoku" (Special issues on overcoming modernity), *Bungakukai*, September and October 1942. The papers and proceedings were republished as a book, *Kindai no Choukoku* (Tokyo: Sougensha, 1943). Takeuchi's words are are cited from his postscript to an enlarged new edition, *Kindai no Choukoku* (Tokyo: Fuzanbo Hyakka Bunko, 1979), 274. The following quotations on the symposium are from this postwar edition. Takeuchi Yoshimi (1910–77) was a leading scholar of Chinese literature before and after World War II. Because of his sympathy with Chinese nationalism, Takeuchi was critical of Japan's invasion of China since the 1920s. After the Pacific War erupted, however, he welcomed "the Great East Asia War" as an opportunity for Japan and China to cooperate for the liberation of Asian people from the history of humiliation. See Tsurumi Shunsuke, *Takeuchi Yoshimi* (Tokyo: Libroport, 1995).

13. Tsumura Hideo (1907–85) was a leading film critic during the war years.

14. Tsumura Hideo, "Nani o Yaburu Beki ka" (What should be torn up?), in *Kindai no Choukoku*, 135–36.

15. Symposium, ibid., 258.

16. Tsumura, "Nani o Yaburu Beki ka," 129.

17. Watsuji Tetsuro, *Nihon no Shindo/Amerika no Kokuminsei* (The way of Japanese subjects/American national character) (Tokyo: Chikuma Shobo, 1943). The two articles in this pamphlet are respectively included in *Watsuji Tetsuro Zenshu* (Collected works of Watsuji Tetsuro), ed. Abe Nosei et al. (Tokyo: Iwanami Shoten, 1961), 14:295–312 and 17:451–81.

18. See Karube Tadashi, *Hikari no Ryoukoku: Watsuji Tetsuro* (The realm of light: Watsuji Tetsuro) (Tokyo: Sobunsha, 1995).

19. Watsuji, "Amerika no Kokuminsei," 481.

20. Ibid., 457–59.

21. Ibid., 459–61.

22. Ibid., 464–72.

23. Ibid., 477.

24. Newton quoted in the *Black Panther* (newspaper), May 11, 1969, 4.

25. Watsuji, "Nihon no Shindo," 307–11. See Robert Bellah, "Watsuji Tetsuro ron" (A note on Watsuji Tetsuro), in *Watsuji Tetsuro*, ed. Yuasa Yasuo (Tokyo: San-ichi shobo, 1973), 69–106.

26. Sakai Naoki, "Bunkateki sai no bunsekiron to nihon to iu naibusei" (Analyses of cultural distinctions and Japan as a closed system), *Jokyo*, December 1992, 82–117.

★ ★ ★ ★

★ **The Promise of Freedom, the Friend of Authority**

★ *American Culture in Postwar France*

This is a story about cultural exchange. It is meant to make several suggestions. The first is that some of the culture that Americans take to be indigenously American is a hybrid, a product of international interpretation, but this hybridity is usually hidden in the nationalist narratives that accompany it. The United States participates in a North Atlantic culture— not exclusively a North Atlantic culture, of course, but during the early Cold War, which is when this story is set, that was the relevant context. A second point is that what reads as anti-American in the United States can be read as American in other countries. Dissent that is taken for weakness in the United States can be taken for strength in places where dissent is dangerous or illegal. This is a circumstance that complicates efforts at cultural diplomacy since it entails the thesis that showing a country at its best may involve showing it at somewhere close to its worst.

A final point is that the concept of Americanism is not meaningful without the concept of anti-Americanism. Americanness would not be a condition requiring a concept if it were not for the existence, imaginary or otherwise, of anti-Americanism. In America, a characteristic mode of anti-Americanism is "true" Americanism. This is why "Civil Disobedience" and the "Letter from a Birmingham Jail" are canonical texts, not heretical ones. Americanism and anti-Americanism are names for two sides of one coin. This paradox has something to do with a feeling some people had during the war in Vietnam and, later, the war in Iraq, which is that it is possible to be a patriot and a dissident at the same time. The question this story ends with is whether that feeling is, at some level, a form of self-deception.

The story concerns American relations with France. The notion that France is an inveterately anti-American country, which is a notion endorsed even in France by two recent books critical of French anti-Americanism, *L'Obsession anti-américaine* by Jean-François Revel and *L'ennemi américain* by Philippe Roger, is highly misleading. American culture had a major impact on France in the twentieth century, and the French response to it has a good deal to do with what has been, since the 1960s, America's idea of itself. For twenty years after World War II, the American government attempted to control the content of much of the culture it sent abroad. Some of this control was exercised in the form of official censorship and intimidation, some in the form of covert subvention, but most often it came about through agencies and institutions whose relations with the state were more symbiotic than legal, such as the Motion Picture Association of America. "Control" is a negative term, especially applied to art and ideas, but it is a fact of life: most things worth doing are conditioned by real or imagined external pressures. These pressures are not, ipso facto, objectionable—even when they emanate from the state or from commercial organizations. It is another fact of life that art and ideas that are subjected to external control mutate in unanticipated ways. They produce backlashes, cultural antibodies that proceed to colonize the very structures that were set up to keep them at bay. The cultural history of the Cold War is in many ways a story of unintended consequences. Cold War actions and policies set in motion changes in art and ideas and even institutions that seemed, at the time, unrelated to Cold War actions and policies.

In the early years of the Cold War, the American government made the conquest of elite opinion in Europe a priority. The creation of the Congress for Cultural Freedom, with the support of the CIA, was one result of this policy. The aim of securing European opinion was also the reason that the United States required Britain and France to open their markets to Hollywood movies as a condition of postwar loans and the forgiveness of war debt. The government wished to export what it regarded as the "culture of freedom." Today, American commercial culture, whether we call it the culture of freedom or the culture of consumption, is dominant in the world. Part of the ideology of that culture is that it is autochthonous—that it expresses indigenously American tastes and values that have, at the same time, universal appeal. But this is not quite how it worked. American culture, as it came to be conceived of in the second half of the Cold War, was largely a European discovery.

When Jean-Paul Sartre gave his famous lecture on existentialism in October 1945, the philosophical movement was already a vogue in Paris. Sartre had published his first novel, *Nausea*, in 1938 and his major philosophical work, *Being and Nothingness*, in 1943. Although he had not put himself in danger during the Occupation, he had become known, by the end of the war, as the voice of the Resistance. In 1945 he came under attack from French Communists, who condemned existentialism as a philosophy of bourgeois individualism, and from Catholics, who condemned it as a philosophy of despair. Sartre intended his lecture as a reply to those critics. He delivered it in a small hall under the auspices of a group called Club Maintenant—"Club Now," the right venue, one feels, for a talk on existentialism. Though the event was not highly publicized, hundreds of people turned up, and the room was so crowded that Sartre needed fifteen minutes to get to the stage. People fainted. Chairs got broken. Sartre spoke extemporaneously for an hour, making it a point never to take his hands out of his pockets, and then he left. The next day, he found that he had become a celebrity.

The lecture was widely reported in the press. Sartre wrote out what he remembered saying, and in 1946 *L'Existentialisme est un humanisme* appeared as a book in France. In 1947 it was published in the United States, under the title *Existentialism*. Because it is short and nontechnical, it is one of the few philosophical works on the subject that many people interested in existentialism actually read, and Sartre's book therefore had a good deal to do with the general understanding of the subject. The author himself did not think that "Existentialism Is a Humanism" was a particularly good essay; he was embarrassed by the attention it received and eventually tried to repudiate it. Its inadequacies are due partly to the fact that it was written in the spirit of nonpartisan solidarity that had characterized the Resistance and of the feeling that anything was possible that flourished briefly in Paris after the Liberation. As the moral complexity of France under the Occupation became known, and as the reality of life as a second-rate power sank in, Sartre's essay began to seem politically naïve and philosophically simplistic. But most Hollywood movies are politically naïve and philosophically simplistic, too, and it is useful to think of "Existentialism Is a Humanism" as an effort to do philosophy in what the French called *le style américain*.

Le style américain was introduced to France by a French expatriate named Maurice-Edgar Coindreau. In 1923, when he was thirty-one, Coindreau took a position as an instructor in Spanish at Princeton. He had been living in Madrid, teaching at a lycée and translating Spanish plays into French, and while he was there, he had met, more or less by chance, John Dos Passos. When Dos Passos's novel *Manhattan Transfer* was published in 1925, Coindreau decided to translate it into French. He thought that this might be a useful exercise for improving his English.

Dos Passos, who was still in his leftist phase, was then living in New York City. Every two weeks or so, Coindreau went in to see him. It was during Prohibition, so they would meet in a speakeasy, where the beer, as

Coindreau later remembered it, "prenait saveur de péché"—took on the flavor of sin.[1] Coindreau would show Dos Passos what he had done, and Dos Passos, whose French was quite good, would correct mistakes and help Coindreau with idiomatic terms. After they finished the first chapter, Coindreau asked about seeing whether a French publisher was interested. Dos Passos consented, and Coindreau sent the chapter to Gaston Gallimard, in Paris. Gallimard liked it and commissioned the rest; and in 1928 Coindreau's translation of *Manhattan Transfer* came out in France. It caused a sensation. In 1928 *Ulysses* had not yet been translated into French. *Manhattan Transfer*'s kaleidoscopic technique—the interposition of fragments of multiple narratives, somewhat similar to Joyce's method in the "Wandering Rocks" section of *Ulysses*—seemed a thrilling and original way to represent the modern city as a palimpsest of simultaneous but discontinuous experiences.

Gallimard realized that he had a good thing in Maurice Coindreau, and he encouraged him to continue to find ways of improving his English. So every summer Coindreau took a boat to France with a new translation of an American novel in his suitcase, and Gallimard published it. In 1932 it was Ernest Hemingway's *A Farewell to Arms*; in 1933, *The Sun Also Rises*; in 1934, William Faulkner's *As I Lay Dying*; in 1935, *Light in August*; in 1936, Erskine Caldwell's *God's Little Acre*; in 1937, *Tobacco Road*; in 1938, *The Sound and the Fury*; in 1939, John Steinbeck's *Of Mice and Men*. Sophisticated French readers gave the books an enthusiastic reception. Gallimard commissioned translations of other works by the American authors Coindreau had introduced him to, and he published many of the volumes with prefaces by leading French writers. Faulkner's *Sanctuary* appeared in 1933 with a preface by André Malraux, who had just published *Man's Fate*. The preface to *A Farewell to Arms* was written by Pierre Drieu la Rochelle; the preface to *The Sun Also Rises* was by the poet Jean Prévost (who had once enjoyed the mixed fortune of boxing with Hemingway, who cheated). *As I Lay Dying*—a title that gave Coindreau fits: he finally came up with *Tandis que j'agonise*—had a preface by Valéry Larbaud, a friend of Joyce and the man who supervised the French translation of *Ulysses*.

Coindreau was not simply creaming off the top of the American bestseller lists. When Coindreau introduced him to France, Faulkner was largely disregarded in the United States—he was treated, as Coindreau put it, like the village idiot. Coindreau was, in short, a canon maker, and his effect on French literary culture was enormous. The 1930s became known as the "age of the American novel." "The greatest literary development in France between 1929 and 1939," Sartre later wrote, "was the discovery of Faulkner, Dos Passos, Hemingway, Caldwell, Steinbeck."[2] And he said elsewhere: "La littérature américaine, c'était la littérature Coindreau."[3]

What did the French find so compelling about these novels? The French thought that American fiction had eliminated psychology. The characters in American novels never seem to reflect on their conduct, and neither does the author. "Hemingway never enters inside his characters," Sartre wrote, in 1946, in an essay called "American Fiction in French Eyes." "He describes them always from the outside. . . . The heroes of Hemingway and Caldwell never explain themselves. They act only."[4] Even in Faulkner's novels, Sartre thought, we are shown the inside only in order to prove that there is nothing there. There is no secret code to conduct; character is simply the sum of its actions. The American novel seemed to have completely rejected what the French novel, culminating in Proust, had made its specialty: introspection and analysis—which is why the French found Coindreau's American authors so modern and exciting.

French critics had an explanation for the absence of explanation in American fiction. They thought that American writers were imitating the movies. This is the argument of the most important critical study in France of American fiction, Claude-Edmonde Magny's *The Age of the American Novel*. Magny claimed that the new techniques in modern writing were literary adaptations of cinematic techniques. She talked a lot about montage and ellipsis, but, at the most basic level, the French thought that the influence of film could be seen in the atomization of action—the *and then, and then, and then* effect—in writers like Hemingway and Dos Passos. What we are presented with is simply a sequence of actions, without commentary. A scene in Hemingway or Dos Passos is like a scene in a film: the camera does not add to what is there, and it does not compress, either. The cinema does not generalize.

French writers talked about "le style américain," but of course there was more than one style represented in "la littérature Coindreau," and different French writers responded to different styles. Jules Romains admired Dos Passos, who he thought had discovered a narrative technique for representing collectivity, for making the spirit of the city the protagonist of the novel. Simone de Beauvoir was influenced by Faulkner. Camus wrote *The Stranger* in the style of *The Sun Also Rises*. Sartre published some influential essays on Faulkner, but in the end he found Faulkner too fatalistic for a philosopher of freedom. "I like his art," he said, "but I don't believe in his metaphysics."[5] On the other hand, Sartre thought that Dos Passos was "the greatest writer of our time,"[6] and he modeled the crisscrossing narrative of his trilogy *The Roads to Freedom* on Dos Passos's trilogy *U.S.A.*

American books, along with American movies, were banned in Occupied France, although there was a black market in American fiction in Paris, for which the Café de Flore, the haunt of Sartre and Beauvoir, served as headquarters. Reading an American novel was regarded by some of those who did it as an act of resistance. After the Liberation, Coindreau resumed bringing translations to Gallimard, and Gallimard began publishing them again. But then Gallimard started another line, just as serendipitous in its origins, and even more successful. The man who handed this series to him was Marcel Duhamel.

Duhamel was a friend of the surrealists, in particular of Jacques Prévert and Henri Filipacchi. He had got to know Gallimard during the Occupation, when he managed to come up with large supplies of paper, which the publishing house was badly in need of. Duhamel loved English and American fiction, and in 1944, shortly after the Liberation, he translated three hard-boiled detective novels by two British writers, Peter Cheyney and James Hadley Chase. He took them to Gallimard, who decided to publish them as a series. Gallimard's art director proposed a cover featuring little green flowers against a white background. Duhamel was disgusted. He got his wife to design an all-black cover, and he asked his friend Prévert to come up with a name for the collection. Prévert looked at the cover design and came up with *série noire*—a pun since the phrase also means "a run of bad luck." (There was also, possibly, an association with the American magazine *Black Mask*, which published detective fiction.) The first translation, of Peter Cheyney's *Poison Ivy*, featuring a secret agent named Lemmy Caution, came out in September 1945. It was a great success, and Duhamel was in business. By 1948 he was bringing out two books a month. Most were British and American hard-boiled crime novels in the tradition of James M. Cain, Raymond Chandler, and Dashiell Hammett (translations of whose works were reissued by Gallimard), though they were often gorier and sexually more lurid, as in the case of Jim Thompson's and Mickey Spillane's books. After 1948 Duhamel started commissioning work by French writers as well (though they were made to use American pseudonyms). Rival series sprang up at other publishing houses. Postwar France was awash in pulp.

Duhamel was a Frenchman and a comrade of the surrealists. He was therefore not the sort of person who would publish a series without issuing a manifesto, and in 1948 he did so. Fans of Sherlock Holmes, he explained, would not find much to enjoy in the novels of the *série noire*.

One sees in [*série noire* novels] detectives more corrupt than the criminals they pursue. The sympathetic detective does not always solve the mystery. Sometimes, there is no mystery. Sometimes, there is not even a detective. But then? Then we are left with action, with anxiety, with violence—in all their forms, and particularly the most evil—beatings and massacres. As in good movies, the state of the soul manifests itself in gestures, and readers fond of literary introspection are obliged to perform an inverse mental gymnastic. There is also love, preferably bestial, unruly passion, hate without mercy. In short, our goal is to prevent you from sleeping.[7]

The *série noire* novel was to the traditional detective novel, in other words, what Hemingway and Faulkner were to the *roman d'analyse*. They were antipsychological, narratively discontinuous, cinematic.

Duhamel was perfectly justified in comparing *série noire* fiction with movies. In fact, it was precisely his intention to publish novels that could be adapted for the screen. Film had always held a great fascination for the surrealists; as a young man, in the 1920s, Duhamel had often attended film society screenings with Prévert and other friends. He knew that crime fiction and the movies had had a collaborative relationship since the beginning of the sound era—arguably, almost since the beginning of the movies. Modern crime fiction, with its preference for action over plot and its stichomythia, seemed almost to have been composed for the screen. By 1945 there had been two movie versions of Hammett's *The Glass Key*, three movie versions of *The Maltese Falcon*, three of William Riley Burnett's *High Sierra*, four of *The Asphalt Jungle*, and four of *The Postman Always Rings Twice*. Duhamel strove to maintain this tradition, and he succeeded. Of the 250 volumes published in the *série noire* between 1945 and 1955, more than 180 were made into movies. The dialogue in two famous French gangster movies of the mid-1950s, Jules Dassin's *Rififi* and Jean-Pierre Melville's *Bob le Flambeur*, was written by a *série noire* author, Auguste Le Breton. Melville, of course, took his name from the American writer.

The popularity of the *série noire* was enhanced by the return of Hollywood. In 1946 France and the United States signed an agreement on the terms of American loans for postwar reconstruction and economic modernization. The agreement was tied to a provision concerning a single American commodity, movies. The stipulation was the outcome of discussions between the motion picture industry and the State Department that had been carried on since 1942. The industry had argued that the movies would be an ideal vehicle for the dissemination of pro-Americanism in postwar Europe, and it had many friends in the State Department who agreed, and who saw to it that any settlement on loans would be contingent on the lowering of trade barriers to American films. Both France and England, despite protests from their own film industries, were compelled to submit to this requirement. Since no American movies had been seen in France during the Occupation, there were more than two thousand Hollywood movies poised to descend on French screens. And on July 1, 1946, the day the trade agreement went into effect, the descent began. That summer, dozens of American movies opened in Paris, including *Citizen Kane*, *Double Indemnity*, *Laura*, *The Maltese Falcon*, and *Murder, My Sweet*. By August, French critics had named a new cinematic style, *film noir*. The name, very likely, derives from the Gallimard series.

The first critic to use the term for this new American genre was Nino Frank, in the journal *L'Ecran français*. Frank defined *film noir* in the same way Duhamel defined hard-boiled fiction. These are not detective stories, he explained. The mystery no longer matters: "The essential question is no longer 'who-done-it?' but how does this protagonist act?"[8] Discussions of *film noir* quickly grew to industrial strength in French film criticism, culminating, in 1955, with the first book-length study of the genre, *A Panorama of American Film Noir*, by Raymond Borde and Etienne Chaumeton. Borde and Chaumeton were associated with the film journal *Positif*, which had a strong surrealist element in its aesthetic; the introduction to their book was written by the publisher of the *série noire*, Marcel Duhamel. This was the transplanted American popular culture out of which the French New Wave emerged. François Truffaut's *Shoot the Piano Player* and Jean-Luc Godard's *Pierrot le Fou*, *Band of Outsiders*, and *Made in U.S.A.* were all adaptations of *série noire* novels; Godard's *Alphaville* features the hero of the first volume in the *série noire*, Peter Cheyney's secret agent, Lemmy Caution, played by the actor who had played Caution in previous *série noire* adaptations, Eddie Constantine.

French enthusiasm for American culture was a highbrow phenomenon. The most popular genres among the movie-going public in postwar France were musicals and comedies; in polls, most people expressed an aversion to gangster movies and to any films showing violent or immoral content. But it was highbrow opinion at which the United States was aiming—something that is often missed in critiques of cultural imperialism. Sartre and Duhamel, Borde and Chaumeton, André Bazin, who was the co-founder of the *Cahiers du cinéma*, Godard, and even, in his autodidactic way, Truffaut, were intellectuals and sophisticates. Their under-standing of popular forms was continuous with their understanding of modernist forms: that is, they theorized both in the same way, as expres-sions of a de-psychologized culture of action. The response to violence in art was an educated response. In 1949 the Harvard professor Perry Miller toured European universities, lecturing on American literature. He re-ported enthusiasm, wherever he went, for American writing, provided it was violent. "As long as a book flaunted the stigmata of American vio-lence," Miller wrote after he returned, "it was accepted uncritically as the real thing. . . . Almost anything which pretends to be 'tough' will be read."[9] He found that he could not get Europeans excited about the Henry James revival.

In an article in the *Atlantic Monthly* in 1946, Sartre suggested that French writers might adopt American literary techniques and, in the postwar spirit of cultural exchange, send them back to the United States, refined and improved, for the further use of American writers. This did not hap-pen. Alain Robbe-Grillet's *The Erasers*, which was published in 1953, might be understood as a *série noire* detective story written at stylistic degree zero, but the impact of the *nouveau roman* in the United States was not great. The French interpretation of American culture was reimported in a different form. It came back as philosophy.

During his brief time in the French army, in 1940, Sartre recorded in his diary a fantasy of becoming a man of unreflective action. Such a man, he wrote, would be

> handsome, hesitant, obscure, slow and upright in his thought; [he would] not have any acquired grace, but only a silent spontaneous kind. I saw him . . . as a worker and hobo in the Eastern u.s.a. How I should like to feel uncertain ideas slowly, patiently forming within me! How I should have liked to boil with great, obscure rages; faint from great, motiveless outpourings of tenderness! My American worker (who resembled Gary Cooper) could do and feel all that. I pictured him sitting on a railway embankment, tired and dusty; he'd be waiting for the cattle-truck, into which he'd jump unseen—and I should have liked to be him . . . [a man] who thought little, spoke little, and always did the right thing.[10]

Sartre seems to have confused the eastern and western parts of the United States, and it is entertaining to imagine him, not the tallest of men, as Gary Cooper, jumping into a cattle truck, whatever that is. Sartre had never been to the United States when he wrote these words. He was plainly taking his idea of America and "the American" from the movies. But it made sense for him to do so: he was trying to analyze his way out of a culture of analysis without recourse to analysis. He was trying to do philosophy by pictures.

In *Being and Nothingness*, Sartre frequently uses dramatic vignettes to accompany his philosophical arguments. He illustrates the concept of bad faith, for example, with a story about a woman who fails to respond to a pass made by the man she is on a date with. In fact, female sexual indifference was a favorite symptom of bad faith for Sartre. Elsewhere, he argues that female frigidity is a consciously chosen condition: the woman knows that she is experiencing pleasure and denies it in order to be able to say to herself that she has no pleasure. He uses the same dramatizing technique in "Existentialism Is a Humanism."

"Existentialism Is a Humanism" defines existentialism as "an attempt to draw all the consequences of a coherent atheistic position."[11] The chief consequence is that man is born in a condition of radical freedom—in the now well-known aphorism, which Sartre had already used in *Being and Nothingness*, man's existence precedes his essence. Because of this, Sartre argues, "there is no reality except in action. . . . Man . . . exists only to the extent that he fulfills himself; he is therefore nothing else than the ensemble of his acts, nothing else than his life."[12] What saves this formulation from tautology, what gives it some normative bite, is the requirement that all acts be freely chosen, or, as Sartre also puts it, that all acts be chosen in the name of freedom. This relegates both acts of passion and acts of refusal or resignation—things we do because we can't help it and things we do in denial of our own wishes—to the realm of bad faith. It also rules out all forms of determinism, since attributing an act to forces over which you have no control is just another form of bad faith. "Every man who sets up a determinism," Sartre says, "is a dishonest man."[13] A choice freely made in the name of freedom is therefore by definition always the right choice. And (Sartre is explicit about this) the same choice unfreely made is by definition always wrong. You get no credit for lucking out.

The dramatic illustration Sartre uses in "Existentialism Is a Humanism" is drawn, he says, from real life. Sartre is approached by a student seeking advice. The student's brother has been killed by the Germans; his father has collaborationist tendencies; he, the student, is the only source of solace left to his mother. His dilemma is whether he should join the Free French forces in England, avenging his brother and fighting for France, or stay home to tend to his mother, who, if he were killed, would be desolated. No ethical system, Sartre says, Christian, Kantian, or otherwise, can point the student the way out of this dilemma. Any philosophy can be used to legitimate either choice. The student suggests that perhaps he should be guided by his feelings: if his love for his mother is great enough, then he will stay with her. Sartre points out, though, that we can deceive ourselves about our feelings. The student might unfreely choose to remain with his mother and then develop the feeling that justifies his choice afterward—just as, presumably, the frigid woman denies herself pleasure in order to allow herself to claim that she cannot experience it. What is the student to do? "I had," Sartre concludes, "only one answer to give: 'You're free. Choose; that is, invent.' No general ethics can show you what is to be done; there are no omens in the world"—that is, something that can be taken as a sign, from above, pointing to the right choice.[14] Rightness has to be created.

The significance of the student's dilemma is the manner in which it is framed. Sartre is not really saying (although he pretends otherwise) that all ethical systems are indeterminate on the problem the student faces. There are plenty of ethical systems available that will resolve the dilemma one way or the other. What Sartre is saying is that a choice made in accordance with a priori principles cannot be a free choice. There is no difference, after all, between a belief system that dictates a particular line of conduct and an unconscious desire or an uncontrollable urge.

In order to make the student's dilemma perform its heuristic function properly, Sartre has to make it seem as though the choice the student faces is a choice between equivalent alternatives. He presents the story as a version of the old philosophical problem of the rational donkey. If you place a perfectly rational donkey between two equidistant piles of hay of equal size, the donkey will starve to death. The student's dilemma is existential only if there are no rational grounds for resolving it—only if the choice between mother and country, between love and duty, is, philosophically, arbitrary. You have to get yourself out there over the abyss before you can say that you have chosen freely; and once you have acted, there is no need to explain. You chose because you had to choose. There was, after all, an abyss. "The heroes of Hemingway and Caldwell never explain themselves. They act only." Sartre's reading of American fiction maps perfectly onto his account of existentialism.

But Sartre was probably not thinking of American fiction when he told the story of the student's dilemma. When he delivered the lecture, in 1945, Sartre had just returned from his first visit to the United States. He had spent four months there, a good deal of the time in Hollywood, where he attended screenings of movies that had been made during the war. He was therefore one of the first Frenchmen to see *Casablanca* and *The Maltese Falcon*; and both of those films are, in the end, about a choice between love and duty. Bogart, of course, chooses duty each time. But how do we know it's the right choice? Because he might, each time, with our approval, have chosen love instead. Duty is the right choice only because love is also the right choice. Love and duty, the girl and the social order, are exactly equivalent haystacks. Analysis leads nowhere, except to more analysis. The thing is simply to jump into the cattle truck. Sartre's postwar existentialism belongs to the same embrace of American cultural forms as Coindreau's translations and Duhamel's detective series. It is a French idea of Americanism.

And yet Americans did not read it that way. Sartre interpreted a literary and film culture characterized by anxiety, violence, discontinuity, godlessness, and psychological emptiness as, in fact, a culture of humanism and radical freedom, but that is now how Americans received existentialism. In 1946 Sartre, Beauvoir, and Camus all came to the United States. Their visits were prominently covered in *Time* and *Life*. They attracted the interest of intellectuals at *Partisan Review*, to which they all contributed. For two or three years, existentialism was a buzz word in the United States, but, in the end, its impact was small. "*Existentialism means that no one else can take a bath for you*" is how Delmore Schwartz summed it up in 1948,[15] and by then serious American interest in Sartre had waned. But the most striking thing about the American reception of French existentialism is that it was regarded by everyone, even by its admirers, as distinctly un-American. Even William Barrett, whose little book *What Is Existentialism?* in 1947 introduced many Americans to the subject, and whose later work *Irrational Man* was widely considered the definitive account of existentialism in the United States, wrote that "existentialism was so definitely a European expression that its very somberness went against the grain of our native youthfulness and optimism."[16] Sartre may have imagined that he was returning an American idea to America, but in 1950 nothing looked more European to Americans than existentialism.

When the term "existentialist" appears in American publications in the 1940s and 1950s, it is associated either with a philosophy of pessimism and atheistic despair (as in the popular understanding of Beckett's plays, for example) or with fashionable bohemianism—the jazz scene, for instance. The art critic Harold Rosenberg, whose account of abstract expressionism as "action painting" seems taken almost directly from "Existentialism Is a Humanism," refused to call himself an existentialist and always claimed that he was not influenced by Sartre. American artists and writers in the 1940s and 1950s who did speak of themselves, vaguely, as existentialists— Mark Rothko, Arthur Schlesinger Jr. (in *The Vital Center*), Norman Mailer— generally had Kierkegaard in mind rather than Sartre. Kierkegaard's works had been available in the United States, in Walter Lowrie's translations, since 1944, and Kierkegaard was not influenced by *le style américain*. The line of Christian existentialism that runs from Kierkegaard through Dietrich Bonhoeffer, Rudolf Bultmann, Martin Buber, and Paul Tillich had much greater appeal in a Cold War culture in which Reinhold Niebuhr was a dominant theological thinker than the atheism of Sartre did.

Then, in the mid-1960s, this changed. People started referring to Herman Melville as an existentialist. At the same time, thanks largely to the French New Wave's recycling of American gangster pictures in movies like *Breathless*, which came to the United States in 1961, and *Shoot the Piano Player*, which came in 1962, Americans discovered *film noir*. The first time an American critic seems to have used the term *film noir* was in 1970, almost twenty-five years after Nino Frank coined it in *L'Ecran français*. In 1965, around the time of a Bogart revival, Knopf reprinted five of Hammett's novels. In 1969 Knopf brought out three James M. Cain novels, in a one-volume edition, with an introduction by Tom Wolfe. In 1967 Hazel Barnes published *An Existentialist Ethics*, in which she explained that William James was an existentialist. The United States took its culture back from Europe. It was away so long we hardly recognized it.

What was going on? In the 1940s and 1950s, Americans were a culturally insecure people. Even well-educated Americans were extremely wary of being caught slumming in the realms of mass culture—of enjoying things that they were supposed to be too cultured to enjoy. But when Europeans took the mass culture the United States exported in the 1940s and 1950s and returned it in the 1960s in the form of a hip and sophisticated pop art, Americans began to feel comfortable with their own culture. It was a form of validation. This was true to some degree of American fiction, although American critics did not have too much trouble writing intelligently about Hemingway and (after 1946) about Faulkner. Hemingway and Faulkner were modernists, and it was a modernist canon. The movies are a much more straightforward case: the transformation of Hollywood movies in the 1970s can be traced straight back to the French reception of American film in the 1940s.

The best-known case of cultural recycling is pop music. Very few Americans over eighteen listened to or thought seriously about rock and roll music until the Beatles arrived in the United States, in 1964. The Beatles had no idea why they made such a hit, though, since in their minds they were simply imitating music already performed by Americans. Why would Americans want something from abroad they already had at home? But the Beatles made rock and roll seem stylish, witty, and even deep, and this sent Americans back to Elvis Presley with new ears—just as Godard and Truffaut sent Americans back to Nicholas Ray and Robert Aldrich with new eyes. There is a suggestive parallel in the case of the revival of American pragmatism in the late 1970s, when Richard Rorty assimilated John Dewey to Jacques Derrida. French poststructuralism revealed the uses that could be made of American philosophy: Derrida showed Americans how to read James and Dewey. This is how myths of cultural autochthony are born. It takes an outsider to explain to insiders who they are.

One irony in the globalization of American culture is that the products that had the most success in presenting a positive image of the United States abroad were perceived as negative images at home—as, in effect, anti-American. In 1946 Barney Balaban, the president of Paramount, told the *New York Times* that it was important to send abroad "only those pictures that accurately reflect our national life, even if this means lessening the profits of certain pictures which might create a distorted impression. There is no need for us to do otherwise and help to foster the impression that America is a country of gangsters."[17] But it was the gangster pictures that captured the European imagination. Sartre tried to explain how this worked. "When the Vichy newspapers published an extract from the American or English press severely criticizing some Allied military operation, or loyally recognizing some Allied defeat, they thought they would discourage us," he wrote in 1946. "They provoked on the contrary among most of us a profound respect for Anglo-Saxon democracy and bitter regret for our own. 'Such people,' we told ourselves, 'have confidence in their rights.' . . . The harsh criticism that your writers made against your social regime we took in the same way. It never disgusted us with America—on the contrary, we saw in it a manifestation of your liberty."[18] Perry Miller, too, addressed the question of whether a literature critical of America was a credit to America. He concluded, in Sartrean language, that "because this is a literature of criticism in the name of the fundamental man, it is a literature of freedom."[19]

But is freedom precisely what the existentialist vision proposes? The story of the student's dilemma, in Sartre's lecture, had resonance because it could easily be made to stand for a choice, at the beginning of the

Cold War, between East and West. In this respect, Sartre *was* like William James. A person may believe in God, James argued, in "The Will to Believe" and elsewhere, without being able to provide reasons, because as long as the belief makes a difference in the world for that person, that belief will be, pragmatically, true. This was the rationale Sartre eventually used to choose to support the Soviet Union while, at the same time, refusing to join the Communist Party: since he had freely *chosen* to believe in Communism, he could try to make it "true," in the Jamesian sense. And because it was a belief freely chosen, it could freely be renounced as well. Existentialism is a philosophy of freedom, but it provides no grounds for *choosing* freedom over something else. It was when the *Partisan Review* writers figured this out that they got over their enthusiasm for existentialism.

But the student's dilemma can also be made to stand for many other things. The separation of love and duty into two separate haystacks is more significant than the method of resolution that Sartre proposes. This separation does more than split loyalty; it splits identity under the illusion of keeping it together. Not son *or* soldier, but son and, nevertheless, soldier. Protestor and, nevertheless, patriot. Hedonist and, nevertheless, moralist. Rebel and, nevertheless, conformist. Something like this condition is characteristic of Cold War culture—*noir*, Beat, pop, existentialist. That culture served as a kind of "nevertheless." It was a mental reserve against all the things that being a citizen in a superpower made ethically fraught. It was the other haystack.

The hope that these identities might be compatible at the end of the day, that by choosing rebellion one is not rejecting loyalty, and that by choosing loyalty one is not closing the door on rebellion, is the characteristic hope of intellectuals living in a superpower. Humphrey Bogart sends Mary Astor to prison at the end of *The Maltese Falcon*; that does not mean (apparently) that he does not love her. It is a tricky proposition, but we buy it. Europeans, unsurprisingly, understood the contradiction better than Americans did. The emblematic representation of America in Cold War–era French film is Patricia, the character played by Jean Seberg, in Godard's *Breathless*. She is the American girlfriend who ends up betraying Michel and turning him in to the police—an echo of *The Maltese Falcon*. She is the promise of freedom and, nevertheless, the friend of authority. "C'est vraiment dégueulasse," Michel murmurs as he dies: it's truly disgusting that it worked out this way. "Il dit que vous êtes vraiment une dégueulasse," the cop mistranslates: he says you're really a bitch. It is the split image with which American culture confronts the world.

NOTES

1. Maurice-Edgar Coindreau, *Mémoires d'un traducteur: Entretiens avec Christian Guidicelli* (Paris: Gallimard, 1974), 37.

2. Jean-Paul Sartre, "American Novelists in French Eyes," *Atlantic Monthly*, August 1946, 114.

3. Quoted in Coindreau, *Mémoires d'un traducteur*, 9.

4. Sartre, "American Novelists in French Eyes," 117.

5. Quoted in Stanley D. Woodworth, *William Faulkner en France (1931–1952)* (Paris: Minard, 1959), 53 (my translation).

6. Jean-Paul Sartre, "A propos de John Dos Passos et de *1919*" (1938), in *Situations* (Paris: Gallimard, 1947), 25.

7. Quoted in Pierre Boileau and Thomas Narcejac, *Le Roman policier* (1975; repr., Paris: Presses Universitaires de France, 1994), 85.

8. Nino Frank, "A New Kind of Police Drama: The Criminal Adventure" (1946), in *Film Noir Reader 2*, ed. Alain Silver and James Ursini (New York: Limelight, 1999), 16.

9. Perry Miller, "Europe's Faith in American Fiction," *Atlantic Monthly*, August 1951, 53.

10. Jean-Paul Sartre, *War Diaries: Notebooks from a Phoney War, 1939–40*, trans. Quintin Hoare (London: Verso, 1984), 273–74.

11. Jean-Paul Sartre, *Existentialism*, trans. Bernard Frechtman (New York: Philosophical Library, 1947), 60–61.

12. Ibid., 37–38.

13. Ibid., 53.

14. Ibid., 33.

15. Delmore Schwartz, "Does Existentialism Still Exist?" *Partisan Review* 12 (1948): 1361 (italics in the original).

16. William Barrett, *What Is Existentialism?* (New York: Partisan Review, 1947), 20.

17. Thomas M. Pryor, "Mission of the Movies Abroad," *New York Times*, March 24, 1946.

18. Sartre, "American Novelists in French Eyes," 116.

19. Miller, "Europe's Faith in American Fiction," 56.

ROB KROES

★ French Views of American Modernity

★ *From Text to Subtext*

This essay could be flippantly called a study in Occidentalism. Taking my cue from Edward Said's seminal exploration of Orientalism as a repertoire of European representations concerning "the Orient," I propose to look at "America" as similarly an object of the European imagination. Much like the Orient, the Occident—since way before the historical discovery of the Americas—has been a European invention. It has served as the screen for the projection of a wide range of European dreams, utopian as well as dystopian. Among the many repertoires in which "America" figured as the quintessential counterpoint to Europe, representing everything that Europe was not or not yet, would never be or wanted to become, modernity was one important point of reference. In spite of the many congruences among European constructions of "America," irrespective of national setting, there have also been characteristically national discourses concerning "America." In the following I look at one national setting and explore French views of "America," seen as the site of the modern, politically and culturally.

Establishing a Repertoire

"America" and "modernity" are two words that when used in conjunction will most likely conjure up images of a twentieth-century America in its heyday as an industrial power, ushering in a new era of mass production and mass consumption. To the European gaze such images have offered the distant mirage of a Promethean technical prowess, of energy unleashed in many directions, going skyward in its high-rise architecture, going westward in its unbridled conquest of open space, going global through its penetration into new markets for mass entertainment. Nor, in the end, was this America only distant; in our century it has become a presence in Europe, seen as either threatening or liberating, opening vistas of a new world as so many versions of "the New World." The sense of "the modern," so strongly centered in the late nineteenth century on bourgeois societies in Europe, now found its favorite site in America. In a Promethean act of cultural robbery, America had taken over Europe's leadership role in defining what modernity was all about.[1]

Yet the association of modernity with America as an advanced technical civilization is not the only one that Europeans have tended to make. There are earlier views that cast America in the light of the modern, contrasting it to a Europe seen as mired in the past. Metaphors of America as having moved beyond Europe, having entered a new plane of history, may be traced back to the use of biblical prophecy by the early Puritans, yet in their secular versions at the time of the Revolution and of the early Republic they clearly echoed the Enlightenment hopes of the day in Europe. Again, though, in spite of the continuity, there was at the same time—much as in the case of the Puritans—a widespread sense, voiced loudly, that it was for Americans to realize these hopes.

From early days onward, there have always been French voices contributing to a discourse that has conceived of America as a counterpoint to Europe. The contrasts that we shall focus on have played on underlying dimensions of new versus old, the future versus the past, the modern versus the antiquated. In these contrasts America has appeared in essentially three different constructions. One is political, focusing on America as a successful Republican experiment; a second is humanist, focusing on "the American" as a "new man"; the third is what we might call, for want of a better term, existential, focusing on America as empty space.

An early French voice, heard widely at the time in many European countries, then forgotten until Americans rediscovered it more than a century later, turning it into one of their canonical definitions of American nationhood, was Hector St. John de Crèvecoeur's. Born into the *petite noblesse* in Normandy, he had fought the British in North America under Montcalm and after the defeat of the French had moved south to take up farming in the province of New York. In his *Letters from an American Farmer*, published in 1782, he asked the now famous question: "What, then, is the American, this new man?" The very choice of words is telling. The American is seen not simply as representing yet another different nationality, adding to a European pattern of national differences. He is new in the sense of transcending the European pattern. The transcendence is of two kinds. Americans may be of European descent, yet, so Crèvecoeur argues, they have left Europe's internecine differences of nationality behind them: "From this promiscuous breed, that race now called Americans have arisen." And he continues: "He is an American, who, leaving behind him all his ancient prejudices and manners, receives new ones from the new mode he has embraced, the new government he obeys, and the new rank he holds. He becomes an American by being received in the broad lap of our great Alma Mater. Here individuals of all nations are melted into a new race of men, whose labours and posterity will one day cause great changes in the world." And in a vein of historical predestination, echoing the old repertoire of the westward course of empires, he goes on to say: "Americans are the western pilgrims, who are carrying along with them that great mass of arts, sciences, vigour, and industry which began long ago in the East; they will finish the great circle."[2]

But, as I have said, there was a second sense in which the American was new. He had overcome other European differences that worked to keep Europe divided against itself. Religious difference and strife had resolved themselves into a pluralism of coequal denominations, happily coexisting on American soil. But, more important, the American had overcome European social inequality. "Europe," in the words of Crèvecoeur, "contains hardly any other distinctions but lords and tenants." American society in contrast does not consist "of great lords who possess everything, and of a herd of people who have nothing."[3] Not only does America tend to level such differences; in doing so it elevates all those involved. America, "this great asylum," has accepted the poverty stricken from all across Europe and turned them into citizens. Crèvecoeur speaks of a metamorphosis worked by America's intrinsic regenerative power: "Everything has tended to regenerate [the immigrants]; new laws, a new mode of living, a new social system; here they are become men."[4] Given the fact that these words were written in an age when language was not yet gender free, we may read the statement as applying to human beings in general.

Crèvecoeur provides, then, an amazing early statement of America's modernity, in the sense of its offering fulfillment of that essentially Renaissance humanist dream that saw individuals as their own free agents, capable of taking charge of their own lives and molding their own private and collective destiny as they saw fit. America, rather than Europe, was the historical stage for this humanist transformation. And, daringly, Crèvecoeur made the point by posing as an American farmer himself, the proud yeoman-citizen who typified the new social order of free and equal human beings.

A second variety of modernity as projected onto America was linked to its great experiment in republicanism. That was how Alexis de Tocqueville and a younger generation of French liberals during the Second Empire chose to look at America. In the very preface to his *Democracy in America*,

Tocqueville had already admitted to the act of projection, to conceiving of America as showing what the future might have in store for Europe: "I admit that in America I have looked for more than America; I have been in search of an image of democracy itself . . . if only to know at least what we might have to hope or fear from it."[5] Tocqueville's approach foreshadows later Weberian methodology. He turns America into an ideal-type of democracy with a view to gaining more general insights into the workings of democracy irrespective of its precise historical setting. As we know, his final view of democracy was never one of total civic bliss. He did find grounds for both hope and fear, as he had set out to do. In his insights into democracy in America, he was always keenly aware of rival forces kept in tenuous balance, such as liberty and equality, individualism and conformism, political participation and civic apathy. His single most important contribution may have been to the theory of republicanism. The inherent instability of republics, representing a form of political order that critically hinged on a politics of distinterestedness, of civic virtue, had engaged political philosophers ever since Greek antiquity. Tocqueville was aware of the American answer to this quandary. He knew the Enlightenment views of the American Federalists, who had sought to rein in human self-interest through the countervailing arrangements of constitutional checks and balances. Yet, according to Tocqueville, the true American genius that could account for the stability of its republican order was not political; it was social. The pluralism of its social life, the freedom it allowed Americans to engage in manifold associations, was the key to understanding America's political stability. This view made Tocqueville a father of modern political sociology. But at the same time it made clear what was truly modern about America, which Tocqueville saw as a society whose central organizational vectors were freedom and equality.

The third view of American modernity focuses on America as empty space, providing an exhilarating contrast to a Europe that had reached the Malthusian limits of marginal existence. Again, the view was central to the American celebration of its Manifest Destiny,[6] but visitors could not escape sharing in this prevailing mood. New techniques of mechanical reproduction, such as the chromolithograph, were powerful mediators in transmitting the iconography of an American civilization vibrantly engaged in its westward march. The imagery of a never-ending renewal of life in America's infinite western expanse fired the imagination of Americans and foreigners alike. It was not long before this iconic repertoire would be made to serve yet another version of American modernity, if not postmodernity:

America's advertising wizardry. In its endless capacity to resemanticize reality, at an early stage advertising transformed the West into an imaginary realm, to be vicariously experienced by anyone who bought a particular product. Early posters from the 1870s and 1880s for tobacco brands like Westward Ho use the same repertoire of the West as empty space, where anyone could be a pioneer for as long as it took to smoke a pipe or cigarette.

French liberals, traveling to America at the time of the Second Empire, give us occasional glimpses of this infatuating cultural climate. Visitors like Jean-Jacques Ampère, Adolphe de Chambrun, Oscar Comettant, Ernest Duvergier de Hauranne, and Xavier Eyma commented on a wide range of aspects of life in the American Republic, but all, in one way or another, connected the energy and dynamism, "le goût du progrès," to the grand project of civilizing a continent while conquering its empty space, spreading the values of liberty, democracy, and hard work.[7]

The French travelers were not uncritical. They noted the rapaciousness and greed, the coarseness of manners, the rape of the land attending the westward march, yet at the same time they appreciated the boundless energy, the technological feats, and most of all the democratic quality of life emerging on the western frontier. America, they found, was in a state of continual transition. As Ampère put it, precisely there lies the poetic quality of American life. The America of Atala no longer exists, he concluded; it has made way for an America propelled by grandiose visions of its future.[8]

If American modernity has more faces than that of a Promethean technical civilization—as I have argued above—it is clear at the same time that even in the earlier views the technical dimension is already present. By the mid-nineteenth century there was an astute awareness that America was assuming the features of a technical civilization. World's fairs, on both sides of the Atlantic, were powerful transmitters of this new face of America. They could inspire panegyrics, as in Walt Whitman's case, or a more brooding sense of spiritual loss, as in the case of Henry Adams. Abroad, the impact would be equally dual. Modernizing entrepreneurial elites would see America as involved in a project parallel to theirs. In the case of others, though, the view of America as a technical civilization would provide them with the ingredients of a discourse of cultural anti-Americanism. The very word *américanisation* in French dates from those times. It was Baudelaire who, on the occasion of the Exposition Universelle de Paris, in 1855, spoke of modern man, set on a course of technical materialism, as "so Americanized . . . that he has lost the sense of differences characterizing the phenomena of the physical and the moral world, of the natural and the supernatural."[9] And at the time of the second Exposition, in 1867, the Goncourt brothers remarked in their journal about "the universal exposition, the last blow in what is the Americanization of France . . ."[10] Industrial progress, as these critics saw it, ushered in an era in which quantity would replace quality and in which a mass culture feeding on standardization would erode established taste hierarchies. There are echoes of Tocqueville here, yet the eroding factor is no longer the egalitarian logic of a mass democracy; it is, rather, the logic of industrial progress. In both cases, though, whatever the precise link and evaluating angle, America had become the metonymy for modernity.

American Modernity in the Twentieth Century

Following two world wars, the global context in which France and the United States found themselves had drastically changed, affecting the sense of psychological distance that French intellectuals experienced toward the United States. From a remote fledgling civilization, intriguing precisely because it was so distant, America was now on its way to becoming the new hegemon on the world stage, and a little too close for comfort in the eyes of many Europeans. Ever since America's rise as an economic, cultural, and political force in the first half of the twentieth century, there had been a new shrillness to critical views about America, marked by an urgent call to arms in defense of European cultural values, as in the interbellum writings of Georges Duhamel and André Siegfried in France and of like-minded cultural conservatives in other European countries. The reaction in their case was antimodern, directed against modernity as it presented itself in its American guise. They set a tone that would continue into the post–World War II era.

Through its victorious presence in Europe, more strongly than ever before America confronted Europeans with its protean modernity. Europeans now had to respond to the American challenge in more than one area. The response could move between rejection and reception, but it was never solely cultural. To a Europe in search of new directions, America held out the example and provided guidance in the economic field, emphasizing economic growth and industrial efficiency, weaning Europe away from its protectionist instincts and old-fashioned managerial traditions. Politically, the United States sponsored the idea of a larger Atlantic community whose universe of discourse centered on democratic values and civil liberties. Militarily, in terms of collective security, it willingly entered into an "entangling alliance" under its hegemonic leadership, establishing a "Pax

Americana" that—at least within its sphere of dominance—also worked to transcend age-old European rivalries. And finally, to return to the cultural domain, through its physical presence in Europe as much as through cultural artifacts—such as Hollywood films, consumption goods, records, and advertising—America transmitted to Europe the tempting image of a mass-consumption society, the image of a "democracy of goods."

Given the plethora of options, people were often of more than two minds about the impact of American modernity. In search of cultural renewal, they could enthusiastically endorse the freedom they found in forms of American mass culture, or envy the informality and mobility of American social life, while at the same time begrudging America's political dominance. Others could welcome American leadership in political and economic life, while deploring the impact of American mass culture on European societies. In addition, over time these positions could change and sometimes merge. Then a rejection of America in one area could lead to a more general anti-Americanism.

An interesting case is that of Jean-Paul Sartre and Simone de Beauvoir. Both had visited the United States in the immediate postwar years, before the dividing line of the Cold War had hardened. Both were on the political left, in a rather anarchist vein; they were as yet unaffiliated to a political party, and they did not vote. They were antiauthoritarian and anticapitalist. Yet both were fascinated by America. They loved jazz, Hollywood movies, and the great American modernists in literature. Both loved the metropolitanism of New York. As Louis Menand wittily argues in his contribution to this volume, precisely this fascination facilitated a peculiarly French construction of the American as "this new man," a liberating antidote and alternative to Europeans mired in traditions of decadent introspection. As unreflecting men of action, Americans inspired a French construction of American culture and Americanism as almost prototypically existentialist. Yet, time and time again, there was the censorial voice of their left-wing conscience to rein in their enthusiasm. There is an ambivalence to their early views about America that is often reminiscent of the older repertoire that we have explored above.

Thus Beauvoir, having established her left-wing credentials by saying that America to her is the country where capitalist oppression has most odiously triumphed, goes on in this vein: "Nonetheless, beyond the good and the bad, life over there has something gigantic and unchained, which fascinated us."[11] In her choice of metaphors, using words like "gigantic" and "unchained," she clearly evokes two faces of American modernity: the towering one of a technical civilization, proudly representing itself in its skyscraping architecture (however corporate its auspices may be), and the one of America as empty space, sucking in Europeans while at the same time liberating them from the shackles of their home cultures.

Ever the dialectician, Sartre returns to old Tocquevillean ground when he tries to fathom how Americans manage to reconcile conformism and individualism: "Conditioned by a propaganda which does not emanate from the state but from society as a whole, cast in the framework of a collectivity that educates him constantly in being a pure American, the individual acts naturally like all the others." That dialectic allows the American "to feel at the same time the most rational and the most national; in showing himself at his most conformist he feels most free."[12] This is not a totalitarian condition; Sartre emphasizes, rather, the universalism of it all, which opens the culture to everyone of whatever background and nationality. It is a "homeless" rationalism, reinforced and further universalized by the very mobility of a mechanized society. Thus, to Sartre, "the Americans are conformists in liberty, depersonalized by rationalism, merging into one cult universal Reason and their particular Nation." Money and success, in this context, are not the mere product of cupidity. They are the symbolic means by which someone can "place himself, when faced with the mass of others, as an individual person."[13] Americans can always hope to regain their autonomy and to reach "an almost Nietzschean individualism symbolized by the skyscrapers in the clear sky of New York." This may not be exactly consonant with Crèvecoeur's thinking, yet there are similarities, in the sense that individual autonomy is seen as a daring modernist endeavor.

At the same time, if there are echoes here of Tocqueville's darker explorations of the tyranny of a majority in mass democracies, Sartre also presents observations that are more in line with the positive views of Tocqueville. Sartre notes, for example, that "the exterior signs of class are nonexistent" and that there exists "a truly human kindness that presides over the relations among classes."[14]

If Sartre managed to keep a sense of distance and balance, Beauvoir, in her *L'Amérique au jour le jour*, tends more clearly toward criticism. That may be due to her coming to America a year later, in 1947, when a climate of anti-Communist repression was building. There are many moments of rapture in her book, where the pace and energy of American life draw her along, yet throughout a censorial voice calls her back, a voice equally reminiscent of Marx and Tocqueville:

In this profusion of dresses, blouses, skirts, and coats, a French woman would be hard put to make a choice and not offend her taste. And then one begins to notice that underneath their multicolored wrappers all chocolates have the same taste of peanut, all bestsellers tell the same story. And why choose one toothpaste rather than another? There is an aftertaste of mystification in all this useless profusion. A thousand possibilities are open: yet they are all the same. A thousand choices allowed: all equivalent. Thus the American citizen will be able to consume his liberty inside the life that is imposed on him without so much as noticing that such a life itself is not free.[15]

Beauvoir's is a critique of American conformism that denounces America's vaunted republican liberty as a sham, its individual consumers as so many dupes of capitalism, and its industrial production as capable of producing nothing but spurious variety.

But for Sartre and Beauvoir, as well as for the French left-wing intelligentsia more generally, it was not until the 1950s that America would assume its place in a Manichaean world as an empire of evil. Interestingly, the dark side of Tocqueville's vision of America was picked up again in France with a vengeance. The rediscovery of his work in the United States had not only inspired the consensus view of a benign pluralism; it had also influenced the return of the theme of conformism to American social criticism, as exemplified by David Riesman's *The Lonely Crowd*, which presented the Americans of of the postwar era as "other-directed," as subordinate to peer-group guidance. Riesman's findings and those of other American critics, such as C. Wright Mills and William H. Whyte, led Beauvoir to reject Americans as a "nation of sheep," who were indeed "extéro-conditionnés" (French for "other-directed").[16]

It was not all Manichaeism on the French left, though. Michel Crozier, a self-described "pro-American leftist," had first visited the United States in 1946. As a sociologist whose work was mostly in the area of industrial sociology and human relations, he was well connected with the American academic world. He too would return to Tocquevillean concerns about the workings of the American Republic. In 1980 he published *Le mal américain*, which examines the country's plight following its many setbacks during the postwar era, from the Kennedy assassination to the Tehran hostage crisis. Several of Crozier's observations focus on the role of interest groups. For Tocqueville, such groups fulfilled a crucial function in preserving republican order. From Crozier's point of view, however, the United States today is no longer the country Tocqueville described: "Its voluntary associations have ceased to be a mainstay of a democracy constantly on the move but are now simply a means of self-defence for various interests. . . . This breakdown of community structures is what has made America a country full of anxiety."[17]

Given the year of publication, Crozier's gloomy analysis is something of an exception. Since the 1970s views of America among the French intelligentsia had undergone a remarkable change for the better. Not only had one pole of intellectual attraction—Soviet Russia—lost its force, but America had also redeemed itself through the way it handled its many torments. It had shown remarkable regenerative power as a republican order at the time of the Watergate crisis, and it clearly became a model to be emulated elsewhere in the world when in the 1980s it could claim renewed success in combining political and economic liberalism. Having shed their infatuation with the closed world of ideological thinking, French intellectuals were ready to appreciate the unideological cast of mind of the Americans. America had regained its power to exhilarate—culturally, politically, and economically.

In 1978, as almost a Crèvecoeur *redivivus*, another French nobleman, originally named Sanche de Gramont, published a personal memoir, *On Becoming American*. American modernity in its humanist version, promising individual regeneration, is central to Ted Morgan's narrative. "Americans are the true existentialists. An American is the sum of his undertakings. . . . He makes himself and is responsible for himself." Morgan asserts that "in old societies, people knew who they were, they were given cards of identity at birth, and they were expected to remain in their allotted compartments. In a new society, people asked themselves who they were and what they might become. It was a matter of finding one's natural place rather than an assigned place." Morgan is impressed by the eagerness with which Americans still join voluntary associations. Yet, unlike Tocqueville, who had chosen to see them as a stabilizing force amid the buzzing energy of America, Morgan sees "pure process; it is an open-ended system. . . . We are a people in transit." Morgan thus appears to merge two older varieties of American modernity into one: the promise of individual regeneration and the existential qualities of being open ended, ever offering empty space to be filled by new projects.[18]

The rediscovery of America as an existential counterpoint to Europe inspired more French authors. Edgar Morin may have set the tone in his *Journal de Californie*, published in 1970. Californian pop culture and the counterculture of the 1960s are the background to a rapturous existential travelogue: "I feel great bliss being in California . . . , it is also the exaltation of being inside the reconnaissance center of spaceship earth, of witnessing the decisive here-and-now of Man's adventure . . . here I am at home: here where new possible worlds take shape, where the guiding forces of humanity spring forth, where what in exaltation I might call the biological Genius is fermenting, a world in gestation."[19] Morin's exalted views verge on the postmodern, where Star Trek and similar space imagery are more evocative of "America" than anything "real" and down to earth.

If there is such a thing as a postmodern rendition of America as the site of the modern, Jean Baudrillard's book *Amérique*, published in 1986, comes close to filling that bill. In an era that has announced the death of the author, America has no more founding fathers. In an era of deconstructionism that has announced the total freedom of the reader, "America" has become a text that anyone is free to read at will. Baudrillard uses this freedom to the fullest possible extent. America has become pure space, sidereal, a realm for the imagination to roam free in.

If, to a visiting European intellectual, America still offers a shocking sense of alienation, Baudrillard now appraises it as a fountain of youth, a sacred fount. To him, Europe has become mired in its heritage of intellectual rituals, caught in rigid conceptual frames, decadent, incapable of an unmediated, direct confrontation with reality. America offers liberation from that conceptual imprisonment. "We will always remain nostalgic utopians, torn between the ideal and our reluctance to realize it. We declare everything to be possible, while never proclaiming its realization. Precisely the latter is what America claims to have achieved." Baudrillard goes on to say: "It is we who think that everything culminates in its transcendence and that nothing exists without first having been thought through as concept. Not only do they [the Americans] hardly care for that at all; they see the relationship in reverse. They don't care to conceptualize reality, but to realize the concept and to implement the ideas."[20]

We cannot but hear old echoes resounding in this statement. Baudrillard, after all, is not the first to hold that America has had the audacity to implement what had been thought out and dreamed of in Europe. It has shed off the old Europe, burdened by history, caught up in unreal structures of thought. Thus America was able to become the authentic expression of modernity, while Europe, in Baudrillard's words, will never be more than its dubbed or subtitled version. But there is more to Baudrillard's argument than this. In a sense, he seems to return to the 1960s, hankering for the libertarian rapture, the sense of instant gratification, unmediated by the intellect, which to so many at the time was the appeal of the counterculture. Much as he was on the left himself, as an ideologue he had missed out on the excitement of the moment. It took the disenchantment of the French left during the 1970s, its sense of ideological bankruptcy, for Baudrillard to become susceptible to the lure of American culture.

And once again, before our eyes, a romance unfolds, a game of cultural adultery, which so many French intellectuals have indulged in. They have a keen eye for all that is banal and vulgar in America, yet at the same time more than anyone else they are tempted by the vital élan, the shameless authenticity of American culture. These romances have one basic plot. It is always a case of a tired, elderly European turning toward America in the hope of regeneration, if not rejuvenation. America is unspoiled, primitive, youthful. It is unaware of itself. It is just there. It is Eden before the fall. Europeans have tasted the forbidden fruit—they are obsessed by knowledge and reflection—yet hope to lose themselves in America. Baudrillard is in a sense a twentieth-century Crèvecoeur, reaffirming America's regenerative potential. With all his metaphors and associations, he is still busy weaving America into an argument and a structure of concepts. He is still quintessentially the European, involving America in a world of preoccupations that are typically those of a French intellectual.

American Modernity in French Eyes: From Text to Subtext
Europeans, French observers included, have always been perplexed by two aspects of the American way with culture, two aspects that to them have represented the core of America's cultural otherness. One is its crass commercialism; the other, its irreverent attitude of cultural bricolage, recycling the culturally high and low, the vulgar and the sublime, in ways unfamiliar and shocking to European sensibilities. As for the alleged commercialism, what truly strikes Europeans is the blithe symbiosis between two cultural impulses that Europeans take to be incompatible: a democratic impulse and a commercial one. From early on, American intellectuals and artists agreed that for American culture to be American it would have to be democratic. It should appeal to the many, not the few. Setting itself up in contradistinction to Europe's stratified societies and the hierarchies of taste they engendered, America proclaimed democracy for the cultural realm as well. That in itself was enough to make Europeans frown. Could democratic culture ever be anything but vulgar, ever be more than the most common denominator of the people's tastes? Undeniably, there

were those in Europe who agreed with Americans that cultural production in the United States could not simply follow in the footsteps of Europeans and who were willing to recognize an American Homer in Walt Whitman, the country's poet of democracy. But even they were aghast at the ease with which the democratic impulse blended into the commercial. What escaped them was that in order to reach a democratic public, the American artist found himself in much the same situation as a merchant going to market. Particularly in the age of mechanical reproduction, when the market had to expand along with the growth in cultural supply, American culture became ever more aware of the commercial calculus. And, by the same token, it became ever more suspect in the eyes of European critics. Something made for profit, for money, could inherently never be of cultural value. This critical view has a long pedigree and is alive and well today.

The other repertoire of the European critique of American mass culture focuses on its spirit of blithe bricolage, of its anticanonical approach to questions of high culture versus low culture, or to matters of the organic holism of cultural forms. Again, some Europeans were tempted, if not convinced, by Whitmanesque experiments in recognizing and embracing the elevated in the lowly and the vulgar in the sublime, or by his experiments in formlessness. They were willing to see in this America's quest for a democratic, if not demotic, culture. But in the face of America's shameless appropriation of the European cultural heritage, taking it apart and reassembling it in ways that went against European views of the organic wholeness of their hallowed heritage, Europeans begged to differ. To them, the collage or reassemblage attitude that produced Hearst Castle, Caesar's Palace, or the architectural jumble of European quotations in some of America's high-rise buildings seemed proof that Americans could only look at European culture in the light of contemporaneity, as if it were one big mail-order catalog. It was all there at the same time, itemized and numbered, for Americans to pick and choose from. It was all reduced to the same level of usable bits and pieces, to be recycled, reassembled, and quoted at will.

Many European critics have seen in this an antihistorical, antimetaphysical, or antiorganicist bent of the American mind. Where Europeans tend toward an aesthetics that values closure, rules of organic cohesion, they see in Americans a tendency to explode such views. If Americans have a canon, it is one that values open-endedness in the recombination of individual components. Americans prefer constituent elements over their composition. Whether on television or in American football, European ideas of flow and continuity get cut up and jumbled: in individual time slots, as on television, or in individual plays, as in football. Examples abound, and many will likely come to the reader's mind. Now, potentially, the result of this bricolage view of cultural production might be endless variety. Yet what Europeans tended to see was only spurious variety, fake diversity, a lack of authenticity. This litany kept resounding in a long chorus of French voices, from Georges Duhamel and François Mauriac in the interwar years to Jean-Paul Sartre and more particularly Simone de Beauvoir after World War IIand into the 1950s. Such French views are far from dated yet. They still inform current critiques of contemporary mass culture. Yet, apparently, the repertoire is so widespread and well known that often no explicit mention of America is needed anymore. America has become a subtext. In the following I propose to give two examples, both of them French. One illustrates the dangers of commercialism in the production of culture; the other, the baneful effects of America's characteristic modularizing mode in cultural production, its spirit of bricolage.

Commercialism and Culture

In our present age of globalization, with communication systems such as the Internet spanning the world, national borders have become increasingly porous. They no longer serve as cultural barriers that one can raise at will to fend off cultural intrusions from abroad. It is increasingly hard to erect them as a cultural "Imaginot" line (forgive the pun) in defense of a national cultural identity. Yet old instincts die hard.

At every moment in the recent past when the liberalization of trade and flows of communication has been discussed in international meetings, the French have raised the issue of cultural protection. They have repeatedly insisted on exempting cultural goods, such as film and television, from the logic of free trade. They do this because, as they see it, France represents cultural "quality" and therefore may help to maintain diversity in the American-dominated international market for ideas. The subtext for such defensive strategies is not so much the fear of opening France's borders to the world as it is the anxiety about letting American culture wash across the country. Given America's dominant role in world markets for popular culture, as well as its quasi-imperial place in the communications web of the Internet, globalization to many French people is a Trojan horse. For them, globalization means Americanization.

During the late 1990s, as attempts were made to start a new round of negotiations on the further liberalization of world trade, France was up in arms again. The French minister of culture published a piece in the French daily newspaper *Le Monde*, once more making the French case for a cultural exemption from free trade. A week later one of France's leading intellectual lights, Pierre Bourdieu, joined the fray in a piece published in the same newspaper.[21] It was the text of an address delivered on October 11, 1999, to the International Council of the Museum of Television and Radio in Paris. Bourdieu chose to address his audience as "representing the true masters of the world," those whose control of global communication networks gives them not political or economic power but what he calls "symbolic power," that is, power over people's minds and imaginations gained through cultural artifacts—books, films, and television programs—that they produce and disseminate. This power is increasingly globalized through international market control, mergers and consolidations, and a revolution in communications technology. Bourdieu briefly considers the fashionable claim that the newly emerging structures, aided by the digital revolution, will bring endless cultural diversity, catering to the cultural demands of specific niche markets. Bourdieu rejects this out of hand; what he sees is an increasing homogenization and vulgarization of cultural supply driven by a logic that is purely commercial, not cultural. Aiming at profit maximization, market control, and ever larger audiences, the "true masters of the world" gear their products to the most common denominator that defines their audience. What the world gets is more soap operas, expensive blockbuster movies organized around special effects, and books whose success is measured by sales, not by intrinsic cultural merit.

It is a Manichaean world that Bourdieu conjures up. True culture, as he sees it, is the work of individual artists who view their audience as being posterity, not the throngs at the box office. In the cultural resistance that artists over the centuries have put up against the purely commercial view of their work, they have managed to carve out a social and cultural domain whose organizing logic is at right angles to that of the economic market. As Bourdieu puts it: "Reintroducing the sway of the 'commercial' in realms that have been set up, step by step, against it means endangering the highest works of mankind."

Never in his address does Bourdieu rail against America as the site of such dismal modernity, yet the logic of his argument is reminiscent of many earlier French views of American culture, a culture emanating from a country that has never shied away from merging the cultural and the commercial (or, for that matter, the cultural and the democratic). Yet blood runs thicker than water. Great artists, and Bourdieu lists several writers and filmmakers, "would not exist the way they do without this literary, artistic, and cinematographic international whose seat is [present tense!] situated in Paris. No doubt because there, for strictly historical reasons, the microcosm of producers, critics, and informed audiences, necessary for its survival, has long since taken shape and has managed to survive." Bourdieu thus manages to have his cake and eat it too, arrogating a place for Paris as the true seat of a modernity in high culture. In his construction of a global cultural dichotomy lurks an established French *parti pris*. More than that, however, his reading of globalization as Americanization by stealth blinds him to the way in which French intellectuals and artists before him have discovered, adapted, and adopted forms of American commercial culture, such as Hollywood movies.

In his description of the social universe that sustains a cultural international in Paris, Bourdieu mentions the infrastructure of art-film houses, of a *cinémathèque*, of eager audiences and informed critics, such as those writing for the *Cahiers du cinéma*. He seems oblivious to the fact that in the 1950s precisely this potent ambience for cultural reception led to the French discovery of Hollywood movies as authentic examples of the "cinéma d'auteur," of true film art showing the hand of individual makers, now acclaimed masters in the pantheon of film history. Such works are held and regularly shown in Bourdieu's vaunted *cinémathèque* (the famous Paris film archive) and his art-film houses. They have therefore been perceived, like much other despised commercial culture coming from America, within frameworks of cultural appropriation and appreciation more typically French, or European, than American. They may have been misread in the process as works of individual "auteurs" more than as products of the Hollywood studio system. That they were the products of a cultural infrastructure totally at variance with the one Bourdieu deems essential may have escaped French fans during the 1950s. It certainly escapes Bourdieu now. This should only make us more intellectually cautious before we accede to facile readings of commercial culture as necessarily a threat to things we hold dear.

The Modularizing Mind and the World Wide Web

Among other dreams, the Internet has inspired those of a return to a world of total intertextuality, of the reconstitution of the full body of human thinking and writing. It would be the return to the "City of Words," the labyrinthine library that, like a nostalgic recollection, has haunted the human imagination since the age of the mythical library of Babylon. Tony

Tanner has used the metaphor of the city of words to describe the central quest inspiring the literary imagination of the twentieth century.[22] For Tanner, one author who epitomizes this quest is Jorge Luis Borges. It is the constructional power of the human mind that moves and amazes Borges. His stories are full of the strangest architecture, including the endless variety of lexical architecture to which humans throughout history have devoted their time—philosophical theories, theological disputes, encyclopedias, religious beliefs, critical interpretations, novels, and every other kind of book. While having a deep feeling for the shaping and abstracting powers of the mind, Borges also has a profound sense of how nightmarish the resultant structures might become. In one of his stories, the library of Babel is referred to by the narrator as the "universe," and one can take it as a metaphysical parable of all the difficulties of deciphering humanity's encounters. On the other hand, Babel remains the most famous example of the madness in the human rage for architecture, and books are only another form of building. In this library every possible combination of letters and words is to be found, with the result that there are fragments of sense separated by "leagues of insensate cacophony, of verbal farragos and incoherencies." Most books are "mere labyrinths of letters." Since everything that language can do and express is somewhere in the library, "the clarification of the basic mysteries of humanity" is expected. The "necessary vocabularies and grammars" must be discoverable in the lexical totality. Yet the attempt at discovery and detection is maddening; the story is full of the sadness, sickness, and madness of the pathetic figures who roam around the library as around a vast prison.[23]

What do Borges's fantasies tell us about the Promethean potential of a restored city of words in cyberspace? During an international colloquium in Paris at the Bibliothèque Nationale de France, held on June 3–4, 1998, scholars and library heads discussed the implications of a virtual memory bank on the Internet, connecting the holdings of all of the great libraries in the world. Some saw it as a dream come true. In his opening remarks Jean-Pierre Angremy referred to the library of Babel as imagined by Borges, while ignoring its nightmarish side: "When it was proclaimed that the library would hold all books, the first reaction was one of extravagant mirth. Everyone felt like holding an intact and secret treasure." The perspective, as Angremy saw it, was extravagant indeed: all the world's knowledge at your command, like an endless scroll across your computer screen. Others, like Jacques Attali, spiritual father of the idea of digitizing the holdings of the new Bibliothèque Nationale, took a similarly positive view.

Whatever the form of the library, real or virtual, it would always be "a reservoir of books." Others were not so sure. They foresaw a mutation of our traditional relationship with the written text, whereby new manipulations and competences would make our reading habits as antiquated as the reading of papyrus scrolls is to us. As Michel Melot, a longtime member of the Conseil Supérieur des Bibliothèques, pointed out, randomness becomes the rule. The coherence of traditional discursive presentation will tend to give way to what is fragmented, incomplete, disparate, if not incoherent. In his view, the patchwork or cut-and-paste approach will become the dominant mode of composition.[24]

These darker views are suggestive of a possible American imprint of the Internet. They are strangely reminiscent of an earlier cultural critique in Europe of the ways in which American culture would affect European civilization. Particularly the contrast seen between the act of reading traditional books and that of reading texts downloaded from the Internet recalls a contrast between Europe and America that constitutes a staple in the work of many European critics of American culture. Europe, in this view, stands for organic cohesion, for logical and stylistic closure, whereas America tends toward fragmentation and recombination, in a mode of blithe cultural bricolage, exploding every prevailing cultural canon in Europe. Furthermore, we recognize the traditional European fear of American culture as a leveling force, bringing everything down to the surface level of the total interchangeability of cultural items, oblivious of their intrinsic value and of cultural hierarchies of high versus low.[25]

Yet in the views presented at the Paris symposium, we find no reference to America. Is this because America is a subtext, a code instantly recognized by French intellectuals? Or is it because the logic of the Internet and of digital intertextuality have a cultural impact in their own right, similar to the impact of American culture, but this time unrelated to any American agency? I would suggest a Weberian answer. It seems to be undeniably the case that there is a *Wahlverwandtschaft*—an elective affinity—between the logic of the Internet and the American cast of mind, which makes for an easier, less anguished acceptance and use of the new medium among Americans than among a certain breed of Europeans.

After reviewing these two exhibits of cultural anti-Americanism as a subtext, taking French attitudes as its typical expression, what conclusions can we draw? One is that fears of an American way with culture, due to either its commercial motives or its modularizing instincts, arise from attitudes that are too narrow, too hidebound. As I have noted, time and time again French artists and intellectuals, after initial neglect and rejection, have discovered redeeming cultural value in American jazz, in American hard-boiled detective novels, in rap music, in Disney World, and other forms of American mass culture.[26] Typically enough, they developed critical lexicons, constructing canonic readings of American cultural genres. Making forms of American culture part of a European critical discourse, and measuring them in terms of European taste hierarchies, is a kind of cultural appropriation. It is a process of subtle and nuanced appropriation that takes us far beyond any facile, across-the-board rejection of American culture due to its commercial agency.

How about the second reason for rejection, America's blithe leveling of cultural components to the level of interchangeable bits and pieces? As I argued in my review of the second exhibit, America may have been more daring when it ventures out in this field, yet we can find parallels and affinities with Europe's cultural traditions. A catalytic disenchantment of the world, as part of a larger secularization of Europe's Weltanschauung, had been eating away at traditional views of God-ordained order before Americans joined in.[27] Again, facile rejections of what many mistakenly see as Americanization by stealth, when confronted with more radical manifestations of the modularization of the world, miss the point. I suggested the possibility that what the World Wide Web brings us in terms of endless digital dissection and reassemblage of "texts" may have more to do with the inherent logic of the digital revolution than with any American agency. A more or less open aversion to this happening should be seen, therefore, as antimodernity rather than as anti-Americanism. It reveals a resentment against the relentless modernization of our world that has been a continuing voice of protest in the history of Western civilization.

It is a resentment, though, that should make us think twice. Clearly, we are not all Americans. We do not all freely join their Promethean exploration of the frontiers of modernity. If Europeans give voice to trepidation when confronting the emergence of new forms of modernity, America today is often only a tacit reference. But not always, as in the case of America's neoconservative project to bring democracy to Iraq. Perhaps it is for Europeans to play Epimetheus to the American Prometheus and reflect on history before dashing forward into the future. Among French observers, Albert Camus and Jean-Paul Sartre commented on the absence of a sense of the tragic in America, the sense of noble pursuits turning into their opposite. It may be for Europeans to remind Americans of the price of hubris and of the old Greek wisdom that the gods strike with blindness those they wish to ruin.[28]

NOTES

1. A good illustration of this angle of perception is Serge Guilbaut's *How New York Stole the Idea of Modern Art: Abstract Expressionism, Freedom, and the Cold War*, trans. Arthur Goldhammer (Chicago: University of Chicago Press, 1983).

2. J. Hector St. John de Crèvecoeur, *Letters from an American Farmer* (London: J. M. Dent & Sons, 1912), 39, 42.

3. Ibid., 40.

4. Ibid., 39.

5. Alexis de Tocqueville, *De la démocratie en Amérique*, 4 vols. (Paris: Librairie de C. Gosselin, 1835–40), 1:5.

6. Strictly speaking, my use of the concept of Manifest Destiny is a bit of an anachronism. The term would not be introduced until 1845 by John O'Sullivan in his *New York Morning News*. Yet it may well serve to capture a mood that was already prevalent at the time of Tocqueville's observations and reflections.

7. Jean-Jacques Ampère, *Promenade en Amérique; États-Unis—Cuba—Mexique*, 2 vols. (Paris: Michel Lévy frères, 1855); Charles Adolphe de Pineton, marquis de Chambrun, *Impressions of Lincoln and the Civil War: A Foreigner's Account*, trans. Aldebert de Chambrun (New York: Random House, 1952); Oscar Comettant, *Voyage pittoresque et anecdotique dans le Nord et le Sud des Etats-Unis d'Amérique* (Paris: A. Laplace, 1866); E. Duvergier de Hauranne, *Les Etats-Unis pendant la Guerre de Sécession: Récit d'un journaliste français* (1866) (Paris: Calmann-Lévy, 1990); Xavier Eyma, *Les deux Amériques, histoire, moeurs et voyages* (Paris: D. Giraud, 1853).

8. *Atala*, a Romantic epic by the French author François-Auguste-René de Chateaubriand, was published in 1801 and widely read on both sides of the Atlantic. It evokes life among American Indians, seen as "noble savages," at a time in the early eighteenth century when the decline of their civilization was near.

9. Quoted in Denis Lacorne, Jacques Rupnik, and Marie-France Toinet, eds., *L'Amérique dans les têtes: Un siècle de fascinations et d'aversions* (Paris: Hachette Littérature, 1986), 61.

10. Ibid., 62.

11. Simone de Beauvoir, *La force de l'age* (Paris: Gallimard, 1960), 160.

12. Jean-Paul Sartre, *Situations III* (Paris: Gallimard, 1949), 82.

13. Ibid., 96.

14. Michel Contat and Michel Rybalka, *Les écrits de Sartre* (Paris: Gallimard, 1974), 122.

15. Simone de Beauvoir, *L'Amérique au jour le jour* (1948) (Paris: Gallimard, 1954), 27.

16. Simone de Beauvoir, *La force des choses* (Paris: Gallimard, 1963), 130–33; C. Wright Mills, *White Collar: The American Middle Classes* (New York: Oxford University Press, 1951); David Riesman, *The Lonely Crowd: A Study of the Changing American Character* (Garden City, N.Y.: Doubleday, 1953); William H. Whyte, *The Organization Man* (New York: Simon and Schuster, 1956).

17. Michel Crozier, *The Trouble with America*, trans. Peter Heinegg (Berkeley: University of California Press, 1984), 85.

18. Ted Morgan, *On Becoming American* (1978; repr., New York: Paragon House, 1988), 4, 72, 310.

19. Edgar Morin, *Journal de Californie* (Paris: Seuil, 1970), 250.

20. Jean Baudrillard, *Amérique* (Paris: Editions Grasset, 1986), 156, 167.

21. Pierre Bourdieu, "Questions aux vrais maîtres du monde," *Le Monde* (sélection hebdomadaire), October 23, 1999, 1, 7.

22. Tony Tanner, *City of Words: American Fiction, 1950–1970* (New York: Harper Collins, 1971).

23. For the Borges quotations, see Tanner, *City of Words*, 41.

24. For my summary of the proceedings at the Paris colloquium, I have used a report published in *Le Monde* (sélection hebdomadaire), June 20, 1998, 13.

25. For a fuller analysis of the metaphorical deep structure underlying the European critique of American culture, see my *If You've Seen One, You've Seen the Mall* (Urbana: University of Illinois Press, 1996).

26. Again, I would like to refer the reader to Louis Menand's chapter in this volume.

27. I argue this more at length in the concluding chapter of *If You've Seen One, You've Seen the Mall*, which is titled "Americanization: What Are We Talking About?"

28. American foreign policy under President George W. Bush may have caused the resurfacing of a much more articulate and open anti-Americanism. From subtext it has moved back to being the text in a spate of recent French publications. See, among other books, Philippe Roger, *L'ennemi américain: Généalogie de l'anti-américanisme français* (Paris: Le Seuil, 2002), and Emmanuel Todd, *Après l'empire: Essai sur la décomposition du système américain* (Paris: Gallimard, 2002).

★ ★ ★ ★

★ **Suffering Sisters?**

★ *American Feminists and the Problem of*

★ *Female Genital Surgeries*

In 1985, when I was a student in Cairo, I went to hear a visiting American lecturer. Angela Davis was in town, speaking to an audience of about fifty women and men, under the sponsorship of the Arab Women's Solidarity Association. Near the end of her lecture, Davis explained that she was in Egypt to research her contribution to an anthology commemorating the United Nations Decade for Women (1975–85). Each essay was assigned to a different feminist from around the world who would focus on the condition of women in a country other than her own: Egyptian feminist Nawal El Saadawi would write about "women and education" in England; Germaine Greer would cover "women and politics" in Cuba; and Davis had agreed to write about "women and sex" in Egypt.

When Davis explained the purpose of her visit, there was an immediate outcry. Much of the audience was furious that Davis had agreed to focus on *sex*. They protested that feminists from the West, and American feminists in particular, were so obsessed with the veil, female circumcision, and sexual matters in general that they were distorting the real struggles of Egyptian women and their sisters in Africa and the Arab world. Though Davis insisted that she intended to take a critical view of the topic, to connect sexual issues to larger concerns, her listeners were not convinced, or, rather, it did not matter. By the mid-1980s they had grown deeply frustrated by this "interest" on the part of American women. As Davis eventually reported, one woman at a similar meeting minced no words: "Women in the West should know that we have a stand in relation to them concerning our issues and our problems. We reject their patronizing attitude. It is connected with inbuilt mechanisms of colonialism and a sense of superiority. Maybe some of them don't do it consciously, but it is there. They decide what problems we have, how we should face them, without even possessing the tools to know our problems."[1]

Davis tried hard in her essay to be sensitive to the issues of cultural domination that were so much on the minds of Egyptian women. In addition to writing on work, education, and divorce laws, she gave attention to women activists who organized against U.S. economic and political influence in their country. But, obedient to both her assignment and the dictates of the larger discourse about "Muslim women," she also wrote in detail about the increasing practice of veiling and the decreasing practice of clitoridectomy. In doing so, Davis, an African American Communist, also implicitly took a stand that marked her in the eyes of Egyptian activists as American, as Western, perhaps even as imperialist.

What Davis well knew, and what the anger of the women in Cairo made clear, was that any focus on female circumcision and veiling placed her in the middle of the heated debate between first and third world feminists about the global politics of feminism. In the 1970s and 1980s, American and European feminists were increasingly riveted by the practice of what is today generally referred to as "female genital cutting"—practices that alter the labia major, the labia minor, and/or the clitoris.[2] For more than thirty years—from the early 1970s, when *Ms.* magazine began reporting the "outrage" of clitoridectomy, concern about the sexual oppression of women in the Middle East and Africa has been a consistent issue for U.S. feminists. Ideas about the nature of Islam have never been far from this discussion, since, as I outline below, popular analyses in the United States and Europe have often linked Islam with the practice of clitoridectomy, even though it is not practiced in most Muslim countries outside of Africa. More broadly, the genital cutting debates have been conducted in the context of a general perception among Americans that Islam is particularly oppressive to women, so that a concern about women's rights is often part of discussions of U.S. relationships with the Muslim world—from the fascination with the harem in the early part of the twentieth century, to the hostility provoked by the Iranian revolution in 1979, to the shocked reaction to the veiling and extreme seclusion of women in Afghanistan, which in 2001 became one central argument for the overthrow of the Taliban.

Scholars have written a good deal about the horror and outrage expressed by Western women and the angry or ambivalent reactions of women's rights activists in Africa and the Middle East. But far less explored is *why* the topic of clitoridectomy became a major issue for American feminists in the 1980s.[3] Those practices were hardly new. In this essay, I argue that the issue captured the imagination of feminists in the United States for reasons that emerged from particular intellectual and political debates within U.S. feminism as much as from a new global consciousness about women. At the very least, the two developed hand in hand, in ways that cannot be fully untangled.

Two kinds of transnational encounters were most relevant to this developing concern. First were literal encounters at the international women's conferences sponsored by the United Nations from 1975 to 1985, when a self-conscious international women's movement emerged. Second were a set of indirect but significant cultural encounters made possible by particular structures of feminist reading—that is, the embrace in the United States of particular Arab women writers as emblematic of this emerging "global sisterhood."[4] Those writers became popular among American feminists precisely because they seemed to speak to, and authenticate, concerns that were animating feminist debates about sexuality in the United States. That popularity had a price, however, as Arab and Muslim feminists frequently found that their larger concerns about international politics and religious stereotyping were being ignored.

During the 1970s and 1980s, the question of imperialism was at the heart of debates about feminism, both within and outside the United States. In this context, "Americanism" should be understood as more than just a national identity, or a belief in the superiority of American democracy. Rather, it marks an assertive sense of that identity as an ideology, a way of life that is both peculiarly American and eminently exportable. This ideology often includes an implicit or explicit representation of "other" women as extraordinarily oppressed, and of Muslim women, in particular, as subjugated by their culture and creed.

This is not to say that American or Western women were inevitably imperialist or that Arab or Muslim women always resented them. In fact, this was a period of productive engagement, as U.S. feminists struggled with their counterparts around the world to achieve a broader vision of women's liberation, one that took into account the realities of race, global capitalism, and cultural difference.

Yet American feminists also played a role—sometimes challenging, often complicit—in constructing the image of Muslims and Arabs that has framed U.S. policies and actions in the Middle East, which have incurred great anger and frustration in the Arab world. For U.S. feminists, it was precisely in their attempts to think globally that they were often confronted with their own Americanism, in all its problematic assumptions about the exemplary nature of American values—in particular, the value of American feminism. As a result, the politics of u.s. feminism and the dangers of "Americanism" have never been entirely separate.[5]

Starting in the late 1970s, a number of American feminist writers—including Angela Davis, Kate Millet, Mary Daly, Andrea Dworkin, Marilyn French, and Alice Walker—took up the topic of female circumcision. It was, they declared, a violation of women's basic rights to control their own bodies. In important ways, this interest was part of a genuine attempt to construct a more globally conscious feminism. Many u.s. feminists had first worked as activists in the movement against the Vietnam war, or in the Student Nonviolent Coordinating Committee (sncc) and other civil rights organizations, which gradually identified themselves with anticolonial struggles in Africa and elsewhere. They were convinced that all politics must in some sense be global: civil rights were human rights, and human rights were under attack all over the world.

This vision was not unique to feminists. In fact, female circumcision was brought to international attention just at the moment when a larger human rights movement was gathering steam.[6] With the founding of Amnesty International in the early 1960s, the un "Declaration of Universal Human Rights" (1948) found a new kind of grassroots, activist support. Soon the language of human rights was taken up across the political spectrum. In the late 1960s sncc redesignated itself a "human rights" organization, as a way of signifying its anticolonial commitments.[7] At about the same time, Alexander Solzhenitsyn published the extraordinary *Gulag Archipelago*, which helped make the oppression of "human rights" in the Soviet Union an international issue, one that was quickly taken up by anti-Communists on the right and in the center of American politics.[8] In the presidential campaign of 1976, Jimmy Carter made the promotion of human rights a main goal of the foreign policy he proposed. Thus, by the mid-1970s the groundwork for thinking of women's rights as "universal"—because they were "human rights"—was very much in place.[9]

When Robin Morgan, one of the founders of *Ms.*, published *Sisterhood Is Global* in 1984, she did so out of the belief that American feminism was desperately needed to promote the human rights of women around the world. The bulk of the book was a collection of essays about women's lives in dozens of different countries, written by activists and writers from each of the nations represented. But the intellectual heart of the book was Morgan's introduction—a tour de force of angry, self-confident, globe-spanning manifesto-making. Morgan acknowledged that some people had tried to define feminism as "Western" or "imperialist." But she dismissed those arguments with quotes from the book's contributors, all of whom were self-defined feminists from outside the United States. Morgan made a broad set of assertions about the universal nature of women's oppression, grounded in fairly simple, sometimes simplistic, ideas about the nature of "patriarchy." In Morgan's view, all women struggled with versions of the same issues, and it was the power relation of gender that underlay and enabled all other relations. If the promotion of human rights was a necessary goal, gender equality had to be central to that project.

Morgan's anthology, with all its flaws and bold hopes for a universal vision of women's liberation, was a prime example of how a significant strand of American feminism was aiming to become something else—not *American* feminism so much as the American branch of a global movement. But by the mid-1980s that vision had already been severely strained by the experiences of U.S. feminists who attended a highly visible series of gatherings on global women's issues—the multiple UN "Decade for Women" conferences that began in the mid-1970s and extended into the 1990s. These conferences became a central site for negotiations over the definitions and priorities of an emerging transnational women's movement, a movement that, in many cases, did not actually define itself as feminist. From the beginning, the UN-sponsored events were freighted with diverse constituencies and competing agendas, including the relative importance of economic development and debates over such issues as apartheid and the Israeli occupation of the West Bank. But, inevitably, questions of sexuality were key, in large part because women activists disagreed strongly about whether those issues should be on the agenda at all.

Some delegates from the global South argued that, for the vast majority of women, poverty, illiteracy, and impure water were far more significant issues than what one representative called "luxury issues," such as equal pay for equal work or women's rights to their own bodies.[10] The U.S. delegation in particular was consistently accused of being aggressive in pushing gender equality and issues of sexual liberation and of being out of touch with women from poorer countries. The lines were not always as stark as some of the rhetoric suggested: many women, including Americans, agreed on the need to improve women's health, to foster economic cooperatives, and to boost literacy.[11] Still, tensions were palpable. In one workshop in 1975, where Western feminists were criticized, an angry American stood up and asked, "Have I been put down by the men in my country for fifty-two years only to be put down again here by all of you?"[12]

Nothing so polarized first and third world women at the conferences as clitoridectomy.[13] By 1980 the practice was already a hot issue for U.S. feminists. In March of that year, *Ms.* published a detailed cover story on the "crime of genital mutilation," written by editors Robin Morgan and Gloria Steinem. The authors put forth a typology of various forms of genital surgery, from the "Sunna" practice of cutting off the tip of the clitoris to the more severe forms of infibulation in the Sudan and other parts of Africa, in which the entire clitoris and labia were cut away. For the editors of *Ms.*, female circumcision was part of a global continuum of the sexual oppression of women that included the veil, enforced virginity, sexual abuse, marginalization of women's pleasure, and the media's commodification of women's bodies.[14]

At both the 1980 and 1985 UN conferences, multiple workshops were devoted to the subject of "genital mutilation." The sessions were attended by scores of American and European women, many of whom, according to one observer, "seemed visibly shocked" to learn of the practice.[15] Several Arab and African feminists, including the novelist Nawal El Saadawi, spoke at these workshops, arguing that women like them had to speak out about the health dangers and sexual consequences of clitoridectomy. Nonetheless, Arab and African women were frustrated by the fact that women activists from the United States and Europe flocked to the meetings and walked out expressing outrage and horror. One group of African women issued a statement condemning the "new crusaders," arguing that Western women were exploiting third world women's lives for their own agendas. They called on women from the West to stop focusing on circumcision and described the workshops as "ill-timed interference, maternalism, ethnocentrism, and misuse of power." At the same time, they also called on women from the third world to "drop the veil of modesty" that prevented them from critiquing traditional practices.[16] Thus it was that female circumcision or female genital mutilation—even the terms revealed competing interpretations of the practice—caused anger and recrimination on all sides. Even El Saadawi, who was unstinting in her critique of the practice, referred pointedly to ways in which American feminists in particular seemed to exude a "feeling of superior humanity" and a "glow of satisfaction" when they encountered third world women.[17]

Most U.S. feminists defended themselves against such charges, arguing that they were not ethnocentric or nationalist, but appropriately internationalist. In their view, if threats to justice and the full recognition of women's status were everywhere due to patriarchy, such threats should be met everywhere by struggles for women's rights, and those struggles would be fundamentally similar. This internationalism should not be construed as merely nationalism in disguise; these first world feminists argued that all women, not just Americans, must achieve a consciousness of liberation. But their presumption was profoundly *un*conscious of power dynamics among women, including the international power of the United States that made it possible for American feminists to set the terms of the international feminist debate.

The commitment of American feminists to a universalist vision of sexual liberation had its origins in the heady days of the new women's movement of the late 1960s, when political theorizing and sexual experimentation went hand in hand. Writers such as Anne Koedt demolished the "myth of the vaginal orgasm" and called for more attention to the specifics of female pleasure, including its potential autonomy from men.

But the exploration of women's sexuality was divisive as well as empowering because sexual liberation came to mean quite distinct things to different groups of feminists. By the early 1980s the politics of sexuality was the most hotly contested issue for American feminists, and the "clitoris," in particular, had taken on a profoundly political status, as feminists argued about the relative status of "pleasure" and "danger" in the sexual experiences of women.

As this debate deepened, activists and thinkers on both sides of the pleasure/danger divide—a conflict between "pro-sex" feminists and "anti-porn" feminists—came to see the clitoris as a kind of feminist icon, a generalized signifier for women's sexual, and thus personal, autonomy. The issue was ripe for export, and many u.s. feminists were all too ready to have the clitoris—and the question of whether it was mutilated or intact—stand in for the status of Muslim women (or African and Arab women) writ large. Before long, the bodies of Arab/African/Muslim women, transformed into signifiers of sexual oppression, would figure centrally in the iconography of feminist sexual politics in the United States. American feminists' investment in the politics of genital cutting must be seen in the context of the deep divisions over how to define and create a workable sexual politics for themselves. Arriving on the global stage, they were conflicted and angry about a range of issues, but they found in their shared outrage over female genital cutting a rare source of common ground.

In 1982 a group of American feminists held a now famous, or infamous, conference at Barnard College called "Towards a Politics of Sexuality."

That conference and the book that emerged from it were interventions in an already highly charged debate. Many U.S. feminists believed it was crucial for women to refuse sexual objectification yet still claim their sexual power by exploring various types of experiences—lesbianism, non-monogamy, and sex with men that was more oriented to female desire. Conference organizers wanted to develop a "pro-sex" position that did not ignore the dangers of rape or pornography or the larger critique of heterosexuality as the only "normal" institution. What they hoped to create, as Carol Vance wrote in her introduction to the conference anthology, was a movement "that spoke as powerfully in favor of sexual pleasure as it did against sexual danger."[18]

For these women, the celebration of the clitoris as the site of female sexuality meant that heterosexuality was no longer mandatory; feminists could and should form a new sexual order based on their own experiences of desire and fulfillment. As historian Jane Gerhard puts it: "Clitoral stimulation resulted in orgasm for women, and this clitoral orgasm, whether stimulated by men or women, became the marker of 'the feminist.' "[19] Female sexual pleasure made its home on a remapped female body, and that home was joyfully reoccupied by sex-positive feminists, both gay and straight.

Some activists, however—those who would later be defined as "cultural feminists"—argued that the enthusiasm for untrammeled sexual liberation was naive. Women, in their view, were fundamentally different from men: less aggressive and competitive, more focused on connection with others, less "goal-driven" than "process-oriented." Women's sexuality was also different: the male-defined focus on orgasm denied a more female-defined focus on intimacy and love. One manifesto, for example, argued that the focus on more and better orgasms was "anti-political liberal sexual propaganda" that ignored the problem of male domination.[20] The clitoris still mattered; it was proof of an authentic female difference and a site of pleasure not defined by men. But for feminists like Kate Millet, Andrea Dworkin, Mary Daly, and Marilyn French, what Dworkin called the "political nature of male sexuality" was the key issue; it operated on a continuum that included control of women's bodies, narrow definitions of beauty, pornography, mutilation, violence, and rape.

The heated debates about sexuality among American feminists often seemed merely a domestic matter, mostly contained inside national boundaries (with a few French and British theorists added to the mix). Erica Jong's heroine in *Fear of Flying*, the popular feminist sex novel published in

1973, might travel abroad with her lover and try to "find herself" in Paris, but her sexual quest was clearly defined as that of a middle-class white American woman with as many choices as problems. Similarly, the charge that women's liberation was becoming too focused on sex was often made by American women of color about white feminists. Writers and activists including Audre Lorde, Cherrie Moraga, Alice Walker, and Gloria Anzaldua wrote a great deal about sexual freedom, but they also argued that white feminists too easily presumed that gender definitions and sexual politics— not racial discrimination or poverty—were the foremost problems affecting the majority of women.[21]

Still, no one in this debate maintained that sexuality was unimportant. American feminists of all races kept returning to questions about the "universals" of gender: Was sexual domination by men inevitable? Did women value intimacy over orgasm? Did feminists in other countries highlight issues of female desire? Those questions led Americans to look outward, to compare the diverse realities of women's lives in the United States with those of women in other parts of the world.

In particular, they looked to the Middle East, where issues of sex and power seemed, at least to American eyes, to be both highly visible and symbolically charged. A central source was writings of and about Arab women, which soon became part of the required reading of a feminist education. In the 1980s and early 1990s, scores of popular and academic books on the subject were published. There were outraged and one-sided tracts like Julie Minces's *The House of Obedience: Women in Arab Society*, as well as more serious works that presented the "voices" of Middle Eastern women, and a range of academic studies, some of which crossed over into the popular press.[22]

Interest grew particularly intense in the wake of the hostage crisis in Iran. When Islamists under the Ayatollah Khomeini overthrew the shah of Iran in 1979, and then took more than fifty Americans hostage, the U.S. media were consumed by the return of the veil and limits on women's public activities in Iran. The news reports often served, implicitly or explicitly, as evidence of the moral corruption of the Islamic government and as justification for the previous American support for the secular shah.[23]

American feminists soon turned to the novels, memoirs, and analytical essays of their counterparts in the Arab and Muslim world. Books by the Moroccan theorist Fatima Mernissa and the Lebanese novelist Hanan al-

Shaykh were widely reviewed in the mainstream and feminist press and became best sellers in women's bookstores. Both wrote about the inhibitions and limitations imposed on women in the Middle East; they embraced female sexuality and criticized aspects of Islam. Although their portraits were far more nuanced than most U.S. reviewers acknowledged, they spoke the language of American feminism, sold well, and gained international recognition.

It was Nawal El Saadawi, however, whose books most fully captured the imagination of a generation of American feminists. El Saadawi became for Americans an exemplary—perhaps *the* exemplary—Arab and Muslim feminist. In her writings, U.S. feminists who were looking outward found an ally. Female sexuality and clitoridectomy were central themes in her work, and her novels featured tough, uncompromising heroines who challenged male power. Just as important, El Saadawi's work addressed sexuality in ways that spoke to both "sex-positive" and cultural feminists in the United States. She thus became a shared icon for feminist thinkers and writers increasingly divided around issues of sexuality.

El Saadawi was introduced to an American audience in 1980 by a cover story in *Ms.* about the "crime of genital mutilation." Accompanying the article was a sidebar highlighting an excerpt from her book *The Hidden Face of Eve*, which appeared in English later that year and soon became an international best seller. El Saadawi depicted female circumcision as an act of terror and aggression toward girls. She described her own clitoridectomy at the age of six—a description that would, by the mid-1980s, become so widely quoted by American feminists as to make it almost a cliché. She told of the fear she and her sister felt, the harsh grip that held her down and pulled her legs apart, the sharp, metallic sound of the knife as it cut her, the terrible pain. Not knowing, at first, what was happening, El Saadawi and her sister soon learned that "we were born of a special sex, the female sex. We are destined in advance to taste of misery, and to have a part of our body torn away by cold, unfeeling hands."[24]

El Saadawi was a key figure in the Egyptian left, and part of her authority as a writer, particularly in the Arab world, derived from her impressive credentials as an activist for the rights of women in her own country. She had also been a practicing physician and was the director of public health in Egypt before being fired for writing as she did about women and sexuality. In the 1970s Anwar Sadat imprisoned her, along with 1,500 other intellectuals, for criticizing the government. Thus when El Saadawi wrote about the politics of sexuality, she did so as someone committed to a broad vision of women's liberation, in which international relations and women's issues were intertwined.

Over the course of the 1980s, at least ten of El Saadawi's books were translated into English. Ignoring her involvement in larger political movements, reviewers and journalists in the United States consistently hailed El Saadawi as a lone pioneer, an isolated feminist cry in the undifferentiated, reactionary wilderness of the Arab and Muslim world. In 1993 a reviewer summarized a decade of American responses when he wrote that El Saadawi "creates an anthem for all those nameless millions who died the outer or inner death, sentenced by fundamentalist Islam's cruel and unjustified repression of women."[25]

Cultural feminists and sex radicals found El Saadawi's work compelling for different reasons. Cultural feminists used El Saadawi's writings to buttress their own view that the female sensibility about sex was fundamentally distinct from that of men. These activists were particularly concerned about such issues as rape, sexual violence, and pornography, which they saw as paradigmatic symptoms of a patriarchal culture that linked sex and violence and ignored the sensuous, emotion-centered nature of female sexuality. Their critiques of sexist practices were often presented through sweeping accounts of male power that claimed to spare no historical period and no part of the world.

One prominent example was Marilyn French's 1985 book, *Beyond Power*, a global history of patriarchy from ancient times to the present. At first glance, her approach seemed even handed. French ferociously criticized the Christian church's treatment of women in the medieval and early modern periods, while she also traced ways that women challenged or revised interpretations of their faith.[26] However, she singled out Islam as uniquely oppressive to women. French pronounced that, in Islam, "the continued subjection of women is part of both practice and principle. . . . Unlike Christianity, however, [Islam] is fully totalitarian: it does not believe in separation of church and state, insisting the two be merged in a theocracy."[27] French went on to quote El Saadawi's already famous description of female circumcision as proof of the tyrannical nature of Muslim societies. Though El Saadawi had repeatedly argued that Islam did not sanction clitoridectomy, this did not prevent French from making the charge. Nor did she recognize the discrepancy in chronicling Christian women's creative rewriting of their tradition while denying agency and interpretive power to Muslim women.

The American feminists who wrote most powerfully about sexual danger used their analysis of Islam or female circumcision (or both) to strengthen their arguments about Western women's sexual oppression. They often linked pornography and rape in Western societies to other horrific practices across the globe. That link served, however implicitly, as a kind of authenticating device—proof that something like pornography was not a minor issue, but instead part of a deadly continuum, one that "sex-positive" feminists ignored at their peril. As Mary Daly argued in *Gyn/Ecology*, women in the West did not really want to imagine the "condition of their mutilated sisters" in the rest of the world, "not merely because of differences in conditions, but especially because of similarities."[28] By insisting on a universal connection among women, and establishing a relation between genital cutting and current women's issues in the United States, feminist theorists concerned about sexual danger tried to challenge complacency and perhaps incite greater outrage at what was happening at home.

Nawal El Saadawi was so valuable a source for cultural feminists in the United States because her vivid description of the removal of the clitoris seemed to disclose the tipped hand of patriarchy. The removal or alteration of the clitoris, she wrote, "goes hand in hand with the brainwashing of girls, with a calculated, merciless campaign to paralyze their capacity to think and judge and to understand."[29] For feminists like French and Daly, the lesson was clear: if this was happening to them, it could happen to us; in fact, it does happen to us, but in forms we refuse to recognize. El Saadawi's writings provided some support for the idea that there was a universal continuum of women's oppression. She clearly believed women faced tremendous sexual danger from the deformed desires of men. "It is a well known fact that in our society young girls are often exposed to various degrees of rape," she wrote in *The Hidden Face of Eve*, almost casually asserting what cultural/anti-porn feminists were working so hard to prove, that females of all ages suffered from the threat of male sexual violence. Later in the book, she wrote that, given the environment of violence and constraint, "it is . . . correct to say that most of the relationships that arise between men and women are not built on true love."[30]

At the same time that cultural feminists were writing about the unique nature of female sexuality, Americans who called themselves "sex radicals" were also defining the meaning of the clitoris. These feminists were more likely than their culturalist opponents to embrace El Saadawi's left politics and anti-imperialist views. But their focus was on the underexplored sensuality of women, and they too could find in the writings of the famous

Egyptian feminist support for their concerns. In *The Hidden Face of Eve*, El Saadawi argued that genital surgeries should be condemned precisely because they limited female sexual pleasure. Her novels feature characters who chafe against the restrictions of their culture. In *Two Women in One*, the heroine is a respectable girl who has extramarital sex with a male radical. In *Woman at Point Zero*, the protagonist is a prostitute who refuses to apologize for her behavior or to deny the pleasure she takes in it.[31]

According to El Saadawi, the repression of women occurred because both Islamic thought and Arab culture understood the power of female desire. Although circumcision was not sanctioned by Islam, it developed from the fear that, untrammeled, women's sexuality would be a disruptive force.[32] For El Saadawi, women were indeed deeply sexual beings whose pursuit of pleasure was a threat to *any* patriarchal stricture, including monogamy. Their desire was not so different from that of men, except perhaps in its dangerous intensity. For the American feminists who had produced such writings as "The Myth of the Vaginal Orgasm," *Fear of Flying*, and *Powers of Desire*, El Saadawi seemed to be speaking their language. Like the cultural feminists, pro-sex radical feminists were searching for an Arab/Muslim woman who could validate their approach, and El Saadawi was the perfect candidate.

Both strands of feminism, however, were guilty of misreading El Saadawi's work by highlighting the themes of sexuality and religion at the expense of her larger arguments. El Saadawi consistently argued that Islam was not in itself the source of women's oppression: "In the very essence of Islam, and in its teachings as practices in the life of the Prophet, women occupied a comparatively high position."[33] In her view, it was social and economic systems, not religious ones, that marginalized women. In fact, she described the Islamic revolution in Iran as motivated primarily by anti-imperialism and chastised those who refused to see the manifold ways in which Muslims had used the Qur'an as an inspiration in their struggles for social justice.[34] But when the feminist Vivian Gornick reviewed El Saadawi's *The Hidden Face of Eve* in the *New York Times Book Review*, she focused only on the sections about Arabs and sex. Directly opposing El Saadawi's arguments about the potential of a progressive Islam, Gornick commented that "no culture as religion-dominated as Arabic culture can ever accomplish social or political equality for women. The struggle is difficult enough in secular cultures where lip service is paid to the idea of universal individualism."[35] As the critic Mohja Kahf argues, American feminists tended to see the Arab woman as either a victim of male oppression or an escapee from her native culture.[36] Intent on viewing "other" women as native informants rather than as political analysts, they "read around" the arguments that got in the way of authenticating their own concerns.

El Saadawi also made clear that clitoridectomy was only one issue that Arab and African women needed to address, whereas it was the first issue of interest to many American readers.[37] In this, however, El Saadawi was also at least partially complicit because she agreed to certain key changes in her work that encouraged that kind of narrow reading. As Amal Amireh has shown, most of the material on clitoridectomy published in the English edition of *The Hidden Face of Eve* was not part of the Arabic edition; it was adapted from another text in Arabic and organized under a new section title, "The Mutilated Half." Yet entire sections and some key sentences of the original were also omitted, including the following statement: "It is important that Arab women should not feel inferior to Western women, or think that the Arabic tradition and culture are more oppressive of women than Western culture."[38] Thus, as El Saadawi's most famous book moved westward, it became more focused on clitoridectomy and spoke less to the positive aspects of women's lives in the Middle East.

Not all American feminists read El Saadawi in these ways; some did directly engage questions of "cultural relativism" and the history of colonialism.[39] And an active internal critique arose among American feminists when such black Americans as Angela Davis and Audre Lorde began to point out that white women from the United States and Europe were approaching genital mutilation and other "third world" issues as a "white women's burden." White feminists, it was argued, only focused on women of color when they needed to be "rescued" rather than looking to them as colleagues and peers.[40] Thus the charges of imperialism had traction not only on the world stage but also among American women themselves. As Davis discovered in Cairo, this critique did not exempt women of color from the criticism of feminists from the global South.

For that matter, African American women expressed a range of views about whether clitoridectomy should be a central issue. In 1992 Alice Walker wrote *Possessing the Secret of Joy*, a best-selling novel that portrayed female genital cutting as a uniquely destructive force in Africa. She later appeared prominently in *Warrior Marks*, a video with the same message that circulated widely on college campuses.[41] Walker argued that silence about clitoridectomy was akin to complicity; American feminists who did nothing to halt the mutilation of women of color were guilty of the worst kind of racism.

Given the intense conflicts among feminists internationally that developed in the 1980s, one might well argue that this type of interest in the problems of Arab and African women *caused* as many problems as it resolved. Yet, despite the ways in which it exacerbated the debates about imperialism, and even given the complexities of the racial politics it participated in, the issue of female genital cutting proved productive for American feminists, in a few key respects. Arab, Muslim, and African feminists were right to be wary of how some of their American counterparts contrasted their own personal freedom with the violence and sexual control faced by women elsewhere. But feminists in the United States also engaged the issue of clitoridectomy by weaving a complex web of differentiation *and* connection, as both cultural feminists and sex radicals used Arab women as symbols in their struggle over the direction of the U.S. feminist movement. Debate about the issue partly sutured a painful, destructive division between radical and cultural feminists, allowed both groups to agree that the attacks on women's bodies must be stopped, and joined them in solidarity with their "mutilated sisters." The focus on clitoridectomy challenged the parochialism of an earlier moment by taking U.S. feminism global, albeit in ways both partial and problematic. It also provided a common ground and a profound icon for the link between sexual pleasure and sexual danger, at a moment when the trajectories of U.S. feminist theory and activism had divided them.

For most of the twentieth century, U.S. opinion leaders articulated "Americanism" as a national identity that eschewed imperialism. The cold warriors of the 1950s argued that the United States had never been more than a reluctant imperialist and thus could be trusted to structure the world order in different and better ways than Europeans had once handled the task. One pundit smugly wrote about America's "benevolent supremacy."[42]

This version of American exceptionalism obscured the many connections between U.S. global power and the strategies of earlier world powers, including the tactic of claiming a superior status for women. Public displays of Arab women's oppression in film, news accounts, and popular literature were almost always linked, explicitly or implicitly, to the individual freedoms enjoyed by American women (notwithstanding the norms of heterosexuality and domesticity lauded in popular culture). In Iran after the revolution, the image of the veil marked what was American as much as what was Iranian. In the Gulf War of 1990–91, feminists debated whether the United States should be an ally of Saudi Arabia, a nation that systematically limited the rights of women. More recently, the desire to rescue Middle Eastern women from their particular oppression was integral to the discourse of the war in Afghanistan—a cause taken up by some feminists and challenged by others.[43]

Knowing this history does not resolve the problem of how U.S. feminists should stand on the issue of clitoridectomy, which raises the vexed issues of whether and when feminism is a universalist ideology. Feminists necessarily make certain universal claims: all women's lives must be taken seriously; it is never acceptable to abuse or rape or violate women; women owe each other a certain measure of solidarity. At the same time, any truly global feminist consciousness must contain a strong element of relativism: there is no "women's culture," or women's nature, for that matter; and any movement for and by women will need to define rights and liberation on its own terms. (Of course, those terms will always be contested within any such movement; Middle Eastern and Muslim women are no more united about issues of liberation and sexuality than are American women.)

In my view, it is less important that U.S. feminists resolve these issues than that we be able to see why they remain persistently on the table. If we attend to the context in which clitoridectomy emerged as a global feminist issue, we will necessarily proceed with humility and caution. Scholars in all parts of the world should continue to research and learn about the practices of genital cutting, as part of a larger engagement with the reality of women's lives globally. But it may be time for most Americans—certainly non-Muslim Americans—to put the issue aside as a topic of feminist activism, since its history as an American and European obsession only makes it harder for African and Arab women to address it. This is not a matter of cultural relativism; it is an issue of historical consciousness, and of recognizing the limits of American (feminist) intervention.

Looking at the cultural work done by a particular feminist problem, we can see the ways in which U.S. feminism was both heir to and challenger of a certain kind of U.S. global project—a certain kind of Americanism. At key moments in U.S.–Middle East relations, feminist concerns have been mobilized by some participants, not as part of the search for solidarity with the movements of women around the globe, but to make a case for the use of U.S. power, as part of the long and inglorious tradition of imperial mission.[44] Nevertheless, it has also been in the writings and activism of feminists, both in the United States and abroad, that the critique of this skewed logic has emerged.

In the end, the feminists of the 1970s and the 1980s could save neither their sisters nor themselves from the complexities of sexual politics or the harsh realities of global power. Yet our task is not to dismiss their project; it is to remember its history and extend their hopes.

NOTES

1. Angela Davis, "Sex-Egypt," in *Women: A World Report*, ed. Debbie Taylor (New York: Oxford University Press, 1985), 328.

2. For basic information on female genital mutilation, see the Female Genital Cutting Network and Education Project, <http://fgmnetwork.org/html/index.php>. There is a great deal of scholarship on the representations of Islam and women; see in particular Lisa Lowe, *Critical Terrains: French and British Orientalisms* (Ithaca, N.Y.: Cornell University Press, 1994); Ella Shohat, "Gender and the Culture of Empire: Toward a Feminist Ethnography of Cinema," in *Visions of the East: Orientalism in Film*, ed. Matthew Bernstein and Gaylyn Studlar (New Brunswick, N.J.: Rutgers University Press, 1997), 17–68; Reina Lewis, *Rethinking Orientalism: Women, Travel, and the Ottoman Harem* (New Brunswick, N.J.: Rutgers University Press, 2004); and Lisa Suhair Majaj, "Arab-Americans and the Meaning of Race," in *Postcolonial Theory and the United States: Race, Ethnicity, and Literature*, ed. Laurence Buell (Jackson: University Press of Mississippi, 2000), 320–37. There has been an outpouring of scholarship that, partly in response to these images, attempts to show the diversity and agency of Muslim women. That work is too vast to cite here; one useful starting place is Therese Saliba, Carolyn Allen, and Judith A. Howard, eds., *Gender, Politics, and Islam* (Chicago: University of Chicago Press, 2002).

3. Among the many excellent studies on the topic, see Stanlie M. Jones and Claire C. Robertson, eds., *Genital Cutting and Transnational Sisterhood: Disputing U.S. Polemics* (Urbana: University of Illinois Press, 2002); Bettina Shell-Duncan and Ylva Herland, eds., *Female "Circumcision" in Africa: Culture, Controversy, and Change* (Boulder, Colo.: Lynne Rienner, 2001); Elizabeth Heger Boyle, *Female Genital Cutting: Cultural Conflict in the Global Community* (Baltimore: Johns Hopkins University Press, 2002); and Lynn Thomas, "Imperial Concerns and 'Women's Affairs': State Efforts to Regulate Clitoridectomy and Eradicate Abortion in Meru, Kenya, c. 1910–1950," *Journal of African History* 39 (1998): 121–45. These books highlight the debate around genital cutting in Africa, which is how much of the discussion has been framed since the 1990s. El Saadawi's Egypt can be considered both Middle Eastern and African, and she has worked in both contexts.

4. Amal Amireh's work has been groundbreaking on this issue. See her "Framing El Saadawi: Arab Feminism in a Transnational World," *Signs* 26, no. 1 (Autumn

2000): 215–50. See also Amal Amireh and Lisa Suhair Majaj, eds., *Going Global: The Transnational Reception of Third World Women Writers* (New York: Garland, 2000).

5. For critiques of the failures and false universalisms of U.S. and Western feminists, see, among others, Chandra Talpade Mohanty's influential " 'Under Western Eyes': Feminist Scholarship and Colonial Discourses," *Boundary 2* 12, no. 3/13, no. 1 (Spring/Fall 1984): 338–58; Marnia Lazreg, "The Triumphant Discourse of Global Feminism: Should Other Women Be Known?" in *Going Global*, ed. Amireh and Majaj.

6. The Universal Declaration of Human Rights had been adopted by the United Nations General Assembly in 1948, and the idea of "human rights" as a force in international politics had been widely discussed, especially regarding racial and religious discrimination. But the "human rights movement" was still relatively young. Amnesty International, for example, was founded in 1961; the organization received the Nobel Peace Prize in 1977. Amnesty International took on female genital mutilation as a human rights issue in the 1990s; see Amnesty International, *Female Genital Mutilation: A Human Rights Information Pack* (ACT 77/05/97), <http:www.amnesty.org/ailib/intcam/femgen/fgm1.htm#a3>.

7. Clayborne Carson, *In Struggle: SNCC and the 1960s* (Cambridge, Mass.: Harvard University Press, 1981), 192–98. See also Melani McAlister, *Epic Encounters: Culture, Media, and U.S. Interests in the Middle East since 1945*, rev. ed. (Berkeley: University of California Press, 2005), chap. 3.

8. Solzhenitsyn was one figure in a much larger dissident movement in the Warsaw Pact, including the 1968 Czech uprising. That movement found international support with the Helsinki Accords of 1977, which asserted the collective right of peoples to self-determination and was widely cited by eastern European liberation movements and by Soviet Jews. See Karl Birnbaum, "Human Rights and East-West Relations," *Foreign Affairs* 55 (July 1977): 783–99; Roy Medvedev, "Andrei Sakarov and Alexander Solzhenitsyn," *Social Sciences* 33, no. 2 (2002): 3–18.

9. Elisabeth Friedman, "Women's Human Rights: The Emergence of a Movement," in *Women's Rights, Human Rights: International Feminist Perspectives*, ed. Julie Peters and Andrea Wolper (New York: Routledge, 1995).

10. President Luis Echeverria Alvarez of Mexico, quoted by James P. Sterba, "Equal Rights Vital, U.N. Chief Asserts at Women's Parley," *New York Times*, June 20, 1975.

11. Hanna Papanek, "The Work of Women: Postscript from Mexico City," *Signs* 1, no. 1 (Spring 1975): 215–26. See also Lois A. West, "The United Nations Women's Conferences and Feminist Politics," in *Gender Politics in Global Governance*, ed. Mary K. Meyer and Elisabeth Prügl (Boulder: Rowman and Littlefield, 1999),

177–96; and Mary Jo McConahay, "Trials at the Tribune," *Ms.*, November 1975, 101–4.

12. Quoted in Papanek, "The Work of Women," 217.

13. The other profoundly polarizing issue was the Israeli-Palestinian conflict, as reflected in debates over several resolutions about Zionism and Palestinian rights. I discuss this material in an unpublished essay, "Global Sisterhood or Women as Weapons?"

14. Robin Morgan and Gloria Steinem, "Genital Mutilation: 30 Million Women are Victims," *Ms.*, March 1980, 65ff. See also Nawal El Saadawi, "The Question No One Would Answer," *Ms.*, March 1980, 68–69.

15. See, for example, Charlotte Brunch, "What *Not* to Expect from the UN Women's Conference in Copenhagen," *Ms.*, July 1980, 80–81; and Georgia Dullea, "Female Circumcision a Topic at UN Parley," *New York Times*, July 18, 1980.

16. Association of African Women for Research and Development, "A Statement on Genital Mutilation," in *Third World, Second Sex*, ed. Miranda Davies (London: Zed Books, 1983), 217–18.

17. Nawal El Saadawi, *The Hidden Face of Eve* (London: Zed Books, 1980), xiv.

18. Carol Vance, "Pleasure and Danger: Toward a Politics of Sexuality," in *Pleasure and Danger: Exploring Female Sexuality*, ed. Carole Vance (Boston: Routledge and Kegan Paul, 1984), 3.

19. Jane Gerhard, *Desiring Revolution: Second-Wave Feminism and the Rewriting of American Sexual Thought, 1920–1982* (New York: Columbia University Press, 2001), 107.

20. Ibid., 150, quoting the analysis of a 1974 New York NOW conference appearing in *Off Our Backs*, a feminist news journal.

21. See Combahee River Collective, "A Black Feminist Statement" (1977), in *Words of Fire: An Anthology of African American Feminist Thought*, ed. Beverly Guy-Sheftall (New York: New Press, 1995), 232–40.

22. Julie Minces, *House of Obedience: Women in Arab Society* (London: Zed Books, 1982); Elizabeth Fernea, ed., *Middle Eastern Muslim Women Speak* (Austin: University of Texas Press, 1978); and Nayra Atiya, *Khul Khaal: Five Egyptian Women Tell Their Stories* (Syracuse, N.Y.: Syracuse University Press, 1982). In the 1990s there was a steady increase in the appetite for literature on Middle Eastern and Muslim women among both general audiences and feminists specifically.

23. Edward Said, *Covering Islam* (New York: Pantheon, 1981).

24. El Saadawi, "Question No One Would Answer," 68–69.

25. Paul Roberts, "Novels of an Arab Feminist," *Toronto Star*, May 15, 1993, quoted in Amireh, "Framing Nawal El Saadawi," 227.

26. See, for example, French's discussion of women as an underlying force in the

literature and ideology of courtly love, with its valuation of female moral superiority. Marilyn French, *Beyond Power: On Women, Men, and Morals* (New York: Summit Books, 1985), 178–88.

27. Ibid., 254.

28. Mary Daly, *Gyn/Ecology: The Metaethics of Radical Feminism* (Boston: Beacon Press, 1978), 156.

29. El Saadawi, *Hidden Face of Eve*, 5.

30. Ibid., 74.

31. Nawal El Saadawi, *Two Women in One* (Seattle: Seal Press, 1986), and *Woman at Point Zero* (London: Zed Books, 1983).

32. El Saadawi, *Hidden Face of Eve*, 40; see also chap. 16, "Love and Sex in the Life of the Arabs."

33. Ibid., iii.

34. Ibid., iii–v.

35. Vivian Gornick, "About the Mutilated Half," *New York Times Book Review*, March 14, 1982, 3ff. Amrita Basu responded to the review's one-sidedness in a letter to the editor, *New York Times*, May 2, 1982. See also Robin Morgan's review of *The Hidden Face of Eve* in *Ms.*, March 1982, 47.

36. Mohja Kahf, "Packaging 'Huda': Sha'rawi's Memoirs in the United States Reception Environment," in *Going Global*, ed. Amireh and Majaj.

37. "Arab Women and Western Feminism: An Interview with Nawal El Saadawi," *Race and Class* 22, no. 2 (1980): 175–82, quote on 177. Also quoted in Amireh, "Framing Nawal El Saadawi," 220.

38. Quoted in Amireh, "Framing Nawal El Saadawi," 225.

39. For an excellent review that places El Saadawi's work in the context of a more layered analysis of the Middle East, see Irene Gendzier, "Arab Feminine Mystique," *Nation*, July 19–26, 1980, 90–91.

40. Audre Lorde, "Open Letter to Mary Daly," in *Sister/Outsider* (Trumansburg, N.Y.: Crossing Press, 1984), 66–71; and Angela Davis, *Women, Race, and Class* (New York: Vintage, 1983).

41. Alice Walker, *Possessing the Secret of Joy* (New York: Harcourt, 1992); Alice Walker, *Warrior Marks: Female Genital Mutilation and the Sexual Blinding of Women* (New York: Harcourt, 1993); *Warrior Marks*, produced and directed by Pratibha Parmar (distributed by Women Make Movies, 1993).

42. Charles Hilliard, *The Cross, the Sword, and the Dollar* (New York: North River Press, 1951.)

43. In *Epic Encounters*, I discuss both the idea of "benevolent supremacy" (chap. 1) and the gender politics of the Afghan war (chap. 7).

44. On feminism, women, and foreign policy, see Mary Renda, *Taking Haiti: Military*

Occupation and the Culture of U.S. Imperialism, 1915–1940 (Chapel Hill: University of North Carolina Press, 2001); Kristin L. Hoganson, *Fighting for American Manhood: How Gender Politics Provoked the Spanish-American and Philippine-American Wars* (New Haven, Conn.: Yale University Press, 2000); and Amy Kaplan, *The Anarchy of Empire in the Making of U.S. Culture* (Cambridge, Mass.: Harvard University Press, 2005). See also Cynthia Enloe's groundbreaking *Bananas, Beaches, and Bases: Making Feminist Sense of International Politics*, rev. ed. (Berkeley: University of California Press, 2001).

Contributors

Mia Bay is associate professor of history at Rutgers University. She is the author
of *The White Image in the Black Mind: African-American Ideas about White People,
1830–1925* (2000).

Jun Furuya is professor of American political and diplomatic history at the Faculty
of Law, Hokkaido University, Japan. He was educated at the University of Tokyo
and Princeton University. He is the author of *Americanism: Nationalism and the
"Universalist State"* (2002) and *America between Past and Present* (2004).

Gary Gerstle is professor of history at the University of Maryland. He is the author
of *Working-Class Americanism* (1989) and *American Crucible: Race and Nation in the
Twentieth Century* (2001), winner of the Theodore Saloutos Prize. He is coeditor
of *The Rise and Fall of the New Deal Order, 1930–1980* (1989), *E Pluribus Unum?*
(1989), and *Ruling America: Wealth and Power in a Democracy* (2005).

Jonathan M. Hansen teaches history and social studies at Harvard University.
Author of *The Lost Promise of Patriotism: Debating American Identity, 1890–1920*
(2003), he is now writing a book about the history of the u.s. Naval Base at
Guantanamo Bay, Cuba.

Michael Kazin is professor of history at Georgetown University. His most recent
books include *The Populist Persuasion: An American History* (rev. ed., 1998),
America Divided: The Civil War of the 1960s (with Maurice Isserman; rev. ed.,
2003), and *A Godly Hero: The Life of William Jennings Bryan* (2006).

Rob Kroes is professor emeritus and former chair of the American studies program
at the University of Amsterdam. He is a past president of the European
Association for American Studies (EAAS, 1992–96). He is the author, coauthor,
or editor of thirty-four books. Among his recent publications are *If You've
Seen One, You've Seen the Mall: Europeans and American Mass Culture* (1996),
Predecessors: Intellectual Lineages in American Studies (1998), *Them and Us:
Questions of Citizenship in a Globalizing World* (2000), and *Straddling Borders: The
American Resonance in Transnational Identities* (2004). With Robert W. Rydell he
coauthored *Buffalo Bill in Bologna: The Globalization of the World, 1850–1920*
(2005). A forthcoming book is *Photographic Memories: Private Pictures, Public
Images and American History* (2006).

Melani McAlister is associate professor of American studies and international
affairs at George Washington University. She is the author of *Epic Encounters:
Culture, Media, and u.s. Interests in the Middle East since 1945* (rev. ed., 2005) and
has published numerous articles in academic journals and in the general interest

press. She is currently working on a book about Christian evangelicals, popular culture, and foreign relations.

Joseph A. McCartin is associate professor of history at Georgetown University. He is the author of *Labor's Great War: The Struggle for Industrial Democracy and the Origins of Modern American Labor Relations* (1997) and coeditor with Melvyn Dubofsky of *American Labor: A Documentary Collection* (2004).

Alan McPherson is associate professor of history at Howard University, where he specializes in U.S. foreign relations. He is the author of *Yankee No! Anti-Americanism in U.S.–Latin American Relations* (2003) and *Intimate Ties, Bitter Struggles: The United States and Latin America since 1945* (2006).

Louis Menand is Anne T. and Robert M. Bass Professor of English and American Literature and Language at Harvard University. He is the author of *Discovering Modernism: T. S. Eliot and His Context* (1987), *The Metaphysical Club* (2001), and *American Studies* (2002). Since 2001, he has been a staff writer for *The New Yorker*.

Mae M. Ngai is associate professor of history at the University of Chicago. She is the author of *Impossible Subjects: Illegal Aliens and the Making of Modern America* (2004).

Robert Shalhope is George Lynn Cross Professor of History at the University of Oklahoma. He is the author of five books, of which the most recent are *Bennington and the Green Mountain Boys: The Emergence of Liberal Democracy in Vermont, 1760–1850* (1996) and *A Tale of New England: The Diaries of Hiram Harwood, Vermont Farmer, 1810–1837* (2003).

Stephen J. Whitfield holds the Max Richter Chair in American Civilization at Brandeis University. He is, most recently, the author of *In Search of American Jewish Culture* (1999) and the editor of *A Companion to 20th-Century America* (2004).

Alan Wolfe is professor of political science and director of the Boisi Center for Religion and American Public Life at Boston College. His latest book is *Return to Greatness: How America Lost Its Sense of Purpose and What It Needs to Recover It* (2005). He is writing a book about the quality of American democracy.

Acknowledgments

This anthology would not have been possible without the support and assistance of a number of individuals, and it is our pleasure to thank them here. The book had its origins in a conference held at Georgetown University in March 2003. That gathering came to pass because of the support of Dean Jane McAuliffe; James Collins, who then served as chair of Georgetown's Department of History; and Ed Ingebretsen, who chaired its American Studies program. The support of our colleagues in Georgetown's Department of History has been overwhelming. But we are especially grateful for the active encouragement of our Americanist colleagues: Emmett Curran, Alison Games, Maurice Jackson, Ron Johnson, David Painter, Adam Rothman, and Nancy Bernkopf Tucker. Kathy Buc Gallagher coordinated all of the logistics of the conference with her characteristic skill and wit. Kazuko Uchimura helped splendidly with Professor Furuya's essay. A large part of the funding was provided through a generous grant from the Neff Family Fund. A number of excellent scholars also participated in the 2003 conference. They include Saul Cornell, Lucy Maddox, Adam Rothman, Yossi Shain, Anders Stephanson, and Ronald Walters.

A number of people helped with the preparation of this volume. We are especially thankful to James Kloppenberg for his advice on the organization of the volume and its essays. We would also like to express our thanks to a number of people at the University of North Carolina Press. As editor, Chuck Grench believed in our volume from the beginning and has goaded and encouraged us since then. The help of project editors Pam Upton and Paul Betz was also invaluable.

Finally, we'd like to thank our spouses, Beth and Diane, and our children, Danny, Maia, Mara, and Elisa. Their love and support gives meaning to all our work.

Index

Grammatical Institute of the English Language (Webster), 57, 70 (nn. 19, 21)

Gramont, Sanche de. *See* Morgan, Ted

Gramsci, Antonio, 12, 101

Great Awakening, 26. *See also* Second Great Awakening

Great Depression, 6, 90, 93

Greatest Generation, The (Brokaw), 132

Green Mountain Boys, 56

Greer, Germaine, 242

Gulag Archipelago (Solzhenitsyn), 245

Gulf War (1990–91), 256. *See also* Iraq, war in

Gyn/Ecology (Daly), 253

Haiti, 15; African American opposition to U.S. occupation of (1915), 169, 170, 179–84; Haitian rebels opposing U.S. occupation (1915), 180–81, 190 (n. 46); corvée, 180; racism in, 182–83; educational reform, and black Americans, 183–84, 190–91 (n. 51)

Hall, Hiland, 60, 63, 64, 65

Hammett, Dashiell, 210, 211, 217

Hammond, Charles, 60

Hancock, John, 57, 70 (n. 21)

Handlin, Oscar, 109, 112–15, 116–18, 121–22

Hanks, Tom, 131, 133, 137

Hansen, Jonathan, 14

Harris, Leslie M., 33

Harrison, Earl, 114

Hart, Philip, 118–20, 126 (n. 31)

Hart-Celler Immigration and Nationality Act (1965), 108–11, 115, 118–21, 122–23, 126–27 (nn. 29–32)

Hartz, Louis, 7, 10, 96

Harwood, Hiram, 14, 55–68; ancestry and early life, 56–57; increasing republicanism of, 60–62; and economic life, 65–66

Haswell, Anthony, 57–58, 59

Haynes, Lemuel, 25, 27, 30, 31, 45 (n. 1)

Hemingway, Ernest, 211, 215, 217; novels of, translated into French, 208, 209

Herberg, Will, 154

"Hida Buntaro," 196–97

Hidden Face of Eve, The (El Saadawi), 253, 254, 255

High Sierra (Burnett), 211

Hobbes, Thomas, 199–200

Hobsbawm, Eric, 8, 100–101

Hobson, Laura Z., 98

Hofstadter, Richard, 1, 7, 99

Hollinger, David, 9, 11, 12

Hoover, Herbert, 97, 181, 183, 195

Hornbeck, Stanley K., 97

Howe, Daniel, 66

Hughes, Langston, 183

Humanitarianism, 9

Human rights, 245, 259 (n. 6)

Hutchison, William R., 154

Ideals, of Americanism, 1, 9, 13, 16–18

Immigration, in early twentieth century: and Americanization, 73–74; Progressive intellectual response to, 79–81, 84; Johnson-Reed Act (1924), 84, 109, 123 (n. 2); Asians, 102, 127 (n. 34); immigrants, as foundation of America, 116–17; Japanese, 193

Immigration, in later twentieth century: liberalism and, 14, 111–13, 117, 120, 122; immigration quotas, 108–9, 111, 112–15, 118–19, 121, 123 (nn. 2–3), 127 (n. 34); Hart-Celler Immigration and Nationality Act (1965), 108–11, 115, 118–21, 122–23, 126 (nn. 29–31), 126–27 (n. 32); Asians, 108, 117–18, 124–25 (n. 19), 161–62, 163–64; Latino immigration, 108, 117, 118, 122–23; and citizenship, 111–12, 124 (n. 8); and Jewish Americans, 115–16; Immigration Reform Act (1965), 154, 163; non-Christian, 161

Immigration and Naturalization Service (INS), 114

Immigration Reform Act (1965), 154, 163

Imperialism: beginnings of American (1899), 5, 169–70, 172–75, 178–79; of